ROUGE RIVER REVIVED

ROUGE RIVER REVIVED

How People Are Bringing Their River Back to Life

EDITED BY
John H. Hartig
and Jim Graham

University of Michigan Press
Ann Arbor

Copyright © 2022 by John H. Hartig and Jim Graham

For questions or permissions, please contact um.press.perms@umich.edu

Published in the United States of America by the
University of Michigan Press
Printed and bound by CPI Group (UK) Ltd, Croydon, CR0 4YY

First published September 2022

A CIP catalog record for this book is available from the British Library.

Library of Congress Cataloging-in-Publication data has been applied for.

ISBN 978-0-472-03908-1 (paper : alk. paper)
ISBN 978-0-472-22072-4 (e-book)

Cover photograph by P.A. Rech.

CONTENTS

Foreword
  William Clay Ford, Jr. | vii

Acknowledgments | ix

PROLOGUE
  John H. Hartig and Jim Graham | 1

CHAPTER 1
The Setting: An Urban Watershed
  Alan VanKerckhove | 8

CHAPTER 2
First Peoples of the Rouge River
  Kay McGowan | 16

CHAPTER 3
Putting the Rouge to Work
  Nancy Darga | 23

CHAPTER 4
Henry Ford and the Rouge River
  Brian James Egen and John H. Hartig | 42

CHAPTER 5
Rouge River Restoration: Revival of an Urban River
  Annette DeMaria, Noel Mullett, and John H. Hartig | 61

CHAPTER 6
The Need for Green Infrastructure
   Cyndi Ross | 91

CHAPTER 7
Rouge River Citizen Science
   Sally Petrella | 106

CHAPTER 8
Environmental Education: Realizing Bill Stapp's Vision
   Sally Cole-Misch | 129

CHAPTER 9
The Rouge River Reborn: From Wen to Wonder
   Orin G. Gelderloos, Dorothy F. McLeer,
   and Richard A. Simek | 143

CHAPTER 10
Reconnecting with Our Home Waters:
Rouge River Offers Growing Number
of Recreational Opportunities
   Kurt Kuban | 159

CHAPTER 11
Rouge River Champion—Jim Murray
   John H. Hartig | 174

CHAPTER 12
Reflections
   John H. Hartig and Jim Graham | 185

Contributors | 201

Index | 209

Most people know my great-grandfather Henry Ford as one of America's foremost industrialists, who founded the Ford Motor Company, created an integrated moving automotive assembly line that revolutionized automobile manufacturing, and invented the Ford Model T. He was a visionary and a student of continuous learning and improvement. He saw industry and agriculture as natural partners, and before it was readily accepted, he experimented with using agricultural crops like soybeans to make plastics for automobiles. Today, this is called integrative thinking and a systems approach to improving quality, quantity, and productivity. His thinking back then clearly was a building block for sustainable transportation systems today.

Henry Ford started building the original Ford Rouge complex in 1917 and completed it in 1928. Located a few miles south of Detroit at the confluence of the Rouge and Detroit Rivers, it was the largest industrial complex in the world. Embracing Ford Motor Company's heritage of innovation and business strength, I have made it my life's work to make people's lives better by accelerating our efforts to be the most trusted provider of smart vehicles and mobility services and to be a model of sustainable transportation.

As part of this commitment, a newly reconstructed Rouge opened in 2004 as a 21st century model of sustainable manufacturing. We do not view this as environmental philanthropy but rather a sound approach that balances the business needs of auto manufacturing with ecological and social concerns. This point of view is evident by the Rouge's greenbelt promenade entrance, its 22 acres of sustainable landscaping, and the system of swales and retention ponds on the grounds that is used to treat stormwater. We have also successfully used phytoremediation beds to absorb and neutralize contaminants on site and incorporated renewable energy into the Rouge.

Probably most prominent to visitors of the Rouge is one of the largest living roofs in the world. The roof collects and filters stormwater runoff and helps cool the building, saving energy and money. Also, the plants on the roof absorb carbon dioxide as part of photosynthesis, emitting oxygen and reducing greenhouse gases.

By the 1960s, the Rouge River was considered one of the most polluted rivers in the United States. In 1969, it even caught on fire. Today, communities are controlling the raw sewage coming from many combined sewer overflows, building green infrastructure, stabilizing streambanks, and removing dams to allow fish to reach spawning and nursery grounds. The river, in response, is experiencing a revival, including improved dissolved oxygen levels, the elimination of frequent fish kills, an improved invertebrate community living on the bottom of the river, an improved fishery, and the return of beaver after a 100-year absence.

The Rouge River is the first watershed in the United States to have a stormwater permit for all of its 48 communities. Few people thought this was possible 37 years ago when the river was identified as a pollution hotspot by the International Joint Commission. It is an amazing turnaround, but more will have to be done to achieve our long-term goals.

What impresses me about this effort today is that we have not only a cleaner river, but also a more educated and engaged citizenry; a realization that the river now provides many ecosystem services and benefits that enhance people's lives; a spirit of collaboration; and a growing sense of community pride.

I am a lifelong environmentalist and a long-term champion of restoring the Rouge River, and the Ford Motor Company is very proud of being a partner in that process. As my great-grandfather Henry Ford stated:

To do for the world more than the world does for you—that is success.

I commend this book to you as proof that river revival is possible when communities are committed to making the world a better place, and I encourage you to get involved in caring for the watershed you call home.

William Clay Ford, Jr., Executive Chair
Ford Motor Company
November 29, 2021

ACKNOWLEDGMENTS

It has been 37 years since the watershed effort to clean up the Rouge River started. First and foremost, we would like to acknowledge all the people who have historically and are currently helping bring our river back to life. The many people and partners who have helped revive the Rouge River have truly inspired us to tell this story. Indeed, this book would not have been possible without their contributions.

This book was published on the 50th anniversaries of the Clean Water Act and the U.S.-Canada Great Lakes Water Quality Agreement. We can think of no better way to celebrate this landmark environmental law and international agreement than to tell the story of how the Rouge River has risen from the ashes of its incendiary past to achieve remarkable ecological revival. We acknowledge the important role that the Clean Water Act and the Great Lakes Water Quality Agreement have played in restoring and protecting the Rouge River and the entire Great Lakes Basin Ecosystem.

We also acknowledge the significant contribution of the late Congressman John D. Dingell, who was the author of the National Environmental Policy Act, the Clean Water Act, the Endangered Species Act, the Detroit River International Wildlife Refuge Establishment Act, and many other important environmental laws. He also was instrumental in securing $350 million in federal funding for cleanup of the Rouge River through the Rouge River National Wet Weather Demonstration Project. These contributions cannot be overstated.

We gratefully acknowledge The Colina Foundation and The Americana Foundation that supported placing a copy of *Rouge River Revived* in each library in the watershed and supported a book tour to share this story of environmental hope throughout the watershed. We especially thank the writers for sharing their passion and knowledge of the Rouge River as an inspiration for caring and loving this ecosystem as their home. We thank John Schmittroth for his early efforts in catalyzing this book and helping fund the index, and Scott Hocking for assistance with securing historical images for this book. We also would like to thank Scott Ham, Danielle Coty-Fattal, Kevin Rennells, Paula Newcomb, and the other staff of University of Michigan Press for their contributions to the production process, and the independent reviewers whose comments improved this manuscript.

PROLOGUE

John H. Hartig and Jim Graham

From a resource treasured for its strategic location and other beneficial uses, to one of the most degraded urban streams in America—that has been the fated course of the Rouge River. Today, however, citizen action is bringing the river and its watershed back to life.

The scale of the river cleanup effort has been massive—126 miles through the most densely populated and urbanized area of Michigan, metropolitan Detroit. The cleanup covers four branches—the Main (or Mainstem), Upper, Middle, and Lower Branches of the River Rouge—which collectively empty into the Detroit River at Zug Island (fig. 1). This watershed spans about 466 square miles and is home to approximately 1.4 million people living in 48 communities and three counties. Heavy industry dominates the lower river at its confluence with the Detroit River. Eventually, people came to realize that no one entity, community, or business could do this alone. It would take everyone doing their part, along with considerable education, cooperation, and federal investment to leverage local dollars, to clean up the river. Today, the revival of the Rouge River is recognized as a model for watershed cleanup throughout the United States.

From the very beginning the Rouge River has been recognized for its strategic location and beneficial uses. Native Americans settled along its shores, using it as a source of drinking water and a transportation route, and benefiting from the incredible fishing and hunting. The earliest inhabitants were the Algonquins, followed by the Hurons and Wyandots. These tribes respected and revered the ecosystems within which they lived.

When the French arrived in the late 17th century, they named the Rouge River (*Riviere Rouge*) due to the red water coloring associated with rushes growing along the banks. The voyageurs, *coureurs des bois*,

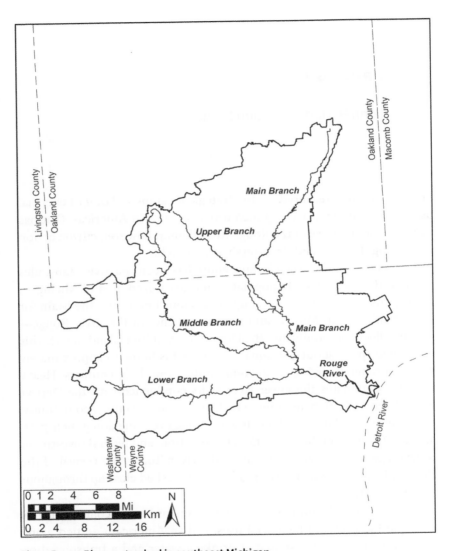

Fig. 1. Rouge River watershed in southeast Michigan.

and fur trappers used the Rouge River as a passage from the Detroit River into the interior. In 1701, the French built a fort and established a permanent settlement in the region.

During the 1700s the Rouge River was a favorite stomping ground of French pony owners. They raced their ponies on the frozen river, from the "first bend" near where the current Henry Ford Estate stands to "World's End" where Fort Street now crosses the Rouge River. Soon after, strip farms were developed along both the Detroit and Rouge Rivers. Later in the 18th century, gristmills would be built on main forks in the river, and shipyards were established on the lower river because of easy access to the Detroit River and Great Lakes. Between 1770 and 1789, twenty vessels were launched along the lower river. Shipbuilding expanded during World War I, when "Eagle" boats were built to fight submarines. These 200-foot submarine chasers were the first ships ever built by mass production.

In the early 1900s the Lower Rouge River was dredged for both Eagle boats and to accommodate automobile manufacturing. Henry Ford consolidated manufacturing operations along the Lower Rouge River into the largest integrated factory in the world at that time. Other industries would follow, and soon the Lower Rouge River became the center of the industrial heartland.

The Lower Rouge River has long had a reputation as a working river that supported industry and commerce. Pollution was considered just part of the cost of doing business. The October 21, 1965, edition of the *Dearborn Guide* includes the headline "Rouge Called State's Most Polluted River" (Gnau 1975). The principal sources of pollution at that time were industrial waste from the Rouge Plant, raw sewage from stormwater and combined sewer overflows (CSOs, the discharge of raw sewage into river systems during rainfall events from a combined storm and sanitary sewer system), and garbage being thrown into the river.

Indeed, the lower end of the river was so polluted with oil and other petroleum products that it caught fire on October 9, 1969 (Hartig 2010). On that infamous day, a welder's torch ignited oil that had been spilled into the water and oil-soaked debris on the lower river. Flames climbed 50 feet in the air and the US Coast Guard had to halt traffic on the river. It took 10 pieces of Detroit Fire Department equipment, including the Detroit Fire Boat, to contain the fire until it burned out.

A study of the Rouge River in the early 1970s reported that approximately 40 miles of the Rouge River had very poor water quality; the evidence was that the invertebrate community living in river sediments was dominated by species tolerant of severe water pollution (Jackson 1975). The 1972 Clean Water Act called for watershed-wide planning throughout the US and for all waters to be "fishable and swimmable" within 20 years. Under Section 208 of the Clean Water Act, municipalities were encouraged to experiment with best management practices to address stormwater challenges, but no broad-based funding for implementation was provided.

Then in the mid-1980s, a major tipping point occurred that would change everything. First, watershed residents of Melvindale and Dearborn, along the Lower Rouge River, could not keep their windows open on warm summer nights because a putrid smell would waft into their bedrooms (Hartig 2010). Residents described it as smelling like rotten eggs. At the time, residents thought that the source of this fetid smell was air emissions from nearby industries. However, after scientific investigations, residents learned that the Rouge River was so polluted with decomposing raw sewage that all the oxygen was being used up in the river. The result was that that the river was releasing hydrogen sulfide gas, which smells like rotten eggs and only forms in the absence of oxygen. The source of the raw sewage was sanitary sewer overflows, CSOs, and illegal discharges. Even the most pollution-tolerant fish, such as carp, were dying due to lack of oxygen (fig. 2). Residents were finally starting to realize that raw sewage was turning the Rouge River into a public health threat.

Concerned citizens from Melvindale and Dearborn started a petition drive in 1984, gathering nearly 1,000 signatures. This petition was sent to the regional administrator of the US Environmental Protection Agency, the Michigan Department of Natural Resources, and the Michigan Water Resources Commission. Residents demanded that something be done immediately to stop illegal raw sewage discharges into the Rouge River and to eliminate the violations of water-quality standards. Public awareness of the pollution was growing, and state and federal agencies were forced to take notice.

A second environmental catastrophe occurred in 1985 when a 23-year-old man fell into the Rouge River, swallowed water, and died of an infection from a rare parasitic, waterborne disease called leptospirosis or rat fever (Diebolt 1985). Even though the local health department

Fig. 2. The concrete channel of the Rouge River in the mid-1980s with decomposing raw sewage and dead carp, Melvindale, Michigan. (Photograph by Larry Caruso.)

news release stated that there was no evidence that the man's illness and death were directly linked to the polluted water, most people believed that the probable cause of death was exposure to raw sewage (Bean et al. 2003). Governments always want to see the "smoking gun" or the human health impact, and now compelling evidence showed that the polluted Rouge River was the source of the waterborne pathogen that likely caused one man's death, and that the river was a public health risk to 1.4 million watershed residents. The health department was obliged to warn the public to avoid contact with the river. The Michigan Department of Natural Resources and its Michigan Water Resources Commission had no choice but to comprehensively address this public health problem.

This book is the story of the response to that mid-1980s "tipping point"—how people overcame apathy and brought their river back from two centuries of human use and abuse. It is a story of people working together. This book includes historical perspectives on the Native American history in the watershed, European settlement, the expansion of industry, and how the Rouge became the most polluted river in Michigan. It also shares stories of how it is being cleaned up and the important role of all citizens. It concludes with reflections on how far the Rouge River cleanup has come, and what still needs to be done to fully realize the benefits of a healthy river ecosystem, one that meets the needs of both the present and future generations. This book combines the writings of a collection of individuals whose daily work gives them an intimate knowledge of the Rouge River's problems and progress, and how it is transforming into a treasured natural resource. We share these stories to inspire and give hope to all who are working to restore and protect watersheds in the places they call home.

LITERATURE CITED

Bean, C.J., Mullett, N., Hartig, J.H. 2003. "Watershed Planning and Management: The Rouge River Experience." In J.H. Hartig, ed., *Honoring Our Detroit River: Caring for Our Home*, 185–98. Bloomfield Hills, MI: Cranbrook Institute of Science.

Diebolt, J. 1985. "Bad Rouge Water May Have Killed Novi Man." *Detroit Free Press*. October 5.

Gnau, T.B. 1975. "Indian Mounds to Dumping Grounds: A History of the Rouge River." *Dearborn Historian* 15 (2): 57–75.

Hartig, J.H. 2010. *Burning Rivers: Revival of Four Urban-Industrial Rivers That Caught on Fire.* Ecovision World Monograph Series. Aquatic Ecosystem Health and Management Society, Burlington, Ontario, Canada. Essex, UK: Multi-Science Publishing.

Jackson, G., 1975. "A Biological Investigation of the Rouge River, Wayne and Oakland Counties, May 17 to October 19, 1973." Michigan Department of Natural Resources, Bureau of Water Management, Lansing.

1   THE SETTING

An Urban Watershed

Alan VanKerckhove

Understanding the setting of this story—the Rouge River watershed—is important, because it gives people the context to better understand how the river became so polluted, and ultimately, what needs to be done to restore its health.

Glacial Origin

North America's most recent ice age is called the Wisconsin Glaciation. It began about 100,000 years ago and ended about 10,000–14,000 years ago (fig. 3). During the peak of the Wisconsin Glaciation about 20,000 years ago, ice completely covered the Great Lakes Basin and the Rouge River watershed.

Glaciers create unique landforms, sediment types, and erosion patterns. They also carry rocks of all sizes great distances. As the Wisconsin Glacier retreated, various materials were deposited to form three distinct landforms in the Rouge River watershed: former lakebeds or lakeplains, moraines, and glacial outwash. Substantial portions of the watershed, particularly Wayne County and southeastern Oakland County, were once the bottoms of lakes and are therefore called lakebeds. Lakebeds in the Rouge River watershed are mostly composed of fine sands and clay. Glacial moraines are prominent features in the northwestern part of the watershed and are characterized by rolling, hilly topography. Moraines are accumulations of dirt and rocks that have fallen onto the glacier surface or have been pushed along by the glacier as it moves. The dirt and rocks in moraines can range in size from powdery silt to large rocks and boulders. Glacial outwash is deposits of sand and gravel carried by run-

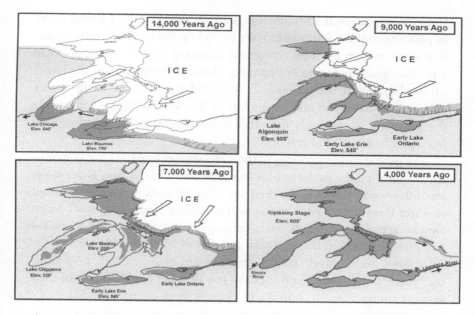

Fig. 3. How the Great Lakes and Rouge River watershed were formed. (Courtesy US Army Corps of Engineers, Detroit District.)

ning water from the melting ice of a glacier and laid down in stratified deposits. These are found predominantly in the northeastern portion of the watershed.

The Rouge River Watershed

The Rouge River flows downhill through a gently sloping landscape. The land surrounding a waterway is called a watershed, which means the land from which water is "shed" into the waterway. The land, air, water, and all living things come together to form an ecosystem. It is important to remember that all are interconnected. How we treat the land affects the water and all life, including humans.

Every river both shapes and is shaped by the landscape it drains. The Rouge River watershed is a fan-shaped basin or catchment consisting of four river branches that drain portions of Wayne, Oakland, and Washtenaw Counties (Rouge RAP Advisory Council 1994; see also fig. 1 in the prologue). The Rouge River has four major branches: the Mainstem, the

Upper Rouge River, the Middle Rouge River, and the Lower Rouge River. In addition to these four major river branches, the basin's extensive surface water system includes numerous tributary streams and more than 400 lakes and ponds. The topography, the surface features of the basin, varies throughout the watershed. The headwaters of the Rouge River, primarily in the north and west areas of the watershed, are hilly, while the southeast is relatively flat. This difference in topography resulted from prehistoric glacial activity.

The geology and hydrology of the watershed define the river system—they determine the patterns of water flow over a landscape. River flows are influenced by both watershed and climatic conditions. The amount of water flowing in a river varies, and scientists study river flows on an annual, seasonal, and daily basis. In some rivers, such as the Manistee and Jordan Rivers in the northern portion of Michigan's Lower Peninsula, flows are relatively stable—they do not change much over time, they rarely flood, and their periods of low flow are less than 80% of their average annual flow. In contrast, the Rouge River is very unstable:

- Peak annual flows are 20–90 times the base flows (the portion of the stream flow that is not runoff).
- Summer base flows are below 10 cubic feet per second.
- Daily fluctuations exceed 500 cubic feet per second after rain events—that is, 50 times the summer-based flow (Beam and Braunscheidel 1998).

These fluctuations in water flow can destabilize riverbanks and increase erosion, transport abnormally large amounts of sediment along the bottom of the river (called "bedload"), destroy and degrade aquatic and riparian habitats, strand and kill organisms, and interfere with recreational uses of the river.

Wiley et al. (1998) have shown that base-flow enhancement has dramatically increased the fishery potential of the Lower Rouge River. These researchers concluded that artificial base-flow enhancement in low-base-flow river systems like the Rouge River may be a particularly useful tool to enhance sport fish populations.

"Gradient" is the drop in elevation over a specified length of a river. It helps determine the energy that river water can exert on its riverbeds and riverbanks. "Stream power" is a product of the combination of gradient and the discharge of water in a river or stream. Steeper gradients increase flow velocity, which can alter channel depth, width, meandering, and sediment transport. The average gradient of the Rouge River Mainstem is 4.9 feet per mile. Average slopes for the Upper Rouge River, Middle Rouge River, and Lower Rouge River are 21.0 feet per mile, 11.2 feet per mile, and 10.9 feet per mile, respectively (Beam and Braunscheidel 1998). Lakeplain areas such as those found in much of the Rouge River watershed have a relatively flat topography, and rivers that drain them have low slopes. Low slopes translate into low flow velocities and a tendency toward flooding when there are large precipitation yields in the watershed, as happens in the Rouge River from late fall through early summer.

Variation of gradients among river reaches is considered good because it creates many different types of channels and therefore different kinds of habitat for fish, invertebrates, and other aquatic life. Rivers that have a wide variety of habitats can support all the different life-history stages of aquatic species. In general, fish and other aquatic life are most diverse and productive in river reaches with gradients between 10 and 69.9 feet per mile (Beam and Braunscheidel 1998).

Unfortunately, such gradients are rare in Michigan due to the relatively flat landscape, and the Rouge River Mainstem has very little slope. Areas of high gradient are also most likely to have been dammed or channelized. The Mainstem of the Rouge River contains only 6.1 miles (13%) of the most desirable gradient. The Upper Rouge River fares better, with 6.2 miles (44%) in this range; the Middle Rouge River has over 7 miles (28%), and the Lower Rouge River has 3.4 miles (14%) (Beam and Braunscheidel 1998). The steepest gradient is usually in areas with the least discharge—the headwaters.

Human Disturbance

The Rouge River watershed was once filled with a myriad of smaller ecosystems and relatively high diversity of species, drawing countless springs into a meandering river. The glacial soils and sloped lowlands provided perfect sites for forests and wetlands alike, where humans could flourish alongside other animal and plant life.

Today, the watershed is heavily urbanized, particularly the eastern portion. More than 50% of the land use in the basin is classified as residential, commercial, or industrial.

Forest and wetlands were historically the dominant land-cover types in the watershed (Roseman et al. 2020). However, the growth of the city of Detroit and its suburbs reduced forest and wetland coverage to less than 20% of the watershed (Beam and Braunscheidel 1998). The forest-cover target for southeast Michigan is 40% (SEMCOG 2020). Twenty-three percent of the Rouge River watershed has been transformed into impervious surface that allows little to no stormwater to infiltrate into the ground (Rouge RAP Advisory Council 2004). This causes both significant runoff problems and loss of habitat. Research has shown that watershed health begins to decline when impervious surface coverage exceeds 10%, and becomes severely impaired if this number climbs beyond 30% of the total watershed area (Arnold and Gibbons 1996).

This large proportion of impervious surface has resulted in the Rouge River becoming "flashy." Hydrologists call a stream or river "flashy" when it experiences a rapid increase in flow shortly after the onset of a precipitation event, and an equally rapid return to base conditions shortly after the end of the precipitation event. Flashiness in a stream can be increased or decreased by a variety of land-use and land-cover changes in the stream's watershed. For example, an increase in impervious surfaces (urbanization) or in agricultural land typically leads to an increase in flashiness. Land-management practices that increase infiltration of precipitation into the soil, such as restoration of native vegetation or implementation of best management practices such as rain gardens, grass swales, and forested riparian buffers, typically decrease stream flashiness. Streams that experience an increase in flashiness undergo a period of channel adjustment to accommodate the increased peak flows. This may include incision (downcutting) and widening of the stream channel, which affects in-stream and near-stream infrastructure as well as stream-adjacent lands.

The "flashy" hydrology is exemplified in the channelized concrete portion of the Rouge River downstream from the Henry Ford Estate Dam, where, as part of a 1962 flood-control project, more than four river miles were reconfigured as a paved V-shaped channel with no flood-plain (fig. 4). Water velocities through this part of the river can be particularly elevated, especially during spring snowmelt, which may limit or deter upstream fish migration for spawning and foraging (Roseman et al. 2020). Conversely, the flows are depressed during dry periods in summer and early autumn because of the straight, smooth river bottom

Fig. 4. A portion of the four-mile concrete channel of the lower Rouge River designed to alleviate flooding. (Photograph courtesy US Army Corps of Engineers.)

in the concrete section. Low flows, coupled with a lack of riparian vegetation, can lead to poor water quality, including low levels of dissolved oxygen and high water temperatures (Beam and Braunscheidel 1998).

The Rouge River has also been highly fragmented by 62 dams: 26 are on the Mainstem and its headwater tributaries, 12 in the Upper watershed, 18 in the Middle watershed, and six in the Lower watershed (Roseman et al. 2020). The majority of these dams are in the headwaters that have the most desirable gradient, water quality, and habitat. Historically, two dams were especially devastating, isolating the watershed from the Detroit River (and the Lake Erie ecosystem)—the Wayne Road Dam on the Lower Rouge River and the Henry Ford Estate Dam on the Mainstem. In recent years, the Wayne Road Dam has been removed and the Henry Ford Estate Dam has been modified for fish passage.

The Rouge River watershed is now dominated by urban and suburban development, with heavy industrial development at the confluence of the Rouge and Detroit Rivers. It is the most densely developed watershed in Michigan. Urban land use has a dramatic effect on aquatic ecosystems through increased erosion, drainage and degradation of wetlands, channelization of streams, destabilization of water flow, and more. Another example of human impact is that the Rouge River is crossed by bridges and other stream crossings (i.e., utilities) approximately 1,950 times (Beam and Braunscheidel 1998). Each crossing can increase sediment runoff—sedimentation, erosion, contamination of the river, and constriction or relocation of the stream channel.

Urban stream deserts are defined as areas in a watershed that exhibit no natural surface stream channels because of human development and population growth. The term "desert" connotes a place lacking something—in this case, natural stream channels. Good examples of urban stream deserts in the Rouge River include:

- The more than four-mile channelized concrete portion of the Rouge River downstream from the Henry Ford Estate Dam (fig. 4).
- Sites of river and stream burial, where portions of waterways are intentionally directed into underground pipes and culverts.
- Places where the natural shape of a stream has been altered—what scientists call "morphometry."

Napieralski et al. (2015) have shown that urban stream deserts exist in 23% of the Rouge River watershed, and these areas accounted for 41% of the watershed population in 2010. The authors suggest that:

- Urban stream deserts should be prioritized for remediation and restoration.
- Additional efforts and resources must be devoted to urban stream deserts to improve environmental literacy and provide environmental education opportunities, especially for young people, with the expectation that they can eventually make informed decisions concerning the environment.

Concluding Thoughts

A river reflects the watershed through which it flows. The Rouge River watershed is a complex urban-industrial landscape, and the natural stream network has been modified; streams have been straightened and buried underground in culverts, dams have been built, and places for underground water retention have been created. This poses particular challenges for river revival. Understanding the watershed setting is fundamental to solving pollution problems. But before this urban river revival story progresses further, we need learn about the First Peoples who lived in the watershed and how they respected their waters and showed reverence for the watershed that sustained all life.

LITERATURE CITED

Arnold, C.L., Gibbons, C.J. 1996. "Impervious Surface Coverage: The Emergence of a Key Environmental Indicator." *Journal of the American Planning Association* 62 (2): 243–58.

Beam, J.D., Braunscheidel, J.J. 1998. "Rouge River Assessment." Michigan Department of Natural Resources, Fisheries Division, Lansing.

Napieralski, J., Keeling, R., Dziekan, M., Rhodes, C., Kelly, A., Kobberstad, K. 2015. "Urban Stream Deserts as a Consequence of Excess Stream Burial in Urban Watersheds." *Annals of the Association of American Geographers,* https://doi.org/10.1080/00045608.2015.1050753

Roseman, E.F., Fischer, J., DeBruyne, R.L., and Jackson, S.A. 2020. "Biological and Habitat Assessment of the Lower Rouge River, Michigan, 2018." US Geological Survey Scientific Investigations Report 2020–5009, Reston, Virginia.

Rouge RAP Advisory Council. 1994. "Rouge River Remedial Action Plan Update." Lansing, Michigan.

Rouge RAP Advisory Council. 2004. "Rouge River Remedial Action Plan Revision." Lansing, Michigan.

Southeast Michigan Council of Government (SEMCOG). 2020. "Green Infrastructure in Southeast Michigan." In Hartig, J.H., Francoeur, S.F., Ciborowski, J.J.H., Gannon, J.E., Sanders, C., Galvao-Ferreira, P., Knauss, C.R., Gell, G., Berk, K., eds., *Checkup: Assessing Ecosystem Health of the Detroit River and Western Lake Erie,* 407–17. Great Lakes Institute for Environmental Research Occasional Publication No. 11, University of Windsor, Ontario, Canada.

Southeast Michigan Council of Governments (SEMCOG) and Michigan Department of Natural Resources. 1990. "Remedial Action Plan for the Rouge River Basin." Detroit.

Wiley, M.J., Seelbach, P.W., Bowler, S.P., 1998. "Ecological Targets for Rehabilitation of the Rouge River." School of Natural Resources and Environment, University of Michigan, Ann Arbor.

2 FIRST PEOPLES OF THE ROUGE RIVER

Kay McGowan

For millennia, First Peoples lived in the Rouge River watershed. They fished in the river, hunted the uplands, built canoes to traverse its waters, and gathered at the water's edge for celebrations and ceremonies. They called the Rouge River *mishqua sibe* or *minosagoink*, both terms meaning Singeing Skin River, referring to the place where game was dressed (Gnau 1975). To them, the river was sacred, their lifeblood (Givens-McGowan 2003). When the Europeans arrived, first during the fur-trade era and then during settlement and the process of becoming leaders of the industrial revolution, the immigrants used and abused these waters until the Rouge River became one of the most polluted rivers in the United States. Today, contemporary society needs to learn from First Peoples that the Rouge River is our lifeblood and that all who live in the watershed are responsible for its stewardship.

Mound Builders

The earliest inhabitants of the Rouge River watershed were the "Mound Builders," so called because they built burial and memorial mounds alongside the river (Givens-McGowan 2003). There were two types of mounds. One type was cone-shaped and used for burial. The second type was shaped like a pyramid, with a flat top. There are twelve known mound sites in Wayne County. The largest mound in Detroit was on the east bank of the Rouge River, about a half-mile from where it enters the Detroit River, and is named "The Great Mound of the Rouge River" (fig. 5). This mound was 200 feet long, 300 feet wide, and 20 feet tall. These mounds were destroyed over time.

The Mound Builders' cultures covered a 5,000-year period, 3500 BCE until the 16th century. The largest mound was located at Cahokia in what is today Illinois, built between 950–1100 BCE.

Fig. 5. The Great Mound of the Rouge River located at the river mouth in the community of Delray in southwest Detroit. (Reproduced from *Archeological Atlas of Michigan*, by W.B. Hinsdale [University of Michigan Press, 1931].)

Burial along the Rouge River was important since Mound Builders' cultures believed that ghosts could not cross water when they died. The "Great Mound" was located in the area known today as Delray at the junction of the Detroit and Rouge Rivers. When it was leveled to make way for development, artifacts of many types were found—arrowheads, chisels, pottery, and axes. Human remains were also found. This site was exploited by "pot hunters" and was destroyed in the search for valuable artifacts left by the Mound Builders. The US Bureau of Ethnology believes there were eight groups of Mound Builders, each with a somewhat distinct culture.

In the 1920s, Professor W.B. Hindale at the University of Michigan began excavation at the sites, which were usually referred to as "Indian forts," although these sites had no military connection. Hinsdale's purpose was to find, measure, and photograph these mounds before they were destroyed completely.

First Peoples' Life along the Rouge River

The natural resources of the Rouge River and the water transportation route between the interior lands and the Great Lakes attracted the
Mound Builders and later the Potawatomi, Chippewa, Odawa, and the
Wyandot. Travel by water was easier than land travel. Canoes could easily move through these waters and protected channels to take advantage
of the abundant aquatic life of the river.

Fish were a major source of protein. Most fishing was done from
dugout and birch-bark canoes. First Peoples used fishing nets, weirs,
harpoons, and hooks-and-lines to catch small fish, and some fishing was
done from the riverbanks. A barbed head that had been whittled and
ground out of bone was attached to a wooden spear for spearfishing.
Hooks were made from wood with a bone barb attached. Bones of lake
sturgeon, primarily from the Detroit River, were often used in making
the barbed heads on spears and fishhooks.

The Rouge River has been a major source of food and a venue for
transportation for centuries. From the earliest times, thousands of years
ago, it was also a site of villages, especially once people began to change
from a nomadic existence to settled agriculture. As First Peoples became
less nomadic, they preferred to live near their major food sources, and
fishing on the Rouge River continued to be important.

The river provided other resources as well. Shells were used as cups,
spoons, scraping tools, and storage containers. They were also used in
art projects. Shells in native societies were perceived as feminine, often
being seen as symbols of birth and good fortune. Many tribes collected
shells, and pregnant women who lived by the Rouge River had an easier
time collecting them because they did not have to go far to find their
"good fortune."

Shells from the Rouge River were also important because they were
used as currency, called "wampum." First Peoples would string them
into jewelry, belts, and eventually use them as a medium of monetary
exchange (Garbarino 1985). Wampum was also important in warfare—
"any warrior who killed an enemy won the right to wear an eagle feather,
and the first to kill on a raid got a wampum belt" (Garbarino 1985).

In the winter months the "People of the Three Fires"—the Potawatomi,
Chippewa, and Odawa—would break up into small family clan-related
villages or hunting camps. They would icefish, but were more depen-

dent on hunting, especially for deer. They also depended on food stored from summer. In the winter food was often scarce, so food storage was extremely important. Storage places had to be suitable to keep fish dry and safe from animals, and had to conceal the fish from people who might try to steal it.

The diet of First Peoples living in the Rouge River watershed included local plants and animals, sunflower oil, and seeds of various kinds. Rabbit, antelope, and squirrel were valued for their meat and skin. Walleye was a favorite fish, as were perch, trout, and catfish.

Many indigenous plants grew along the Rouge River, and First Peoples introduced them to the early Europeans. Corn, the most important plant, was used in many ways. Corn soaked in alkaline solutions was a popular native food, today known as hominy. In different regions of the Americas, native peoples domesticated plants, including potatoes, sweet potatoes, manioc, peanuts, tomatoes, cocoa, squash, pumpkins, pineapple, papaya, and avocados, so First Peoples' foods continue to feed the world—imagine Italy without the tomato, or Ireland without the potato. European Americans successfully integrated these new plants into their diets. Corn, from the Maya of Guatemala and Mexico, was especially important as a major food source. Although inedible, corn husks were also used in many ways, to cover food and give it a good corn flavor, most commonly with tamales.

The most frequent way to travel the Rouge River was by canoe. Birchbark canoes were broad and sat high in the water, so they could be used in deep or shallow water. Lightweight, they were easy to carry when the need arose.

Many native societies used sand paintings as part of their healing rituals. They considered the power of healing to be stored in the paintings. These paintings were created by traditional healers, who poured natural grains of sand on the ground. These shamans passed their knowledge from one generation to the next verbally, because native North Americans had no written language.

The Rouge River was important in a variety of other ways to men, women, and children. Children were taught how to swim very early— their lives depended on it. They were instructed never to go alone into the Rouge River because there would be no one to help if a problem arose.

Natives did not locate their villages on the immediate waterfront because animals would not go down to the river to drink if longhouses and villages were right on the water's edge. First Peoples respected and recognized their dependence on the animals and treated them accordingly. The villages would be located away from the river, but within walking distance.

There is a direct correlation between some of the earliest First Peoples' trails and contemporary roads. The Great Sauk Trail ran west from the Rouge River and terminated at Rock Island, Illinois, on the Mississippi River. The road that exists today is US-12, or Michigan Avenue in the Rouge River watershed (Sewick 2016). The St. Joseph Trail, also called Territorial Road, connected the Rouge River to the St. Joseph River that empties into Lake Michigan on the western side of Michigan. This First Peoples' trail became one of the three great east-west routes crossing Michigan in the pioneer days. It too is today part of Michigan Avenue (US-12) in the Rouge River watershed. Trading posts were located all along the Rouge River, reportedly from as early as 1618 BCE (Garbarino 1985). The site of Farmington, Michigan, in the watershed, was chosen by its founder, Art Power, because it was where the Shiawassee Trail crossed the Rouge River (Sewick 2016). The Shiawassee Trail started just west of Detroit and connected to the Shiawassee River that flows into the Saginaw River and eventually Saginaw Bay on Lake Huron. The region we know today as Detroit was a hub for the continent-wide footpaths worn into the earth by First Peoples centuries before Europeans arrived. Today, some of these trails are modern roads and highways, and stops on these trails became important cities such as Farmington. Today, we can still walk in the footsteps of the First Peoples who came before us.

The Rouge River watershed was once home to ten million beavers (Morgan 2017). The beaver was a food source, but it had a more important function to the Wyandot tribe. The Wyandot believed that people had to be buried in beaver skin to reach the spirit world when they died. Villages were located close to beaver habitat to make burials easier. Beavers were important for their fur, their meat, and their castoreum—a secretion still used today in many products, including perfume, alcoholic beverages, baked goods, frozen dairy products, and chewing gum. The Wyandot used castoreum to cure headaches and back problems, and to help with emotional problems such as anxiety and depression. The Wyandot used it like perfume because of its nice scent, and also to enhance the flavor of food.

The Rouge River was sacred to all First Peoples. Tobacco would be placed on the water as an offering to the water spirits, to thank the water for giving people life. Water is often used as a symbol of purity and of cleansing (Givens-McGowan 2003). Many cultures across the world have ceremonies and rituals for giving thanks for water, which is essential to life. The First Peoples showed their deep appreciation by protecting the water, but Europeans did not practice this protection, and the water was polluted.

First Peoples thrived for thousands of years on the lands and waters of the Rouge River watershed and the Great Lakes Basin ecosystem. They developed a deep understanding of the land, water, and all living things, and the interrelationships among them. This intrinsic understanding of animals, plants, and ecosystems is often referred to as "traditional knowledge." Its core components are the knowledge, practices, and traditions that have been passed down through generations since time immemorial. First Peoples understand their responsibility to the creator to care for all things, including the ecosystems where they live. And they also understand their responsibility for stewardship of these ecosystems to future generations. Much can be learned from First Peoples about watershed protection and management, such as

- How we are all part of an ecosystem, and that what we do to our ecosystem we do to ourselves
- How to show reverence for a watershed that sustains all life
- How to consider the impact of our decisions on the next seven generations, in every watershed deliberation
- How to live in harmony with nature
- How to build respectful relationships for water management based on trust
- How to share responsibilities for stewardship of ecosystems

Concluding Thoughts

Water changes each day, and native people recognized this and marveled at its beauty each day. All life is dependent on water. The Rouge River is important to all 48 of the communities it traverses, for their survival, recreation, transportation, and more, and the plants and the animal life are just as dependent on it. Water must be cared for to sustain plant, animal, and human life over the coming generations. The First Peoples of the Rouge River understood this and respected the water.

This ideology of caring for the water, inherited from the earliest times, must be continued. To be able to fish, swim, boat, and hike along the river requires a reverence and recognition that the river is a lifeway for all species. And this must be taught from generation to generation.

The Rouge River was abused and polluted for many years, particularly during the 1940s through the 1970s. We now know this is not sustainable, and people are trying to clean up the river and recognize all the important ecosystem benefits and services it provides. All who live in the watershed of the Rouge River depend on these waters to sustain life. And all must show reverence for it and care for it as their home.

LITERATURE CITED

Garbarino, M.S. 1976. *Native American Heritage*. Prospect Heights, IL: Waveland Press.

Givens-McGowan, K. 2003. "The Wyandot and the River." In Hartig, J.H., ed., *Honoring Our Detroit River: Caring for Our Home*, 23–34. Bloomfield Hills, MI: Cranbrook Institute of Science.

Gnau, T.B. 1975. "Indian Mounds to Dumping Grounds: A History of the Rouge River." *Dearborn Historian* 15 (2): 57–75.

Hinsdale, W.B. 1931. *Archeological Atlas of Michigan*. Ann Arbor: University of Michigan Press.

Morgan, C.L. 2017. *Ottissippi: The Truth About Great Lakes Indian History and the Gateway to the West*. Published by the author; ISBN 978-0-9993923-2-4.

Sewick, P. 2016. "Retracing Detroit's Native American Trails." *Detroit Urbanism*, January 19. https://detroiturbanism.blogspot.com/2016/01/retracing-detroits-native-american.html

3   PUTTING THE ROUGE TO WORK

Nancy Darga

The French voyageurs who explored the Rouge River would be surprised to learn that the winding river and its many tributaries that they trapped along would become one of the most influential working rivers in America and play a major role in revolutionizing mass production globally. First Peoples made the Rouge River Basin their home, attracted by rich soil for farming, abundant timber, and ample fish. European trappers were similarly drawn to the area by the presence of beaver, muskrat, and the riches their furs promised, leading to the establishment of tanneries and trading centers along the river.

The discovery of deposits of sand, salt, iron ore, copper, clay, and lime would provide resources for manufacturing pharmaceuticals and other products. The location on the chain of Great Lakes and across from Canada provided a strategic advantage for shipping.

Most importantly, flowing water provided a readily available source of power for the numerous mills that would come to dot the shorelines and lead to the settlement of early villages around them. Thus, we see that the Rouge watershed possessed many of the natural ingredients needed to support both settlement and manufacturing, and the area became one of the most significant industrial centers in the nation.

Rich in Natural Resources

Carved out by a glacier, the Rouge River and its tributaries are what remains after the glacial Lake Whittlesey drained off. This lake spanned the area from Lake St. Clair to Lake Erie. When it receded, it formed the straits of Detroit. Lake Erie is all that remains of the lake. After landing in 1701, Antoine de la Mothe Cadillac described the land in his journal as being wet prairies with rich fertile soil, with deposits of clay and minerals. He listed a variety of tree species, such as walnut, white oak, red oak, ash, pine, cottonwood, beech, birch, hickory, maple, elm, butternut, cedar, conifers, and basswood. Such trees were eventually harvested for lumber, and fruit trees were cultivated in orchards, which would be the beginnings of an agricultural economy. The wildlife listed by Cadillac was equally diverse and plentiful.

Trapping for furs by the French voyageurs would be the first commercial activity in the Rouge River watershed. Cadillac had been sent to the straits to set up a French outpost to control the rich fur trade; there was concern about protecting the French fur trade in the Great Lakes from the English and the Iroquois natives. For centuries before Cadillac landed, however, the woodland natives had been trapping and farming along the river and trading the fish they harvested. The tribes that followed these early natives were encamped in the area and were willing to trade (see also chapter 2).

Despite the richness of the land, famine plagued the settlers in the late 1780s. Cadillac introduced French wheat to the farming community, and by 1886 Detroit had collectively exported 26 million bushels of wheat. Early farmers changed their focus from harvesting their crops for consumption and local trade to selling to markets outside the state. Settlers exported crops such as Indian corn, peas, beans, wheat, cornmeal, sunflower oil, tobacco, medicinal roots, squash, melons, apples, pears, and lumber. In the 1800s, Michigan produced more lumber than any other state. Included in the harvest were pine, walnut, oak, maple, hickory, butternut, and ash. Further, in 1819 more than 150,000 pounds of maple syrup were produced and sold. The export of fruits and grain became so significant to the local economy in 1837 that the Agricultural and Horticultural Society—later called the Detroit Horticulture Society—was formed to promote farming techniques (Farmer 1890).

Fur Trade: The Great Export

Fur pelts were greatly desired in the 17th and 18th centuries. French aristocrats and affluent members of the middle class were fond of wearing furs. Because France had become the fashion center of Europe under Louis XIV, the wearing of furs spread to other European countries. Broad-brimmed beaver hats came into vogue in the 17th century—King Louis wore one. Native Americans living in the area exchanged pelts and furs for European goods such as guns, cooking utensils, cloth, and jewelry. Many early immigrants discovered that the fur trade was an easier and more profitable existence than the drudgery of farming. By 1771, Detroit had become the center of the Great Lakes fur trade, with numerous tanneries dotting the shores of the river. The pelts shipped from Detroit included bear, elk, deer, marten, raccoon, mink, lynx, muskrat, opossum, wolf, fox, and of course beaver. Beaver pelts were so valued that the prices for goods in Detroit were expressed in terms of beaver or buckskin. A "buck" referred to a buckskin, leading to the slang for a dollar as a "buck."

Future growth in fur trading became possible when a German immigrant, Traugott Schmidt, brought with him Germany's most advanced methods of fur and pelt processing in 1852. The complex he built near the Detroit River originally consisted of eighteen separate buildings. Traugott Schmidt & Sons became a major trading and manufacturing center, the most active industry at that time. By 1892, the factory was producing 200,000 dressed skins every day. The complex was lost to fire; however, the main fur tannery structure was rebuilt. Traugott died in 1897, leaving the company to his sons, Albert and Edward, and eventually to his son-in-law Arnold Hoffman. The fur trade declined in the late 1800s due to overharvesting. The building was redeveloped in 1983 and is now known as "Trappers Alley," located in today's Greektown area of downtown (Dittrich Furs 2021).

Waterpower

The initial First Peoples to live along the banks of the Rouge River were the Woodland natives, as is evident from the burial mounds they left. The Indian encampments along the river gave way to settlements and French ribbon farms (strips of land that extended a mile and a half inland from the banks of the Detroit River, giving each farm a narrow river frontage). The soils of the Rouge River basin were found to be mostly clay and large sections were swampy. Many early settlers contracted "swamp fever," so there was some reticence about establishing homesteads in the area. The first home built outside of the Fort Pontchartrain stockade was not erected until 1740, by farmer Jean Baptiste Baudry. Homesteading slowly increased, after the Northwest Territories were formed, which includes the area of Michigan, created by an ordinance of the Continental Congress in 1787 (Detroit Historical Society 2021a).

Farming within the Rouge River watershed eventually expanded as the United States opened a land office in Detroit in 1804. A shipyard was built on the Rouge River by the US government and used during the War of 1812. Bricks were made from the clay on the banks of the river to erect twelve buildings in Dearborn, which became the Detroit Arsenal in 1833 (Gnau 1975). Brick-making would become an industry of its own as many brickyards and operations were established throughout the basin.

It was not just the land that enticed settlers up the river—it was the power of the water. The steady flow of the Rouge River was harnessed by mills erected along its shores to grind grains, make cider, and produce lumber. As mills were built along the river, settlements started to grow around them. These mills functioned as community centers and social hubs, with many of them serving additional purposes, such as providing sites for post offices and meeting halls. For this reason, the roads leading to these mills often became stagecoach or mail routes.

Mills located along the branches of the Rouge River prospered due to its constant flow of water. The mill operations were a day's ride by carriage to Detroit markets. The mills along this waterway varied greatly. One of the oldest mills on record was a gristmill built in 1776 by Jacques Duperon Baby at the main forks of the Upper Rouge River. Eventually he had two gristmills at the same site. This practice of sharing mill ponds between mills became common because it was cost-effective and eliminated damming the river at another point. The Coon's Mill built in 1850 by Joseph Coon on the Middle Rouge is of note in that Henry Ford brought his family's grain there to be milled when he was 10 years old (fig. 6). It is thought that this mill spurred his interest in waterpower. During the time of the Civil War, Coonsville had a church, school, and general store. When the mill closed, the settlement around it became a ghost town.

The location that became the best known for its mills was the Northville and Plymouth area, along the Walled Lake branch of the Rouge River. The mills built there were at the highest elevation of the watershed and connected to a tributary, Johnson Creek, that provided cold spring water to power the mills. Many artesian wells in the area could be used commercially. One of the first mills in the upper reach of the Rouge River in the village of Northville was built by John Miller in 1827. The mill used a crude split boulder to grind grain. The next mill at the site was Yerkes Gristmill, followed by a sawmill built by James A. Dubuar in 1890.

Fig. 6. Coon's Grist Mill, where Henry Ford brought his family's grain to be milled, 1850. (Credit: Nancy Darga, personal collection.)

The Dubuar sawmill produced wood for pulleys, wheelbarrows, wood moldings, and air guns. It was bought by Henry Ford in 1919, becoming the first Village Industry Plant (the Ford Valve Plant) in Ford's experimental project; these plants were small parts factories in converted former mills, powered by hydroelectric generators. Ford Motor operated the mill until 1981. Currently the plant is privately owned, and its water wheel has been restored.

The village of Northville would become the home base of numerous mills as the village evolved from farming to manufacturing. The Northville area's importance in manufacturing was second only to Detroit, due to waterpower (Eagle Steam Printing and Engraving 1892). By 1832, Northville had developed a gristmill, sawmill, cider mill, a wood-turning shop, and a foundry.

In addition to mills, innovation birthed many businesses, not only in Northville but throughout the basin. In 1833, Charles T. Roer founded the first commercial milk-condensing plant in the country. In 1873, C.G. Harrington invented the folding school desk. He renamed his foundry the Michigan School Furniture Company, and his products were shipped nationwide. After the plant burned in 1874, it was rebuilt and expanded to manufacture school and church furniture, bells, and refrigerators. With the completion of the railroad to Northville in 1870, worldwide markets became accessible. In 1884, the company was incorporated as the Globe Furniture Company, and their products were shipped internationally to Europe and South America. The company split into three manufacturing entities in 1899—the Globe Furniture Company, the American Bell and Foundry Company, and the American Shade Cloth Company. Bells from the foundry were famous worldwide and were shipped as far away as Egypt and West Africa (*Northville Record* 1899).

The Stimpson Scale and Electric Company manufactured scales from 1902 to 1927, becoming a noted operation on the river. Northville Laboratories, on Johnson Creek, started making extracts and flavorings in 1914. The company still operates on the creek, making and exporting breakfast bars. The water from the artesian wells in Northville was thought to have healing power, and the Deep Spring Water Company, founded in 1917, started bottling it and shipping it to Detroit. With Henry Ford purchasing the old Northville/Dubuar Mill in 1919, business picked up along the Rouge River. Edward A. (Eddie) Stinson purchased the old Stimpson factory in 1927 and manufactured Stinson closed-cabin airplanes (fig. 7). The operation outgrew the site along the Middle Rouge and moved to the Lower Rouge River in the city of Wayne. Thus airplane production began the Rouge River's trajectory to become an artery for the future production of war armaments (*Northville Record* 1932).

Mills were built along the four branches of the Rouge, from Detroit all the way to the headwaters. Some of these mills have had a lasting impact and still exist today. In the prosperous village of Waterford (now Northville Township), three brothers, Marshal, Wadsworth, and Samuel Mead, built and operated Mead's Mill. The original Mead's Gristmill, built in 1837, was once the largest in Michigan, with an eighteen-foot waterwheel producing power for grinding more than 200 barrels of flour per day. The village had several industries: a sawmill, a barrel-stave factory, a sash factory, and an iron foundry.

The mill burned down and was rebuilt twice before the Civil War. Many believe it was burned because it was part of the Underground Railroad—Samuel Mead was a known abolitionist. Nankin Mills, located further downstream, is also believed to have been a station on the Underground Railroad. Marcus Swift, a noted abolitionist working

Fig. 7. Stinson airplane factory, located in the former Stimpson Scale and Electric Company, 1927. (Credit: Northville Historical Society Archive Collection.)

with Samuel Mead, had a farmstead nearby. The foundry closed in 1888. Henry Ford purchased the mill site in 1925 for his Village Industry Plant project.

Newburgh Lake was first created by a settler named Nicholas Bovee when he dammed the Rouge River for his Bovee Cider Mill (Newburgh Mill) in 1870. Newburgh was an important apple-producing area, and the mill produced up to 25,000 gallons of cider per year. In 1889, the Detroit Urban Railway built an interurban rail line that accommodated a type of self-propelled electric trolly, through Newburgh, connecting the eastern villages in Wayne County to the village of Northville. The village of Newburgh was incorporated into the township of Livonia in 1835. The mill was purchased by Henry Ford and rebuilt in 1934 as the last Village Industry Plant along the Rouge.

Transition from Farms to Factories

It is no surprise that the first explorers of the shores of Detroit came by boat—the "Straits of Detroit" is located on the chain of the Great Lakes. Early settlers found the land fertile, rich with timber, wildlife, and fish, but getting their farm products to markets was difficult. Exporting goods was limited to shipping or slow travel over rustic roads at great cost. It took more than a year for exported furs to reach their destination overseas and payment to come back to trappers. National efforts were underway to improve shipping, and being connected to the Great Lakes and located across the Detroit River from Canada gave the Rouge River Basin a unique advantage as it became a hub for shipping.

The dynamics of trade changed as several developments around the turn of the 19th century made it practical to export goods. The Detroit River was declared a "public thoroughfare" by President James Monroe in December 1819, allowing for federal investment in shipping improvements (Burton 2017). In 1818, the *Walk-in-the-Water*, the first steamboat on the upper Great Lakes, made water travel from Buffalo, New York, to Detroit easier (Detroit Historical Society 2021b). A tax was placed on wharves in 1804 to keep them repaired and operational. The first public stagecoaches started in 1822 with a limited run from Detroit. In 1837, coaches started going from Detroit to Chicago, expanding the reach to national markets. Steamboat travel would soon allow passengers and freight to reach the upper Great Lakes (Farmer 1890).

Once the Erie Canal to Buffalo, New York was completed in 1825, one could travel from Detroit to New York in five days. This achievement prompted the opening of the Welland Canal in 1831, connecting Lake Ontario to Lake Erie. This allowed for the shipment of iron and copper to foundries in Detroit (Raso 2021). In 1837, ferryboats on the Detroit River developed the ability to break ice to keep shipping going year-round. These developments shortened shipping times and made it possible to transport perishable goods. By 1850, shipping had become Detroit's biggest industry.

Steady improvements in transporting goods from Detroit gave factories along the Rouge River an advantage in reaching national and international markets. The opening of the Michigan Central Railway Tunnel under the Detroit River to Canada in 1910 and the Detroit Windsor Tunnel for vehicles in 1930 spurred expansion of many industries along the Rouge River. The Ambassador Bridge opened in 1929, and to this day it is the busiest international border crossing in North America in terms of trade volume.

While efforts were being made to improve shipping and the transport of goods between Michigan and Canada, the "Good Roads Movement" took root as the League of American Wheelmen, a club of bicy-clists, began calling for improved roads on which to ride in the 1870s (Kelly 2021). Edward Hines, an avid cyclist, served as the Detroit Wheel-man's (a state affiliate of the League of American Wheelmen) chief coun-cil in 1890 and started campaigning for better roads. He was influen-tial in creating the first state highway commission in 1892 (Trepagnier 1938). He befriended Horatio "Good Roads" Earle and encouraged Earle to become the chair of the Michigan Good Roads Association and the head of the Michigan Highway Department. Hines became one of the founders of the Wayne County Road Commission in 1906; many road-way innovations were made under his direction, including the first mile of concrete pavement on Woodward Avenue in 1909 and the introduc-tion of the "safety stripe," a white line marking driving lanes in 1911. The first below-ground-level limited-access freeway, the Davison Freeway, was built in 1941, with a national interstate system soon to follow. Tre-mendous resources were allocated to road construction and rivers were relocated or straightened to accord with road alignments and bridges. These improvements to transportation and connections to international markets would have a big impact on the creation of an industrial corri-dor along the Detroit and Rouge Rivers. In honor of Hines's impact on the roads in Michigan, as well as his role in the formation of the Wayne County Road Commission, a 17-mile parkway from Dearborn to North-ville along the Middle Rouge River was built in 1949 and named Edward N. Hines Drive.

Commercial Fish Farming Begins

Cadillac's earliest journals in the 1700s indicate that fish were plentiful and diverse in the creeks and rivers flowing through the region. Records kept at the docks in Detroit in the early 1830s indicate that more than 3,500 barrels of fish were exported each year. The types of fish docu-mented in the shipping logs are whitefish, sturgeon, pickerel, pike, perch, black bass, catfish, sunfish, and bullheads. Fish were a common trade item, as both the natives and settlers caught fish for both imme-diate consumption and exchange. The establishment of commercial fish hatcheries in the early 1800s would have an exponential impact on fish-ing as an industry.

The first national fish hatchery was started in Michigan in 1874 by

Ponds, U. S. Fish Hatchery, Northville, Mich.

Fig. 8. US Fish Hatchery along the Rouge River in Northville, Michigan, circa 1880. (Credit: Northville Historical Society Archive Collection.)

Nelson W. Clark, a prominent fish breeder from Clarkston, and his son Frank (Farmer 1890). They moved their operation to the village of Northville in 1876 along the Johnson Creek, a cold-water tributary of the Middle Rouge River (fig. 8). Mr. Clark leased springs above the village. The hatchery covered 17 acres, 5 of which were under water. Nelson Clark died in 1880. The federal government leased the hatchery from his son, Frank N. Clark, until 1890, when it was purchased by the US Fish Commission (Fetch 2021).

Frank Clark, who served as the president of the National Fisheries, died in 1920. William W. Thayer took over as superintendent on Clark's death. He would serve in that capacity for 20 years. The US Fish Commission kept the fish hatchery operating until 1935. The US Fish and Wildlife Service, National Fish Hatcheries, then took over and operated the hatchery until 1957 (Thayer 1957). Later the hatchery operated in a cooperative agreement with the University of Michigan. The last remaining hatchery buildings were razed in 1968. The area is now a public park named Fish Hatchery Park.

Minerals and Mills Give Rise to Manufacturing

From the 1700s to the 1800s, land within the Rouge River basin was cultivated for farming. In the 1800s, many farming efforts evolved into factories as rich mineral deposits were discovered in the soil, aiding the production of goods. Predominant along the river are glacial till and sandy loams with deposits of clay and lime. The sand proved to be of high quality, suitable for the production of glass, leading to the establishment of several glass-manufacturing shops such as the Detroit Glass Works and the American Plate Glass Company. Many natural beds of clay were suitable for plaster and brick. Limestone was also plentiful. The clay was found to have a good consistency for brick manufacturing. John Haggerty built a brickyard on such a deposit in the Dearborn area.

A special deposit of fine-grain clay in the Northville region of the watershed resulted in the construction of a stone pottery facility erected in 1847 by Asa Harmon and his son John. They manufactured tiles in a yard kiln invented by John until 1888, when the clay deposit was depleted (Harmon 1927). Grindstone quarries were mined north of Detroit and on Grosse Ile in the Detroit River. Early settlers used these stones to set up their gristmills. The quarries continued to be mined for other industrial uses.

In addition to natural resources being used in manufacturing, bones from the killing of bison on the plains were used as raw materials. The Michigan Carbon Works Company, established by Deming Larves and William Hooper in 1879, burned and distilled bones into animal charcoal to meet the growing demands of the sugar industry for filtering and purifying sugar. Bone black (used as a pigment in paint and in refining sugar), fertilizer, and gelatin were being produced at peak levels during the late 1880s and early 1890s. The company purchased the Harbaugh Farm in Springwells Township (now part of the Delray neighborhood of Detroit) on the Rouge River to expand operations. This campus was called "Boneville," and it produced 5,000 tons of bone black per year. By 1883, Michigan Carbon Works had become the most extensive and complete carbon works in the United States (*Detroit Evening News* 1885), and by 1892, it was the largest industry in Detroit. The plant covered 100 acres and employed 750 people. Production continued well into the 1920s. When American Agricultural Chemical Company (Agrico) began consolidating bone-char-producing companies, Michigan Carbon Works became a division of Agrico. Ebonex Corporation purchased the operation from Agrico, the division started by Michigan Carbon Works, when they pulled out of Detroit and moved to Melvindale, Michigan; they still produce bone black (Ebonex Corporation 2021).

After a state surveyor discovered iron ore and copper in the Marquette region of Michigan's Upper Peninsula in 1844, that area became the source of materials for manufacturing nationwide. The availability of these metals in southeast Michigan would spur the mass production of parts, machines, motors, and ultimately, the automobile. The "Lake Superior" iron and copper extracted from the mines in the Upper Peninsula proved to have a high grade of purity. Foundries, metal shops, and factories expanded because metal was accessible and the need for metal products and machines kept growing. The Detroit region was the site for most of the largest copper smelting works in the United States. In the 1800s, Michigan's Upper Peninsula had the largest iron mine in the world.

With the outbreak of the Civil War in 1861, the demand for iron grew, and federal funding to build military roads and shipping facilities to transport the metals downstate was a major factor in farms turning into factories. By 1886, the area had multiple furnaces turning out pig iron (Farmer 1890). With the availability of metals and other raw materials, the manufacturing plants blossomed. In 1864, the first Bessemer-type steel was produced at the Eureka Iron Works in Wyandotte, downstream of the mouth of the Rouge River, laying the groundwork for railroad, stove, and automobile manufacturing in the region (Detroit Historical Society 2021c).

By the turn of the century, multiple commercial operations were based in the Rouge River watershed. They are too numerous to list, but they provided products and services ranging from ship building at the John Clark Shipyard and Drydock to railroad-car building at the Michigan Car Company. The capacity to manufacture metal parts and machinery continued to improve. A Detroiter, William Davis, invented the railroad refrigerator car in 1868, giving rise to new industries dealing with perishable goods along the Rouge River.

Numerous metal factories were opening in the basin, such as the Detroit Copper and Brass Rolling Works, Eureka Iron Co., Detroit Steel and Spring Co., Middlebrook & Post Manufacturing, and the National

Pin Company. The area also became known for manufacturing machines and engines, by companies such as the Fulton Iron and Engine Works, the Michigan Galvin Brass and Iron Works, and Detroit Car Wheel (Farmer 1890). Metal production would get more sophisticated as Donald B. McLouth, a Detroit scrap dealer, established McLouth Steel on the Detroit River in 1934; it became the first plant in North America to make steel via the basic oxygen process. Easy access to metal and machine shops helped the Rouge River become a major player in the evolving auto industry.

The Rise of the Auto and Steel Industry

When Brady King drove the first gasoline-powered car down Woodward Avenue and Henry Ford drove his Quadricycle down the streets of Detroit in 1896, automobiles were already being made in Germany. Production vehicles began appearing in 1887 when Karl Benz developed a petrol- or gasoline-powered automobile. Despite Germany's lead, the numerous machine and carriage shops, metal production, and a spirit of innovation would soon create a synergy for motor vehicle production. By 1901 Ransom E. Olds had produced the first practical American car, and Henry Ford started the Henry Ford Company. More than 15 million Ford Model Ts, created in 1908, would be sold worldwide. Manufacturing was being revolutionized with the invention of the automated assembly line at the Ford Motor Company's Highland Park Plant.

The availability of steel was key to mass-producing cars. Near the mouth of the Rouge River, furniture mogul Samuel Zug purchased a 334-acre lot in 1859. The need for industrial land grew tremendously during the early 20th century, and several blast furnaces for steel production were built on the island beginning in 1902. These steel mills have changed hands several times and were at one time owned by the now-defunct National Steel. Now called the Great Lakes Works, the mills are owned by United States Steel. In 2020, US Steel substantially reduced its operations along the Detroit River in the city of River Rouge and in Ecorse. Zug Island is one of only a handful of locations in the United States that produce coke, an ingredient used in making steel (Detroit Historical Society 2021d).

Just up the Rouge River from these steel mills and Zug Island, Henry Ford built the Ford Rouge Complex in 1917. Its operations were so immense that national companies such as Marathon Oil relocated facilities from their base in Houston, Texas in order to better serve the Ford factories of the industrial complex. Explained in detail in chapter 4, the plant had a worldwide impact and became a major force during World Wars I and II.

Arsenal of Democracy

With the availability of raw materials, mass-production practices, and a well-networked distribution system, southeast Michigan became the powerhouse of automobile production worldwide. During World Wars I and II auto plants switched production from cars to military vehicles, planes, and machine guns, earning a name for the region as the "Arsenal of Democracy." The Ford Rouge Complex, shipping via the Willow Run Airport, became a major source of armaments during the wars (see chapter 4).

Car companies and parts shops would not be the only manufacturers involved in war production; the Burroughs Corporation, located along the Middle Rouge in Plymouth, would start manufacturing the Norden bombsight, changing the trajectory of World War II. In 1904, the American Arithmometer Company of St. Louis, Missouri, moved to Detroit and changed its name to the Burroughs Adding Machine Company. It produced and sold adding machines invented by William Seward Burroughs. In 1931, it built a production facility in Plymouth. It was soon the largest adding-machine company in America. During the war years production at Burroughs Machine was restricted to military purposes only. The Norden bombsight was invented by Carl L. Norden, a Dutch citizen and recent immigrant, for the US Navy's Bureau of Ordinance. It improved the accuracy of bombs released at high altitudes. The Plymouth factory started producing the Norden bombsight in 1941, along with other machines for the Army, Navy, and war contractors. Frederick Entwhistle, the Navy's chief of bombsight development, called it revolutionary, and its design was good enough that it would be used throughout World War II and up to the Vietnam War (Norden Bombsights by Moore 2021).

In 1944, the Burroughs Co. was awarded the Army-Navy E "for outstanding achievement for its production of war materials." After the war, Burroughs continued its research and development of electronic devices and technology, leading to the production of computers, which they specialize in today (Burroughs Adding Machine Company 2021).

From Water Wheels to Hydroelectric Power

The Rouge River became a "living laboratory" in one of the most visionary industrial experiments of the 20th century. The auto pioneer Henry Ford, raised on a farm located in the Rouge River watershed, created a system of Village Industry Plants powered by hydroelectric generators, as mentioned earlier. From 1918 to 1944, he converted 32 mills along the Rouge, Raisin, and Huron Rivers into small shops making parts for his factories. Farmers could work in these plants during the winter months and farm during the summer, thus keeping them, as he stated, with "one foot on the soil and one in the factory."

Ironically, even as he was investing in the renovation of these old mills, the Ford Motor Company was building the world's largest integrated factory, the Ford Rouge Complex (see chapter 4). Being a farm boy, Henry Ford wanted to stop the mass migration of farmers to the very factories he was building. This experiment in converting old mills into hydro-powered machine shops, he believed, would provide enough income in the off season to keep the farmers at home working their farms. Many of the dams that powered these mills were no longer operational. Looking for assistance in rebuilding these dams and the roads going to the mills, Henry Ford needed a partner. As a former Wayne County Road Commissioner, Ford was aware that the Road Commission had become a Park Trustee in 1923 and was developing a parkway along the Middle and Lower Branches of the Rouge River. In a mutually beneficial agreement, the Road Commission rebuilt the mill-pond dams of Nankin Mills, Newburgh, Wilcox, and Phoenix (fig. 9). In exchange, the land would be deeded over to the Park Trustees to be incorporated into the parkway, which took place in 1948 after Henry's death.

Each of the mills had made a unique contribution that influenced the development of the state and eventually the nation over the decades. During the Civil War these mills had been part of the route to freedom for escaping slaves. Later, many of them provided electricity to neighboring businesses and residents. During World War II, Ford converted their operation to manufacturing armaments to protect democracy.

At the Phoenix Mill, the plant employed women who fabricated gen-

Fig. 9. The Newburgh Dam was built in a joint effort between the Wayne County Road Commission, the Ford Motor Company, and the New Deal Works Progress Administration, 1934. (Credit: Nancy Darga, personal collection.)

erator parts for the B-24 Bomber and the M7 machine gun, becoming some of the first "Rosie the Riveters" (fig. 10). The Cherry Hill Mill in Canton, Michigan, would provide a peaceful setting for "shell-shocked" veterans to work in. The Waterford Mill would introduce the "Jo-Block," named after Carl E. Johansson. Henry Ford purchased this famous gauge-making operation from Johansson in 1923. This measuring device allowed the joining of sheet metal within an accuracy of micrometers. "Jo-Blocks," or gauge blocks, became a means of length standardization used by industry. All of these Village Industry Mills were a part of the Middle Rouge Parkway (Hines Drive) from 1948 until 2020, when they were sold to private entities for commercial use (Tobin 1985).

The Middle Rouge Parkway Plan

Although the passage of Public Act 90 of 1913 allowed the Wayne County supervisors to institute a county park system, the assemblage of

Fig. 10. Women assembling electrical parts at the Phoenix Mill, 1922. (Photograph courtesy Benson Ford Library.)

parkland did not launch until the Wayne County Road Commission was made a Park Trustee in 1923. Edward Hines was named chairman, William F. Butler secretary, and John S. Haggerty trustee. These men would revolutionize transportation and roadway construction in America, and the preservation of the river lands into a parkway system is one of their greatest legacies.

The greatest achievement of the Road Commission as a Park Trustee was the development of the Middle Rouge Parkway, now referred to as Hines Park. The parkway was started through a gift of property in 1922 at the intersection of Five Mile Road and Northville Road along the Phoenix Lake Mill Pond in Northville. Land acquisition would continue even through the Great Depression years. This parkway encompassed the lands along the Rouge River from the city of Dearborn to Northville. These parcels were acquired over time and strung together like pearls in a necklace, joined together piece by piece. The Park Trustees also continued acquiring lands along the Lower Rouge River, these parcels spanning from the city of Dearborn to Canton Township. After Henry Ford's death in 1948, the Ford Motor Company made good on Ford's promise to deed over to the Wayne County Road Commission, as Park Trustees, the Village Industry Plants and the surrounding land to be incorporated into the Middle Rouge Parkway (Hines Park). This would mark the turn from using the Rouge River solely for industrial uses to preserving it as a community resource.

LITERATURE CITED

Note: All websites accessed over August 22–23, 2021.

Burroughs Adding Machine Company. 2021. Burroughs Plymouth Plant. http://www.burroughsinfo.com/plymouth-plant.html

Burton, C.M. 2017. *The City of Detroit, 1701–1922*. Bayern, Germany: Jazzybee Verlag.

Detroit Evening News. 1885. March 27.

Detroit Historical Society. 2021a. "French Detroit." http://detroithistorical.org/learn/timeline-detroit/french-detroit-1700-1760

Detroit Historical Society. 2021b. "Early American Detroit." https://detroithistorical.org/learn/timeline-detroit/early-american-detroit-1787-1820

Detroit Historical Society. 2021c. "Industrial Detroit (1860–1900)." https://detroithistorical.org/learn/timeline-detroit/industrial-detroit-1860-1900

Detroit Historical Society. 2021d. "Zug Island." https://detroithistorical.org/learn/encyclopedia-of-detroit/zug-island

Detroit Windsor Tunnel. 2021. https://www.dwtunnel.com/history/

Dittrich Furs. 2021. "Fur Industry in Detroit." http://www.dittrichfurs.com/about-us/fur-industry-in-detroit

Eagle Steam Printing and Engraving Company. 1892. "Northville: The Ideal Suburban Village." Northville, MI.

Ebonex Corporation. 2021. "Bone Black Pigments." http://ebonex.com/history.html

Farmer, S. 1890. *History of Detroit and Wayne County*. 3rd ed. Vol. I. New York: Silas Farmer & Co., for Munssel & Co.

Fetch, M. 2011. "Northville Fish Hatchery Gave Northville National Prominence." Patch, Northville, MI. https://patch.com/michigan/northville/fish-hatchery-gave-northville-national-prominence

Gnau, T.B. 1975. "Indian Mounds to Dumping Grounds: A History of the Rouge River." *Dearborn Historian* 15 (2): 57–75.

Harman, F.S. 1927. Northville pamphlet, University of Michigan Historical Collections, Northville File, Ann Arbor.

Kelly, S.C. 2021. "Good Roads Movement." Britannica, www.britannica.com/event/Good-Roads-movement

Michigan Department of Natural Resources. 2021. "Hatcheries & Weirs." https://www.michigan.gov/dnr/0,4570,7-350-79136_79236_80247---,00.html

Norden Bombsights by Moore. 2021. "History." https://nordenbombsightsbymoore.com/norden-bombsight-history

Northville Record. 1899. "History of the Globe Furniture Company." Northville, MI.

Northville Record. 1932. "Death of Eddie Stinson." Northville, MI.

Raso, A. 2021. "The Welland Canal Information Site." https://wellandcanal.com/hist.htm

Thayer, W.W. 1957. "Weekly Work Reports." Northville Historical Society Archives, Northville, MI.

Tobin, J. 1985. "Henry Ford and His Village Industries in Southeastern Michigan." Master's thesis, Department of History, Eastern Michigan University, Ypsilanti.

Trepagnier, W.J. 1938. *Motor News Magazine.* AAA Michigan, Dearborn.

Brian James Egen and John H. Hartig

Most people know Henry Ford as industrialist, innovator, developer of the assembly line, and the man who helped put the world on wheels. He was obsessed with innovation and constantly learning. It has often been said that he had one foot in industry and one in agriculture. Before it was even readily accepted as a potentially fruitful line of research, he experimented with how agricultural crops such as soybeans could be used to make plastics for automobiles. Today, managers call this integrative thinking and practice in management a "systems' approach" to improving quality, quantity, and productivity, and Ford was a systems thinker and innovator before it was fashionable. This chapter investigates the life and times of Henry Ford in the context of the Rouge River watershed, where he grew up, established a home for his wife and family, built the largest integrated factory in the world at that time, and became one of the world's greatest industrialists.

Early Childhood and Formative Years

Henry Ford was born into a farming family, on July 30, 1863—just three weeks after the climactic Battle of Gettysburg. He was the oldest of six children. The family farm was in what is now Dearborn, Michigan, in the heart of Rouge River watershed. He was born during the height of the Civil War, and his family was affected personally by this pivotal moment in America's history. Two of his uncles, Barney and John Litogot, had enlisted in the famous 24th Michigan Volunteer Infantry regiment. John was killed in December 1862 and Barney was wounded at Gettysburg on July 1, 1863.

Early in his childhood, Ford showed some of the characteristics that would make him successful, powerful, and famous. He organized other boys to build rudimentary waterwheels and steam engines. He was fascinated with full-sized steam engines and became friends with men who ran them. At age 13 he started repairing watches. Working on a small bench in his bedroom, he would take watches apart, study them, and learn the rudiments of machine design. Clearly, at a very young age he demonstrated mechanical ability, a penchant for leadership, and an eagerness to learn by trial and error. These traits would become the foundation of his whole career.

For eight years he attended a one-room school, when he wasn't helping on the farm. At age 16 he left home to find work in Detroit's machine shops. From 1880 to 1882, he worked as an apprentice machinist at the Detroit Dry Dock Company, where he learned a great deal about heavy machinery. During his apprenticeship he received $2.50 a week, but room and board cost $3.50, so he had to work nights repairing clocks and watches to make ends meet.

In 1891 Ford became an engineer with the Edison Illuminating Company, and within two and a half years he rose to the position of chief engineer. By 1896 he had completed his first horseless carriage, the "Quadricycle," so called because the chassis of the four-horsepower vehicle was mounted on four bicycle wheels. But Ford was not satisfied—his big dream was to create an affordable automobile for the masses. Receiving backing from various investors, he formed the Detroit Automobile Company in 1899. In 1901, he formed the Ford Motor Company. He would introduce his famous Model T in 1908 and build it for two decades. By mastering the art of mass production with the assembly line, Ford built 15 million Model Ts (fig. 11). It is one of the most important cars in history, because it was one of the first to be sold at an affordable cost, making it easy for people to travel from place to place for business and pleasure. The Model T quickly became prized for its low cost, durability, versatility, and ease of maintenance. Today, historians recognize that the Model T put America on wheels and helped forge a manufacturing revolution. Ford's worldview is captured in the following quote:

> The gifted man bears his gifts into the world, not for his own benefit, but for the people among whom he is placed; for the gifts are not his, he himself is a gift to the community.

Henry Ford is known for many innovations in agriculture and industry, but he is also remembered for his controversial anti-Semitic views.

Fig. 11. Henry Ford with the 10 millionth Model T and the 1896 Quadricycle, 1924. (Photograph courtesy of The Henry Ford.)

In the early 1920s, his newspaper, the *Dearborn Independent*, began to publish anti-Semitic editorials, with every front page reading, "The International Jew: The World's Problem." Tension and pressure from critics mounted. Ford was eventually sued for libel by a leading Jewish activist named Aaron Sapiro, but prior to the trial he closed his newspaper and made a cash settlement (Pavuluri 2015). He would release a formal apology. Although he may most often be remembered as the face of 20th-century innovation, his anti-Semitic views hurt his reputation.

Rouge Plant

Henry Ford had a vision of an ideal automotive "ore to assembly" complex, where every element of production could be processed, manufactured, and assembled in one place. It was a revolutionary idea at that time. To achieve his vision, in 1915 he purchased nearly 2,000 acres along the banks of the Rouge River, just upstream of the confluence with the Detroit River at Zug Island.

Fig. 12. The construction of Ford Motor Company's Rouge Plant was completed in 1928, making it the largest integrated factory in the world. (Photograph courtesy The Henry Ford.)

Ford began construction on the Rouge Plant in 1917 and completed it in 1928. It was the largest integrated factory complex in the world (fig. 12), 1 mile wide and 1.5 miles long. It included 93 buildings with nearly 16 million square feet of factory floor space and 120 miles of conveyors. With its own docks on the lower Rouge River, 100 miles of interior railroad track, its own power plant and ore processing, the Rouge Plant could mass-produce automobiles from raw materials in this single complex. Over 100,000 workers were employed there in the 1930s.

World War I

To combat German submarine attacks on US cargo ships during World War I, the US government needed what they called "submarine chasers,"

Fig. 13. An Eagle boat being launched at the Ford Rouge Plant in Dearborn, Michigan, 1918. (Photograph courtesy The Henry Ford.)

and they needed them quickly. The government immediately thought of Henry Ford because he was at the forefront of mass production of automobiles. He was given the blueprints for a 200-foot steel submarine chaser called an Eagle boat, and he immediately put his engineers to work. They came back with a plan that was, as expected, revolutionary. He would adapt the site on the Rouge River and produce Eagle boats using the same mass-production techniques used for his Model T, but on a larger scale. At the time, his Ford Rouge complex was not even fully developed, yet four months after the company received the order in 1918, the first Eagle boat was launched into a Rouge River boat slip (fig. 13). Although the government had contracted with Ford Motor Company for 100 Eagle boats, only 60 were produced before the war came to an end (Cianflone 1973). Eagle boats were not the only product made by Ford Motor Company to help with the Allied victory in World War I. It also produced helmets, tanks, airplane engines, Model T cars, trucks, ambulances, and Fordson tractors.

World War II

Following the Japanese attack on Pearl Harbor in 1941, the United States plunged into World War II. President Franklin Delano Roosevelt recognized the need to help supply Europe with the implements of war and called for the United States to become the "Arsenal of Democracy" (Blaime 2014). Detroit responded in 1942 by ceasing all civilian production and converting to military production with one single purpose—to win the war. The Ford Rouge Plant was converted to tank production.

In 1943, Detroit-area companies received contracts worth about $14 billion, a massive amount at that time, constituting 10% of all US military output during that year. By 1944, Detroit was the leading supplier of military goods in the United States. Between 1942 and 1945 Detroit produced nearly $29 billion of military output. Approximately 610,000 metropolitan Detroit people were employed in this military production, which produced products ranging from ball bearings to bombers, trucks, and tanks.

Oil Pollution during and after World War II

Today, it is hard to imagine the volumes of oil and other pollutants being discharged into the Rouge River during and after World War II. Remember, there were no regulations at that time. The single goal was to win the war. Oil, heavy metals, and many other contaminants were simply discharged into the Rouge and Detroit Rivers, in unbelievable amounts during the war years. Everyone knows that oil is a significant environmental pollutant that can kill wildlife and cause substantial ecological damage. It is generally accepted that about one gallon of oil will contaminate approximately one million gallons of water. During 1946–48, the US Department of Health, Education, and Welfare (1962), estimated that 5.93 million gallons of oil and other petroleum products were released into the Rouge and Detroit Rivers each year. By extrapolation, this 5.93 million gallons of oil was enough to pollute 5.93 trillion gallons of water. The volume of water in the western basin of Lake Erie is approximately 6.4 trillion gallons. Thus, during 1946–1948, enough oil was being discharged into the Rouge and Detroit Rivers each year to pollute almost the entire western basin of Lake Erie, including all Michigan, Ohio, and Ontario waters.

This massive oil pollution took its toll in the winter of 1948. It was a particularly cold winter, and the Detroit River virtually froze over, leaving only a few areas of open water. As they had done for millennia, migrating waterfowl headed for the open water. It was filled with oil, and the result was a massive kill of 11,000 ducks and geese. Hunters on the lower Detroit River collected the oil-soaked carcasses, threw them into their pickup trucks, drove them to the state capitol in Lansing, and dumped them on the capitol sidewalk and steps in protest. The duck hunters and the Michigan United Conservation Clubs called a press conference at the state capitol, railed against the oil pollution killing ducks and geese, and called for stricter laws and enforcement. Today, this single event has been credited with starting the industrial pollution control program in Michigan (Cowles 1975).

In response to state efforts to control industrial pollution, particularly oil and grease, oil discharges to the Rouge and Detroit Rivers were reduced by 97.5% between the late 1940s and early 1960s (US Department of Health, Education, and Welfare, 1962). Even though this was a great percentage reduction, oil releases and pollution persisted. The US Department of Health, Education, and Welfare reported that during the early 1960s Ford's Rouge Plant discharged 900 gallons of oil per day, representing 97.5% of the oil discharged to the Rouge River (Vaughan and Harlow 1965). During the 1960s the Rouge River was also heavily polluted with "pickle liquor," a waste product from steel processing (Cowles 1975). However, thick oil was floating on top of the orange pickle liquor, so the only time you could see it was when a boat passed, and churned up the water in its wake. In 1960 and 1967, another 12,000 and 5,400 ducks and geese died from oil pollution (Hartig and Stafford 2003).

Rouge Fire of 1969

Adding insult to injury, the Rouge River caught fire on October 9, 1969. That morning, about 1,000 feet downstream from the I-75 freeway bridge near the city of River Rouge boundary with southwest Detroit, smoke billowed over the river (River Rouge Herald, 1969). The Detroit firefighters who extinguished the blaze estimated that flames shot 50 feet into the air. The cause of the fire was sparks from a welding torch, which ignited floating oil and oil-soaked debris.

The Detroit Fire Department deployed 10 pieces of equipment and

65 men to fight this river fire (Hartig 2010). However, it was the Detroit fireboat *John Kendall* that contained the fire and allowed it to burn out. It was reported that the spill began when a gasket on an oil pipe broke, allowing furnace oil to escape from the Shell depot. Some of the spilled oil was pumped into a truck, but wind spread the remainder across the river. The US Coast Guard was called to the scene before the fire started, to position oil-containment booms to keep floating oil from spreading. Despite these efforts, the oil spread across the river and caught fire, the flames spreading upstream and stopping about 500 feet from the culvert where the fire started. The Coast Guard had to halt traffic on the river. In an October 12, 1969, editorial, the *Detroit Free Press* had this to say about the Rouge River fire: "When you have a river that burns, for crying out loud, you have troubles. It happened on Cleveland's Cuyahoga, and now it has happened on the Rouge River."

Earlier in 1967, Ford Motor Company approached Usher Oil Service of Detroit to help clean up oil pollution in the Rouge River. Today, this company is called Marine Pollution Control and is located on the banks of the lower Rouge River across from Zug Island. It is now one of the leading environmental cleanup companies in the world, and it all started on the Rouge River. Following the 1969 Rouge River fire, Ford Motor Company purchased an "oil eating" pontoon boat that operated out of a boat slip at their Rouge Plant.

Renewable Energy from Hydroelectric Power

Henry Ford was always interested in resource conservation, efficiencies, and reliability. This philosophy is manifest in one of his quotes:

> We are entering an era when we shall create resources which shall be so constantly renewed that the only loss will be not to use them. There will be such a plenteous supply of heat, light and power, that it will be a sin not to use all we want. This era is coming now. And it is coming by way of water.

From 1910 to 1920, Ford dammed the Rouge River, to supply power to his mansion, Fair Lane, located in Dearborn, and also to supply hydroelectric power to small Ford factories along the Rouge River. He and his wife Clara had a dual interest in nature and industry, which is reflected in every aspect of their 31,000-square-foot mansion, built on 1,300 acres just a couple miles from where they both were born in Dearborn. Fair Lane was their sanctuary. They hired famed landscape architect Jens Jensen to design the vast gardens and landscapes at Fair Lane and to "green" the hydroelectric dam by making it appear to be natural rapids.

In the 1920s and 1930s, Henry Ford created his Village Industrial Mills (see chapter 3), essentially 17 mini-factories that harnessed hydroelectric power for manufacturing. Famed architect Albert Kahn designed some of them, even as he was designing Ford's much larger factories, and inventor Thomas Edison created some of the hydroelectric systems that powered the mills. Each mill produced auto parts such as valves and rivets, and during World War II some were converted to produce parts for B-24 bombers assembled at Ford's Willow Run plant. Phoenix Mill, located on Phoenix Lake near the city of Plymouth, employed women exclusively during the war. Ford endeavored to develop a sense of "field and factory" in these plants by training rural workers in the latest technological advances, allowing them release time to farm their fields, and paying them "city" wages (Mullin 1982).

Four Vagabonds

Between 1915 and 1924, Henry Ford, Thomas Edison, Harvey Firestone, and John Burroughs, calling themselves the Four Vagabonds, embarked on a series of summer camping trips (Guinn 2019). Everyone knows Edison as an inventor who transformed the world with inventions such as the lightbulb and the phonograph, and Harvey Firestone as the founder of Firestone Tire and Rubber Company. Fewer people know about John Burroughs, who was an American naturalist and famed nature essayist, active in the US conservation movement. Today, the John Burroughs Association gives out a prestigious annual literary award for nature writing.

These Four Vagabonds loved being together, communing with nature, exploring ideas, and acting like boys. An important point is that Henry Ford had a long-standing interest in nature and industry, as evidenced in the design of Fair Lane and his association with Burroughs. These trips started in 1914, when Ford and Burroughs visited Edison in Florida and toured the Everglades. The next year, Ford, Edison, and Firestone joined Burroughs in California for the Panama-Pacific Exposition. They visited

Luther Burbank and then drove from Riverside to San Diego. Can you imagine the discussions these four had?

The Henry Ford

Henry Ford was a man ahead of his time. Although he did not invent the automobile, he believed that an affordable car would give all people the freedom to travel, experience the country, and achieve prosperity. But Ford was also ahead of his time in another way. He could have collected the finest and most expensive art in the world, but instead, he collected commonplace things, such as toasters, farm machinery, kerosene lamps, and steam engines. Ford felt that these everyday objects told a truth not written about in history books. Today, educators call these items "primary sources."

To display his collections, Ford founded the Edison Institute, in honor of his friend Thomas Edison; it was later called Henry Ford Museum and Greenfield Village, and today is often called simply The Henry Ford. It is the world's largest indoor-outdoor history museum. Ford wanted his museum to be a place where people could see how their ancestors lived and worked. The 250-acre museum and village complex celebrate the accomplishments of American innovators such as Ford, Thomas Edison, Rosa Parks, the Wright brothers, George Washington Carver, Abraham Lincoln, and many more.

Today, The Henry Ford, in Dearborn, Michigan, is an internationally recognized history destination that brings the past forward, immersing visitors in stories of ingenuity, resourcefulness, and innovation that helped shape America. This national historic landmark has five unique venue attractions, an on-site high school, and nationally recognized programming and signature events. The Henry Ford's unparalleled collection and expertise further its position as a global resource for American history and innovation.

The Henry Ford's mission is to provide unique educational experiences based on authentic objects, stories of lives that reflect America's traditions of ingenuity, resourcefulness, and innovation. The goal is to inspire people to learn from these traditions to shape a better future. In 1928, a cornerstone was laid at The Henry Ford symbolizing Ford's "one foot in industry and one foot in agriculture" (fig. 14). This symbolizes the union of nature (Luther Burbank's spade) and technology (Edison's sig-

Fig. 14. Laying the cornerstone during the dedication of The Henry Ford, symbolizing the union of nature and technology, 1928. (Photograph courtesy The Henry Ford.)

nature and footprints). That unity is borne out by the block itself, made from Portland cement refined from blast furnace slag at Ford's Rouge Plant—a good example of how Henry Ford approached industry like a good farmer, prohibiting waste. This also was a precursor for sustainable manufacturing and sustainability.

Synergy between Industry and Agriculture

Henry Ford long recognized the need for a synergistic relationship between industry and agriculture. Even before the Great Depression, he was working with staff and scientists, conducting extensive and exhaustive experiments in a search for new industrial uses for agricultural products. He once told a young friend that he expected a time to come "when a good many automobile parts will be grown." He clearly foresaw how plastics would revolutionize the production of automobiles. This also would give farmers a more dependable source of income.

In 1938, the *Dearborn Chronicle* reported that Henry Ford and the Ford Motor Company had 30,000 acres of land under cultivation in southeast Michigan, the principal crop being soybeans. He developed a new process for extracting soybean oil that could be used in a variety of products throughout the country, but particularly in the automobile, paint, varnish, and plastics industries. This did not happen by chance—it was the result of exhaustive, expensive research. In 1932 and 1933, Ford invested $1.25 million in the research and development possibilities of soybeans.

It was always Ford's conviction that industry and agriculture were natural partners. Although he was the first to harvest the "miracle bean"—the soybean—as a basic industrial material, his company had many other firsts. Ford Motor Company was the first automobile company to start growing its own trees (Ford Motor Company 1946). For example, in 1919 Ford purchased a large tract of land in northern Michigan to provide a dependable source of both hardwoods and softwoods. Ford was the first car manufacturer to acquire its own rubber plantations, and to provide its own tung oil for paints and enamels by planting tung-tree groves.

Ford was a systems' thinker and innovator, driven by the goal of continuous improvement. His thinking was clearly a building block for sustainable manufacturing, and a "cradle to cradle" approach to manufacturing things, one that attempts to achieve a circular economy that eliminates wastes and ensures the continual use of resources.

Rouge River Oxbow at The Henry Ford

As a river descends from its headwaters and reaches flatter land near its mouth, it swings from side to side, forming winding bends called meanders. Eventually, a river may take a shortcut, cutting across the narrow neck of the loop, leaving a separated U-shaped oxbow. Historically, there was one such oxbow on the lower Rouge River, adjacent to Henry Ford Museum of American Innovation and Greenfield Village in Dearborn and virtually in the shadow of Ford Motor Company's world headquarters. Over time it was filled in as part of flood control efforts in the 1960s. Back then there was considerable flooding in the communities of Melvindale, Dearborn, Allen Park, and others, and stormwater and wastewater were backing up in home basements and creating a health hazard.

In the 1960s, the US Army Corps of Engineers straightened a significant portion of the lower Rouge River by constructing a 4.2-mile concrete channel to quickly move as much stormwater out of the area as possible. It was as part of that effort that the oxbow was filled in, and all its ecological benefits lost, including providing habitat for fish and wildlife, filtering stormwater, and buffering against flooding. As controls of combined sewer overflows (where stormwater and raw sewage are discharged during heavy rainfall) and urban stormwater runoff were implemented in the late 1980s and 1990s, people began to imagine restoring this historical oxbow as an ecological, educational, and cultural asset.

This oxbow restoration was initiated in 2002 and completed in three phases over 17 years at a cost of over $3 million. Phase 1 included restoring the 2,200-foot channel at 16- to 105-foot widths and 3- to 7-foot depths. In total, 13 acres of wetland and upland habitats were restored in this phase. Phase 2 re-established a partial connection between the oxbow and the Rouge River in 2005. Phase 3 completed full connection with the Rouge River and restored natural flows in 2018–2019. Partners in the project included The Henry Ford, Wayne County, the Clean Michigan Initiative, the Rouge River Gateway Partnership, the Rouge River Advisory Council, the University of Michigan–Dearborn, Ford Motor Company, the city of Dearborn, the US Army Corps of Engineers, the Michigan Department of Environmental Quality, and the US Environmental Protection Agency.

The benefits of restoring this oxbow are wide-ranging. When the oxbow was filled in, fish lost important habitats required to complete their life cycle. Today, the oxbow provides important nursery habitat for many species of fish, including largemouth bass, channel catfish, and bowfin. The natural shoreline and muddy bottom of the oxbow provide much-needed habitat for native amphibians and reptiles, such as basking logs, winter shelter for dormant animals such as snakes, and nesting locations. Naturalists have reported diverse wildlife sightings throughout the restored uplands and wetlands, including coyotes, foxes, raccoons, deer, raptors, owls, bats, ducks, herons, turtles, and frogs.

Students at the Henry Ford Academy, located on the grounds of The Henry Ford, now use the oxbow as a living laboratory (fig. 15); in fact, it is incorporated into the Academy's curriculum. Further, the oxbow is used by scouts for service-learning projects and overnight camping. Trees have regularly been planted in the oxbow area as part of teaching stewardship and sustainability.

Fig. 15. Students using the restored oxbow for environment education. (Photograph by Brian James Egen, used by permission.)

Leadership in Sustainability—Ford's Rouge Plant

"By the time I became chairman of the company, the Rouge Plant had become one of largest dirty manufacturing sites in the country," noted William Clay "Bill" Ford Jr., great-grandson of company founder Henry Ford. Embracing Ford Motor Company's heritage of innovation and continuous improvement, Bill Ford Jr. rebuilt the Rouge Plant in 2000 at a cost of $2 billion. It is now one of the best examples of sustainable manufacturing in the world (fig. 16). "This is not environmental philanthropy," said Bill Ford Jr. in November 2000, when the first steel beam was installed for the new plant. "It is sound business, which for the first time balances the business needs of auto manufacturing with ecological and social concerns."

When Bill Ford Jr. re-envisioned the Rouge Plant, he was influenced by the pioneering environmental work of world-renowned architect and industrial designer Bill McDonough. McDonough guided transformation of the site at every level. All manufacturing processes were designed to minimize waste at all stages. Parts are delivered in reusable

Fig. 16. The Ford Rouge Plant in Dearborn, Michigan, a 21st-century model of sustainable manufacturing. (Photograph courtesy Ford Motor Company.)

bins whenever possible, all paper and cardboard excess is recycled, and waste gases at the paint plant are captured and turned into fuel cells to help power the plant itself. The stamping process was redesigned to collect excess aluminum, such as the cut-out for the windshield, shred that excess material, and immediately return it for reuse by aluminum manufacturers. In the F-150 truck plant, ceiling-mounted light boxes and monitors flood the manufacturing floor with natural light. This innovative daylighting system, together with tempered air, more space, and the application of ergonomics to every task, have greatly changed workers' daily experience.

The entrance to the Rouge complex was turned into a 1.5-mile-long green boulevard with 22 acres of wetlands, trees, and shrubs. A system of swales or landscaped ditches, along with retention ponds, is used to treat stormwater. Ford Motor Company has also successfully used phytoremediation to absorb and neutralize contaminants on site. Renewable energy sources such as fuel cells and solar cells have been incorporated into the Rouge complex.

The Rouge Plant is notable in that it has one of the largest living "green roofs" in the world, which has helped jump-start the early North American green-roof industry. Over 10 acres of assembly plant roofing are covered with sedum, a succulent groundcover, and other plants. The roof reduces stormwater runoff by holding one inch of rainfall, and helps cool the building, saving energy and money. Also, the living plants absorb carbon dioxide as part of photosynthesis, so oxygen is emitted and greenhouse gases reduced. Vines on the side of the plant act as further insulation.

Through the use of "eco-effective" products and processes, Bill Ford has made the Rouge Plant a model for environmentally friendly industrial production. Ford Motor Company has worked with suppliers to "design out" emissions and wastes and to revitalize the area as a "green" place for the community. Interestingly, in 2004 the Rouge Plant resumed factory tours, attracting hundreds of thousands of paying tourists. It has now become both a sustainable manufacturing site and an ecotourism tourist attraction. Henry Ford would be so proud of his great-grandson taking up the torch and leading Ford Motor Company to become a model of sustainable manufacturing in the 21st century.

A spinoff of the sustainable redevelopment of the Rouge Plant was a decision by Roush Industries, an automotive design and engineering firm who built a new facility on the banks of the Rouge River in Allen Park, to make the Rouge River their front door. Historically, all developments were positioned facing away from the Rouge River, making the river their back door. Roush felt that the Rouge River was becoming an asset and intentionally positioned the new facility to face the Rouge River.

Ford and the Future

Thomas Kuhn, an American physicist, philosopher, and historian of science, described and popularized the concept of paradigm shifts—significant changes in perspective that result in a completely new way of thinking about or doing something. Throughout his life, Ford was involved in or led several paradigm shifts. For example, during the shipbuilding paradigm shift, when more ships were built along the Detroit River during the 1890s than in any other city in America, Ford worked at an apprentice machinist at Detroit Dry Dock Company, where he learned about heavy machinery and how to move people and goods by water. Ford was clearly a leader of paradigm shifts for both the automobile that put the world on wheels and in creating the Arsenal of Democracy that helped win World War II.

In Henry Ford's day, there was no term for "environmentalist." But he had a goal of sending zero waste to landfills and believed in innovation and continuous improvement. "If you go way back, my great-grandfather was really an environmentalist," says Bill Ford. Henry Ford railed against the notion of waste in the production process. For instance, the wood from shipping crates for parts received in the plant was stripped and used as either running boards or the sides of "woody" station wagons. The scrap that was left over from that process was compressed into charcoal, for which purpose Henry Ford started Kingsford Charcoal.

Henry Ford also pioneered the use of environmentally friendly materials in the manufacture of cars—from soybeans to wheat gluten. In fact, during the early 1930s, the company developed a soybean enamel that was used to paint cars and oil-casting molds (The Henry Ford 2014). In 1935, Ford Motor Company reported that two bushels of soybeans went into every car—in the paint, the horn button, the gearshift knob, door handles, the accelerator pedal, and timing gears.

Today, the same tenets of innovation, continuous improvement, and elimination of waste live on in Ford Motor Company, as can be seen in its leadership of the sustainability paradigm shift. Ford Motor Company supports increasing clean car standards, while providing flexibility to help offer more affordable options to their customers. They are currently working with the US Environmental Protection Agency, the National Highway Traffic Safety Administration, and the state of California to make advances in this area.

Ford Motor Company believes that it must reduce CO_2 consistent with the Paris Climate Accord. It has worked relentlessly to reduce water use, waste, use of energy, and emissions footprints in its manufacturing plants and vehicles. Just as Henry Ford did during his time, Ford Motor Company is exploring new ideas and technologies to make transportation more efficient, accessible, and affordable. There is no better example of that than Ford's new mobility district, centered in Detroit's old Michigan Central Station in the Corktown neighborhood, which is a hub for autonomous and electric research. The old train station is another instance of Ford as a leader in the sustainability paradigm shift. That would indeed bring a smile to Henry Ford's face.

Henry Ford's entire life was centered around the Rouge River, which was essential to bring in materials and goods to mass-produce automobiles and put the nation on wheels. It also can be argued that the Rouge

River helped win World War II by facilitating efficient delivery of raw materials to produce nearly $29 billion of military output.

Henry Ford also loved the Rouge River and made his home on its banks. He loved nature and was a conservationist at heart. If he were here today, Henry Ford would be proud of the ongoing cleanup of his beloved Rouge River, and that his Rouge plant is now a 21st-century model of sustainable manufacturing. As Henry Ford so eloquently stated, "Coming together is the beginning. Keeping together is progress. Working together is success." All people, communities, industries, and businesses must continue to work together to restore the Rouge River so that it can support healthy communities and a healthy economy.

LITERATURE CITED

Blaime, A.J. 2014. *The Arsenal of Democracy: FDR, Ford Motor Company, and Their Epic Quest to Arm an America at War*. New York: Mariner Books.

Cianflone, F.A. 1973. "The Eagle Boats of World War I." *Proceedings* 99 (6): 844.

Cowles, G., 1975. "Return of the River." *Michigan Natural Resources* 44 (1): 2–6.

Dearborn Independent. 1938. "Small Soybean Patch Has Grown to Vast Industry." The Henry Ford, Dearborn, MI. https://www.thehenryford.org/collections-and-research/digital-collections/artifact/374843#slide=gs-257711

Guinn, J. 2019. *The Vagabonds: The Story of Henry Ford's and Thomas Edison's Ten-Year Road Trip*. New York: Simon & Shuster.

Ford Motor Company. 1946. "1st to Grow Automobile Parts on the Farm." The Henry Ford, Dearborn, MI. https://www.thehenryford.org/collections-and-research/digital-collections/artifact/352600#slide=gs-223753

Hartig, J.H. 2010. *Burning Rivers: Revival of Four Urban-Industrial Rivers That Caught on Fire*. Ecovision World Monograph Series, Aquatic Ecosystem Health and Management Society, Burlington, Ontario, Canada. Essex, UK: Multi-Science Publishing Company.

Hartig, J.H., Stafford, T., 2003. "The Public Outcry over Oil Pollution of the Detroit River." In Hartig, J.H., ed., *Honoring Our Detroit River, Caring for Our Home*, 69–78. Bloomfield Hills, MI: Cranbrook Institute of Science.

The Henry Ford. 2014. "Soybeans: Henry Ford's Miracle Crop." Dearborn, MI. https://www.thehenryford.org/explore/blog/soybeans/

Mullin, J.R., 1982. "Henry Ford and Field and Factory: An Analysis of the Ford Sponsored Village Industries—Experiment in Michigan, 1918–1941." *Journal of the American Planning Association* 41 (https://scholarworks.umass.edu/cgi/viewcontent.cgi?article=1040&context=larp_faculty_pubs; accessed 25 January 2021).

Pavuluri, Rohan. 2015. "Sapiro vs. Ford: The Mastermind of the Marshall Maneu-

ver." *Exposé* 2015. https://projects.iq.harvard.edu/expose/book/sapiro-vs-fo
rd-mastermind-marshall-maneuver

River Rouge Herald. 1969. "Sparks Ignite Rouge River." October 15.

US Department of Health, Education, and Welfare. 1962. "Pollution of the Nav-
igable Water of the Detroit River, Lake Erie and Their Tributaries within the
State of Michigan." Detroit.

Vaughan, R.D., Harlow, G.L. 1965. "Report on Pollution of the Detroit River,
Michigan Waters of Lake Erie, and Their Tributaries." Grosse Ile, MI: US
Department of Health, Education, and Welfare.

5 ROUGE RIVER RESTORATION

Revival of an Urban River

Annette DeMaria, Noel Mullett, and John H. Hartig

The Rouge River has experienced two centuries of human use and abuse (table 1). Metropolitan Detroit was and continues to be the automobile capital of the United States and was considered the industrial heartland and epicenter of the Arsenal of Democracy. Heavy industry has long dominated the lower end of the river near its confluence with the Detroit River. Consequently, the lower river has long had a reputation of being a working river that supported industry and commerce.

Prior to the 1970s, most considered pollution to be just part of the cost of doing business. Oil and other petroleum products, heavy metals, and organic compounds such as polychlorinated biphenyls (PCBs) were discharged by industries and were killing organisms living on the river bottom, causing cancer in bottom-feeding fish, making game fish unsafe to eat, and creating water-pollution problems downstream in the Detroit River. Indeed, the lower end of the Rouge River was so polluted with oil and other petroleum products that it caught fire on October 9, 1969 (Hartig 2010; see chapter 4).

But it was not just the lower river that was polluted—other portions of the watershed were also being affected by urban sprawl. As in many other urban areas, beginning in the 1950s people in southeast Michigan began moving away from the central city, seeking suburban areas with more space. With personal automobiles and cheap fuel they could still drive to their workplaces. Federal tax subsidies for home mortgage interest and property taxes, the expansion of highways, and racial tensions helped fuel this new suburban growth. This outward migration trend accelerated during the 1960s with more people fleeing the central city for outer-ring suburbs, including those in the Rouge River watershed.

Table 1. Examples of Historical Environmental and Natural-Resource Problems in the Rouge River

Time Period	Environmental/Natural Resource Problem
Late 1600s to mid-1800s	During the fur trade era, beaver were trapped and hunted to extirpation in the watershed; the last beaver in the region was reported in 1877.
Starting in 1707	Cadillac began to divide land into long, narrow "ribbon farms" to provide water access to the Detroit River and Lower Rouge River; this resulted in loss of forest land and riparian habitats.
1700s to early 1900s	Logging for timber and to clear land for agriculture and urban development resulted in loss of valuable forest and wetland habitats.
Late 1700s	Gristmills were established on the main forks of the river, altering river hydrology.
Starting in the late 1800s and early 1900s	The Lower Rouge River was dredged to accommodate larger vessels in support of industry, altering river hydrology and destroying river habitats.
1910s and 1920s	Dams were built along the Rouge River for hydroelectric power, and some were built to provide a water supply for firefighting, altering river hydrology, destroying river habitats, and creating barriers to fish passage.
1917–1928	Henry Ford built the largest integrated factory in the world at that time on 2,000 acres along the lower river, eliminating riparian and upland habitats and altering river hydrology.
1932	Logs floating on the river that were being staged for processing by the Detroit Sulfite Pulp and Paper Company near Zug Island caught fire; the fire lasted six days, displacing fish and wildlife from this section of the river.
1948	Oil pollution from industries along the Rouge and Detroit Rivers killed 11,000 ducks and geese in the Detroit River.
1960	Oil pollution from industries along the Rouge and Detroit Rivers killed 12,000 ducks and geese in the Detroit River.
Early 1960s	An estimated 900 gallons of oil per day was being discharged from the Ford Rouge Plant, representing 97.5% of the oil discharged to the Rouge River.
1967	Oil pollution from industries along the Rouge and Detroit Rivers killed 5,400 ducks and geese in the Detroit River.
1969	Oil and wooden debris floating on the river caught fire, displacing fish and wildlife from this section of the river.
1983–1984	Residents of Melvindale and Dearborn complained of a putrid smell near the river. An investigation found that the river was so polluted with raw sewage that all the oxygen was used up through decomposition, resulting in the formation of hydrogen sulfide (source of the smell of rotten eggs) off-gassing from the river.
1985	In a tragic accident, a 23-year-old man fell into the Rouge River, swallowed water, and died of an infection from a rare parasitic, waterborne disease called leptospirosis or rat fever.
2002	A suspicious oil spill of over 100,000 gallons occurred in the Rouge River, resulting in a $7.5 million cleanup on the lower Rouge and Detroit Rivers; 10 ducks and geese died from the oil pollution.

Source: Vaughan and Harlow 1965; Hartig 2010; Hartig et al. 2020.

But there would be unintended consequences of this urban sprawl. Much of the watershed was developed with combined storm and sanitary sewers, a practice no longer followed today. When heavy rainfall exceeded the capacity of the combined sewer and stormwater system, raw sewage and stormwater were discharged into the Rouge River through outlets known as combined sewer overflows (CSOs). By the early 1960s, a total of 168 uncontrolled CSOs were present in the watershed, adding raw sewage and other waste to the river and depleting the oxygen in the water every time it rained. When the dissolved oxygen was used up through decomposition, the river became uninhabitable for many fish and invertebrates.

Adding to the CSO problem, 23% of the watershed had become impervious, covered by roads, parking lots, and rooftops that would not allow stormwater to penetrate the soil. To put this in perspective, ecologists recommend that the impervious surface of a healthy watershed should be less than 10% (Arnold and Gibson 1996). These impervious surfaces increased urban runoff and brought sediment, trash, fertilizers, pesticides, and other pollutants into the river, further degrading it. While it was usually unintentional, nearly everyone was contributing to the pollution problems of the Rouge River.

Despite an October 21, 1965, headline in the *Dearborn Guide* that read "Rouge Called State's Most Polluted River" (Gnau 1975), most people did not care, accepting that pollution was part of the cost of doing business and of suburban living. Industrial jobs, technological progress, and homes in suburbia were the priorities, not environmental protection or justice.

Tipping Point Unites All Levels of Government to the Common Cause of Restoring the Rouge River

As noted in the prologue, a tipping point occurred in the mid-1980s, catalyzed by the odor problem and an accident that resulted in the death of the 23-year-old man (Diebolt 1985). Governments knew that solving the pollution problems of the Rouge River would be difficult and complex. They were fortunate to have a 1980 study of the quantity and quality of CSOs in the entire watershed. This study showed definitively that if the city of Detroit alone implemented necessary CSO control measures in their portion of the watershed at the lower end of the river, the quality of the Rouge River would not be improved one iota (Giffels, Black, and Veatch 1980). It would take all 48 communities in the watershed each doing its part to restore the river. It was decided to build on the strengths of the Michigan Department of Natural Resources, the US Environmental Protection Agency, the Southeast Michigan Council of Governments, and others to restore the river while maintaining local ownership and responsibility.

On October 1, 1985, the Michigan Water Resources Commission—the agency responsible for protecting the waters of the state through establishing rules, issuing permits, and ensuring enforcement—instructed the Michigan Department of Natural Resources to develop a remedial action plan (RAP) and implement a public participation process to decrease pollution in the river. At the same time, the International Joint Commission's Great Lakes Water Quality Board identified the Rouge River as one of 42 Great Lakes pollution hotspots or Areas of Concern— areas where significant pollution existed and remedial and preventive actions were needed to restore beneficial uses. They recommended that a RAP be developed and implemented to restore all impaired beneficial uses, following an ecosystem approach (Bean et al. 2003; International Joint Commission's Great Lakes Water Quality Board 1985). This made the cleanup effort both a state and an international priority.

An Ecosystem Approach and Watershed Partnerships

An ecosystem approach takes into account the interrelationships among air, water, land, and all living things, including humans, and involves all user groups in management (Canada and the United States 1987; Vallentyne and Beeton 1988). It is important to recognize the difference between an environment and an ecosystem, which is like the difference between a house and a home. A house is something external, detached, separate. In contrast, a home is something you see yourself as a part of even when you're not there. A home is where we raise our children, have family meals, celebrate special occasions, and entertain friends. What we do to our home (and ecosystem) impacts everyone who lives in it. A house is just a structure, but when we talk about a home, we take into account the interrelationships and events that occur there, and how every element influences every other.

Think of it like grassroots ecological democracy. An ecosystem approach brings all the watershed stakeholders together to sit around a table and reach agreement on what needs to be done to clean up and care for their ecosystem as their home.

Another good way of visualizing such ecosystem-watershed partnerships is through the analogy with farming, which entails "preparing the ground," "sowing the seed," "tending the fields," and "reaping the harvest" (World Health Organization 2003). Such partnerships are tailored to each specific watershed. In the "preparing the ground" phase of a watershed partnership, it is important to bring potential partners together and reach agreement on mutual needs, a common vision, and shared values. Once the partnership comes together, it can move to the phase of "sowing the seeds." This involves reviewing project options and reaching agreement on a preferred project option or options to be implemented. As part of this phase, it is important to reach agreement on priorities and each partner's roles and responsibilities for implementation. In the next phase, "tending the fields," partners coordinate implementation of the projects within a consensus timeframe and undertake midcourse corrections as necessary to achieve desired outcomes. In the final phase, "reaping the harvest," partners perform assessments to confirm that the desired outcomes have been achieved, and celebrate their achievements in a very public fashion to ensure that partners are satisfied. The Rouge River project was a pioneer in the use of an ecosystem approach and watershed management. In fact, it became a North American leader and innovator in this area.

The Model of Ecosystem-Based Watershed Management

To facilitate collaboration and ensure public participation, in 1985 two local committees were established—the Rouge River Basin Committee and the Executive Steering Committee. The Rouge River Basin Committee included all 48 mayors in the watershed, key legislators, and representatives from the Michigan Natural Resources Commission, the Michigan Water Resources Commission, the International Joint Commission, the Rouge River Watershed Council, the League of Women Voters, Michigan United Conservation Clubs, the East Michigan Environmental Action Council, the Michigan Clean Water Coalition, and the Michigan Manufacturers Association. The executive steering committee included representatives from the Michigan Water Resources Commission, the governor's office, the Michigan Department of Natural Resources, the US Environmental Protection Agency, the Southeast Michigan Council of Governments, the city of Detroit, Wayne and Oakland Counties, the Rouge River Watershed Council, four local government representatives, and one citizen representative. The intent was to structure this institutional framework to ensure broad acceptance of the RAP and local ownership by all stakeholders—the communities, counties, businesses, and citizen groups who would implement it. Also in 1986, as a spinoff to the Rouge River Basin Committee, the Friends of the Rouge (FOTR) was established as a nonprofit organization to help coordinate Rouge Rescue, an annual volunteer river cleanup, to foster environmental education, and to encourage citizen stewardship.

In 1988, the Rouge River RAP was completed, and the following year it was adopted by the Michigan Water Resources Commission (Michigan Department of Natural Resources and Southeast Michigan Council of Governments 1988). The RAP had the goal of restoring all impaired uses within 20 years. There was also a deliberately adopted view that remedial projects ready to be implemented should not be delayed by additional studies. Everyone wanted an aggressive, "move-ahead" action plan. The initial Rouge River RAP focused heavily on controlling raw sewage—notably, the approximately 7.8 billion gallons of combined sewage being discharged annually into the Rouge River during heavy rains. While the 1988 RAP recommendations focused on sanitary sewer capacity and CSO control, it also recognized polluted stormwater from separated storm sewers as a significant problem across the entire watershed. In support of continuous improvement, the Rouge River RAP was updated in 1994, 1999, and 2004 (Rouge RAP Advisory Council 1994, 1999, and 2004).

In 1992, the representatives of the Rouge River Basin Committee were reorganized into the Rouge RAP Advisory Council (RRAC), and in 1993 the Rouge River National Wet Weather Demonstration Project (Rouge Project) was established, initially with $42 million, to help implement CSO controls and the innovative stormwater management techniques called for in the Rouge River RAP (Murray 1994). This funding was provided from the US Environmental Protection Agency to Wayne County's Department of Environment to implement cost-effective control programs in a collaborative fashion with local governments. This initial funding was supplemented with several additional grants, which

Table 2. Projects that Helped Restore the Rouge River, with Financial Support from the Rouge River National Wet Weather Demonstration Project, 1993–2014

Type of Project	Projects Implemented
CSOs and separate sanitary overflows	88
Stormwater control	47
Streambank stabilization, lake restoration, and dam removal	48
Public education and involvement	71
River-based recreation	23
Illicit discharge elimination, water-quality monitoring, and other community projects	106
Total	383

totaled $350 million by 2014. These substantial funds were essential to moving forward on cleanup.

Stakeholders recognized that to be cost-effective, pollution problems in the river must be addressed collaboratively by all the local governments, with flexibility across regulatory programs. Effective policy, programs, and institutional arrangements were consistently emphasized through the Rouge Project (Ridgway and McCormack 1994). For practical reasons, the Rouge River watershed was divided into seven subwatersheds, with distinct watershed advisory groups and subwatershed management plans. Over 380 cleanup, restoration, and preservation projects were implemented by 75 communities and agencies through Rouge Project (table 2) subgrants. Other major accomplishments of the Rouge Project include the state of Michigan's Watershed-Based Stormwater Permit (the first of its kind in the nation) to comprehensively address stormwater pollution, passage of the Watershed Alliance legislation Public Act 517 of 2004 that calls for establishment of watershed alliances, the establishment of the Alliance of Rouge Communities (ARC) in 2003, and the implementation of a comprehensive monitoring program for the Rouge River watershed (Ridgway et al. 1996).

Progress in CSO Controls and Stormwater Management

As industrial point sources of pollution were being addressed during the 1960s and 1970s through both federal and state regulations, it became clear that considerably more effort would have to be targeted on addressing nonpoint sources of pollution—pollution that cannot be traced to a single origin or source, such as stormwater runoff, water runoff from urban and agricultural areas, and failing septic systems (Ridgway and McCormack 1994). The Rouge River was still highly polluted through the mid-1980s as a result of raw sewage being discharged to the river from CSOs and separate sanitary sewer overflows. CSOs and polluted stormwater runoff result in many water-quality problems, including extreme flow variations, streambank erosion, flooding, loss of habitat, high bacteria levels, and low dissolved oxygen. Polluted stormwater run-off contains bacteria, heavy metals, nutrients, oil, and pesticides. Minimizing the impacts from both CSOs and polluted stormwater became a top priority (Ridgway et al. 1996).

Between 1988 and 2014, over $1 billion in federal and local funds was spent on sewer-capacity projects, CSO controls, and stormwater management initiatives, which dramatically reduced pollution (Ridgway et al. 2019). This included a 90% reduction in CSO pollutant loads during most wet-weather events, with all CSOs being fully controlled in Oakland County and continued control efforts being implemented in Wayne County and Detroit. The Rouge River began to respond with improved dissolved oxygen conditions to the point that they rarely violated water quality standards (Ridgway 2010).

Improving Dissolved Oxygen Conditions

Dissolved oxygen is an important parameter in defining the health of aquatic ecosystems. Dissolved oxygen concentrations below 4.0 mg/L have potentially adverse impacts on aquatic life. To provide protection, state of Michigan water-quality standards specify that dissolved oxygen must be always greater than 7 mg/L for streams designated as coldwater fisheries, and must always be always greater than 5 mg/L for streams designated as warmwater fisheries. The Rouge River and its tributaries are designated as warmwater streams except for Johnson Creek, which is designated as a coldwater fishery.

Figures 17A–C present the long-term trends of dissolved oxygen for three subwatersheds of the Rouge River: the Main and Upper subwatersheds in Detroit, which include drainage from 56% of the watershed; the Middle subwatershed in Dearborn Heights, which represents 24% of the watershed; and the Lower subwatershed in Dearborn, which represents 20% of the watershed (DeMaria and Mullett 2020).

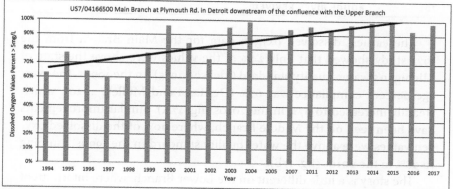

A

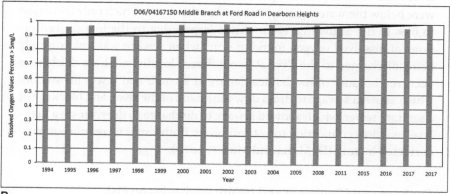

B

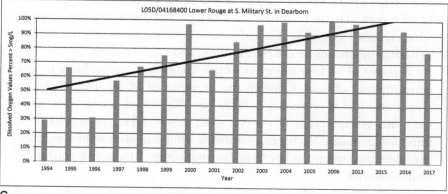

C

Fig. 17. The percentage of dissolved oxygen measurements in the Main and Upper subwatershed (*A*), the Middle subwatershed (*B*), and the Lower subwatershed (*C*) of the Rouge River that exceed the Michigan standard of 5 mg/L for protection of a warmwater fishery.

The earliest dissolved oxygen data for the Main Branch from the 1973 study showed that only 24% of the values were above the state of Michigan's water-quality standard (Jackson 1975). In the 1990s, the average percent compliance was 67% (DeMaria and Mullett 2020), which steadily increased to 97% in the 2010s (fig. 17A). Similar improvements have been seen on the Middle Branch, where 90% of the dissolved oxygen values were above the water quality standard in the 1990s, jumping to 98% in the 2010s (fig. 17B).

The story is a little different on the Lower Branch, where intermittent sanitary sewer problems caused the most recent dissolved oxygen values to be lower than in previous years. On the Lower Branch, 54% of the values were below the water-quality standard in the 1990s, which only increased to 92% in the 2010s (fig. 17C). This is largely due to the low concentrations of dissolved oxygen found in 2017, when sewage was unknowingly being discharged to the river at two different locations. These discharges occurred because of mechanical failure at a combined sewer lift station, which allowed sewage to drain down the bank of the river, and blockage of a sanitary sewer, which allowed sewage to discharge to the river via a high-level overflow connection to a storm sewer. Both issues were subsequently corrected in 2017 (DeMaria and Mullett 2020).

Contaminated Sediment and Health Advisories on Fish

The Rouge River's long history of industrial activity resulted in contaminated sediment in the river bottom. This legacy of contamination, some of which remains today, has resulted in health advisories on fish, the decline of healthy organisms on the river bottom, and loss of aquatic habitat.

Portions of all four branches of the Rouge River are subject to fish consumption advisories due to the presence of PCBs. The Michigan Department of Community Health has also issued a statewide mercury fish consumption advisory for all inland lakes, reservoirs, and impoundments in Michigan. Removing contaminated sediment from the lakes and streams is key to addressing some of these fish consumption advisories.

Contaminated sediment remediation has been a major priority of the Rouge River RAP. Between 1986 and 2020, 519,000 cubic yards of contaminated sediment was cleaned up in the Rouge River, at a cost of $62.75 million (fig. 18; table 3). Additional sediment cleanup is still

Fig. 18. Contaminated sediment remediation in the Old Channel of the Rouge River, 2019. (Credit: US Army Corps of Engineers.)

Table 3. Contaminated Sediment Remediation in the Rouge River, 1986–2020

Location or Site	Nature of Project	Volume of Sediment	Year	Cost
Lower River near Double Eagle Steel	Dredging and disposal	39,239 cubic yards	1986	$1 million
Evans Products ditch	Dredging and disposal	9,548 cubic yards	1997	$750,000
Newburgh Lake	Dredging and disposal	400,233 cubic yards	1997–98	$11 million
Lower River—Old Channel	Dredging and disposal	69,975 cubic yards	2019–20	$50 million

required in the shipping channel of the lower river. This final cleanup is being facilitated by the Michigan Department of Environment, Great Lakes and Energy under a cooperative agreement with the US Environmental Protection Agency.

Contaminated sediment has also been addressed at reservoirs in the watershed, most notably in Newburgh Lake located along the Middle Branch in Livonia, Michigan. Between 1997 and 1998, Wayne County removed 350,000 tons of PCB-contaminated sediment from the lake. Following sediment remediation, 30,000 pounds of contaminated fish were eradicated and removed, and new fish stocked. Post-remediation monitoring of PCBs in fish in 2001 showed nearly an order of magnitude decline in PCB levels.

In 2003, improved sediment and water quality in Newburgh Lake allowed the Michigan Department of Community Health to lift the fish-consumption advisory ban for some species of fish in the lake. This was the first time in over two decades that some fish caught in Newburgh Lake were safe to eat (Hartig 2010).

Progress in Restoring and Conserving Habitats

Loss of fish and wildlife habitat is considered an impaired beneficial use in all branches and tributaries of the Rouge River (Rouge RAP Advisory Council 1994). Based on 1995 land-use cover data, 23% of the Rouge River watershed has been transformed into impervious surface, which results in significant runoff problems and loss of habitat (Rouge RAP Advisory Council 2004). As mentioned earlier, watershed health begins to decline when impervious surfaces coverage exceeds 10% and becomes severely impaired if the number climbs beyond 30% of the total watershed area (Arnold and Gibbons 1996). Clearly, impervious surfaces in the Rouge River watershed impair water quality, and much needs to be done to moderate flows while conserving, rehabilitating, and restoring naturally water-absorbing wetlands and upland habitats.

The Rouge River Watershed Management Plan identifies habitat restoration and preservation as a goal (ARC 2012), including fish and wildlife habitat restoration. Habitat restoration efforts have been undertaken throughout the watershed in the last two decades through partnerships between government agencies, nonprofit organizations, and in some cases, private landowners. These projects range from streambank stabilization to wetland restoration to creation of fish passages around existing dams. These projects, implemented by local governments and partners, include 13 completed projects supported by the RRAC, the stakeholder group that advises Michigan Department of Environment, Great Lakes, and Energy and the US Environmental Protection Agency on restoring beneficial uses in the Rouge River watershed to delist it as an Area of Concern. Thirteen additional projects recommended by RRAC are underway, and several more recommended projects need funding. The largest of these involve making modifications to the concrete channel and adjacent areas to improve habitat for fish and wildlife in this heavily affected area. The complete list of habitat restoration projects supported by the RRAC is provided in table 4.

Figure 19 shows Friends of the Rouge staff and volunteers installing fascines, long bundles of sticks used to stabilize a streambank and enhance habitat in Fairway Park in Birmingham, Michigan.

A larger example undertaken by the ARC and Wayne County is the reconnection of an oxbow to the Rouge River at The Henry Ford (fig. 20). This project was completed in three phases over a period of 18 years and required reconnecting the oxbow through a portion of the river that was lined with concrete (see discussion in chapter 4).

All the large-scale habitat-restoration projects in the watershed have been completed primarily by the ARC and Wayne County with the support of funding from the state and federal governments. Since 2010, most of that funding has been provided by the Great Lakes Restoration Initiative, which has made the cleanup of Areas of Concern a priority.

Response of Invertebrates Living in River Sediments

Benthic macroinvertebrates are bottom-dwelling small spineless aquatic animals and insects that are widely used as indicators of stream health. Spending all or a portion of their lives in streams, they cannot escape pollution, and they vary in their ability to tolerate it. River segments that have a healthy community of benthic macroinvertebrates include sensitive families such as mayflies, caddisflies, and stoneflies. These pollution-sensitive invertebrates are lost as sites become degraded by pollution or loss of habitat caused by excessive stream flow variability.

For 20 years, the Friends of the Rouge have sampled benthic macroinvertebrates in the Rouge River. A comparison of their data with his-

Table 4. Habitat Restoration Projects in the Rouge River Watershed by RRAC and Partners

Status	Project/Location
Completed	• Valley Woods Wetland Restoration, Southfield • Eliza Howell and River Rouge Parks Habitat Improvements, Detroit • Danvers Pond Dam Removal and Stream Restoration, Farmington Hills • Rouge Oxbow Restoration, Dearborn • Carpenter Lake Restoration, Southfield • Kingfisher Bluff Restoration, Dearborn • Fordson Island Marine Debris Removal, Dearborn • Lola Valley Park Habitat Improvements, Redford Township • Newburgh Lake Restoration, Livonia • Wayne County Parks Property Habitat Improvements, various communities • Inkster CSO Basin Habitat Improvements, Inkster • Venoy Park Habitat Improvements, Wayne • Wayne Road Dam Removal and Stream Restoration, Wayne
In Progress	• Henry Ford Estate Dam Fish Passageway, Dearborn • Tamarack Creek Stream and Wetland Restoration, Southfield • Lola Valley Park Wetlands, Redford Township • Bell Creek Park Wetland Restoration, Redford Township • Nankin Lake Restoration, Livonia • Riverview Park Wetlands, Livonia • Johnson Creek Fish Hatchery Park Habitat, Northville • Sherwood Park Wetland Restoration, Westland • Johnson Intercounty Drain Restoration, Northville Township • Venoy Wetlands and Fish Habitat Structures, Wayne • Colonial Park Wetland and Reforestation, Inkster • Lower Rouge River Habitat Restoration, Wayne • Seeley Creek Restoration, Farmington Hills
Not Yet Funded	• Fordson Island and Upland Habitat Restoration (Phases 1 and 2), Dearborn • Patton Park Wetland Restoration, Detroit • Lawrence Tech University Wetland Restoration, Southfield • Fire Fighters Park Sprague Stream Improvements, Troy • Merriman Hollow Wetland and Grow Zone, Westland • Perrin Park Wetlands and Reforestation, Westland • Wallaceville West Wetland Restoration, Dearborn Heights • Wilcox Lake Habitat Improvements, Plymouth • Phoenix Lake Habitat Improvements, Plymouth Township • Inkster Park Wetlands and Fish Habitat Structures, Inkster • Grow Zone Retrofits, watershed-wide • Concrete Channel Modifications/Enhancements, Dearborn • Oakwood Commons Oxbow Restoration, Dearborn • Michigan Avenue/Evergreen Road Stormwater Management and Habitat Restoration, Dearborn

Fig. 19. Friends of the Rouge staff and volunteers installing fascines to stabilize a streambank in Fairway Park in Birmingham, Michigan, 2007. (Photograph courtesy Friends of the Rouge.)

Fig. 20. Final open cut of the concrete channel that reconnects the oxbow at The Henry Ford to the Rouge River in Dearborn, Michigan, 2020. (Photograph courtesy Alliance of Rouge Communities.)

torical data collected by Michigan Department of Natural Resources in 1973–1994 showed an overall improvement in benthic macroinvertebrate communities in the downstream sections of all the major branches, with most sites rating as "fair" (Petrella et al. 2020). Exceptions included continued "poor" communities in Evans Creek and the Middle Branch downstream of the confluence with Tonquish Creek, as well as one site on Tonquish Creek. The Main Branch near Eight Mile had several sites with "good" communities, including sensitive species such as dobsonflies. In most cases, Rouge River benthic macroinvertebrate communities are affected by urbanization and stormwater runoff. Additional projects to reduce stormwater impacts and improve habitat are needed to mitigate the effects of urbanization.

Improving Fishery

Fish are another good measure of a river's health; their presence or absence, abundance, and diversity indicate the functioning of many river variables, including stream flow, water temperature, water quality, and habitat. In general, species richness (the number of fish species) and species evenness (the relative abundance of fish species in the fish community) are good indicators of river health.

Historically, over 60 species of fish were documented in the Rouge River watershed (Beam and Braunscheidel 1998), including northern pike, white sucker, largemouth bass, walleye, channel catfish, white and black crappie, and various sunfishes. In 1995, only 53 species of fish were known to inhabit the Rouge River watershed (Beam and Braunscheidel 1998). Historical species missing included walleye, bass, and pollution-sensitive species such as minnows, darters, and sculpins.

In 2015–18, the Michigan Department of Natural Resources performed a number of fishery surveys in the Rouge River to evaluate the status of the fishery (table 5). Based on these surveys, headwaters' fisheries remain healthy, with species indicative of good water and habitat quality. Johnson Creek continues to support a brown trout fishery despite continued urbanization of its watershed. In 2015, the fishery of Fowler Creek had improved significantly from 1995, as evidenced by the dramatic increase in fish numbers and diversity. This is probably due to improved water and habitat quality. In 2017–18, the fishery at stations in the Upper Branch had high diversity with good numbers of pollution-intolerant species.

Table 5. A Comparison of Recent (2015–18) and Historical (1986, 1993, 1995, and 2002) Fish Survey Data Collected by the Michigan Department of Natural Resources at Selected Stations in the Rouge River

River Segment/Tributary	Description	Survey Findings
Johnson Creek, Washtenaw and Wayne Counties	Coldwater headwater stream that empties into the Middle Rouge River	From 1992 through 2013, Michigan DNR stocked fingerling brown trout to establish a sport fishery, but this stocking stopped in 2013 due to potential harm to the endangered redside dace population targeted for restoration under the Michigan Wildlife Action Plan. In 2017, a fishery survey of Johnson Creek found 14 species and 163 individuals, including three remnant brown trout.
Pebble Creek, Oakland County	Tributary of the upper Mainstem Rouge River	In 2018, the fish abundance was 2.5–6.0 times higher than was found in 1995, due to improved habitat and water quality.
Franklin Branch, Oakland County	Headwater tributary, upper Mainstem Rouge River	In 2018, the fish community and habitat conditions in this stream had been relatively stable with little change in fish diversity over the previous 20 years, although fish abundance may have been somewhat lower than in the past. The presence of fair numbers of blacknose dace, mottled sculpin, and central stoneroller indicated overall good water and habitat quality as these species are considered pollution-intolerant.
Fellows and Fowler Creeks	Headwater tributaries of the Lower Rouge River	In 2015, the fishery of Fellows Creek was considered relatively high quality, with both coolwater and warmwater species, and unchanged for 20 years; the fishery of Fowler Creek improved significantly after 1995, as indicated by the dramatic increase in fish numbers and diversity, probably due to improved water and habitat quality.
Upper Rouge River, Oakland County	Lola Park, Redford	In 2017, Johnny darter and central stoneroller, two species indicative of higher habitat and water quality, appeared for the first time since 1995.

(continues)

Table 5—*Continued*

River Segment/Tributary	Description	Survey Findings
Upper Rouge River, Oakland County	Shiawassee Park, Farmington	In 2017, the fish community was fairly diverse, with 13–16 species found; this fish community diversity is among the highest found in the watershed. A new species found since 1995 was the pollution-intolerant rainbow darter; state-endangered redside dace were found in both 1986 and 1995, but not in 2017.
Upper Rouge River, Oakland County	Nine Mile Road, Southfield	In 2018, the fish community was reasonably diverse with good numbers of pollution-intolerant species, such as central stoneroller and blacknose dace. Fish species composition and abundance were similar to those found during the 1995 survey.
Middle Rouge River, Wayne County	Warren Road, Plymouth Township	In 2018, overall fish abundance based on number of fish per length of stream was more than twice that found in the 2002 survey and an order of magnitude higher than in earlier surveys. Fish diversity improved compared to the historical surveys (9–11 species vs. 6 species historically), but the number of species is still lower than in higher-quality rivers in the area, such as the Huron and Raisin Rivers, which had 24–28 species in recent surveys.
Lower Rouge River, Wayne County	Three stations upstream and two downstream of the former Wayne Road Dam	In 2015, higher fish abundance, greater diversity, and overall fish assemblages in the upper section of the Lower Rouge River indicated better water quality and habitat conditions than in the lower sections. Removal of the dam at Wayne Road opened up new habitats to both resident and migratory species. The appearance of emerald shiner in fair numbers at Ford Field in 2015 (not found in 1995) indicates that some Great Lakes species requiring better water quality are starting to migrate up through the Mainstem Rouge River; a significant increase in species diversity from 1995 to 2015 is probably the result of cleanup and restoration efforts over the last 30 years

Table 5—*Continued*

River Segment/Tributary	Description	Survey Findings
Lower Rouge River, Wayne County	Immediately downstream from the Henry Ford Estate Dam	In 2016, 28 species were collected during the four sampling periods; gizzard shad, emerald shiner, and yellow perch were most abundant, followed by largemouth bass, carp, white sucker, rock bass, and pumpkinseed. Although the total number of species was similar between 1993 (27) and 2016 (28), the types and abundance varied.
Lower Rouge River, Wayne County	Lower Mainstem near Fordson Island, downstream from the Ford Rouge Plant	In 2016, a total of 48 individuals representing eight fish species were collected; the most abundant species were bluntnose minnow, pumpkinseed, and rock bass. Other species caught included largemouth bass, golden shiner, bluegill, and brown and black bullhead; most species found were typical of quiet water habitats, reflecting the extremely broad channel with slow-moving water in this portion of the river.

In the Middle Branch in Plymouth Township, fish abundance more than doubled between 2002 and 2018, and fish diversity improved from 6 species historically to 9–11 species in 2018. In the upper section of the Lower Branch, fish abundance and diversity improved because of improved water quality and habitat conditions, and removal of the dam at Wayne Road (fig. 21), which opened new habitats to both resident and migratory species.

No corresponding improvements have been noted recently in the lower reaches of the Lower Branch. However, in 2018–19, a fish passage was created in the Lower Branch at the Henry Ford Estate Dam in Dearborn (fig. 22). This fish passage is about 15 feet wide and includes riffles and pools mimicking a natural waterway. This fish passage is currently offline allowing vegetation to establish to stabilize the banks, but when opened, it will enable many resident and migratory fish species to access additional habitats and segments above the dam. Together, removal of the Wayne Road and Danvers Pond dams and construction of the fish passage at the Henry Ford Estate will reconnect 50 miles of the main river with 108 miles of smaller tributaries. This will improve and enhance

Fig. 21. Completed dam removal at on the Lower Branch at Wayne Road, Wayne, Michigan, in 2017. (Photograph courtesy Alliance of Rouge Communities.)

habitat for many species of fish, macroinvertebrates, mussels, and other aquatic life.

Angler observations have also shown that steelhead have returned to the lower river in limited numbers, indicating improved water quality. Anglers have reported more northern pike in the lower river. Populations of gamefish were restored in Newburgh Lake following the previously mentioned sediment remediation and habitat rehabilitation, and more species and size classes are safe to eat. Recreational fishing in Newburgh Lake has increased as a result.

The frequent fish kills that occurred in the lower river during the 1960s, 1970s, and early 1980s because of dissolved oxygen depletion, which even included the most pollution-tolerant common carp, have been eliminated. With the rehabilitation of fish habitats—both completed and planned—and the removal of fish barriers, the fishery is poised for additional improvements. Stable flow regimes and further habitat enhancements will help further recovery.

The Role of Post-Construction Stormwater Controls and Green Infrastructure

Through Rouge Project–funded studies and pilot projects implemented across the watershed, the understanding of the critical need for better

Fig. 22. Fishway (*foreground*) constructed in 2020, which bypasses the historic dam at the Henry Ford Estate (*background*) in Dearborn, Michigan. (Photograph courtesy Alliance of Rouge Communities.)

on-site stormwater management practices using green infrastructure has matured. These pilot projects included detention-pond retrofits in Canton Township; installation of a pervious asphalt parking lot at the Southfield Civic Center; conversion of turf areas to deep-rooted native plant prairie landscapes in Eliza Howell Park (Detroit), Rouge Park (Detroit), and in the Lower, Middle, and Upper Rouge River Wayne County Parkways; and the restoration of wetlands including the Valley Woods Nature Preserve (Southfield). These types of pilot projects provided the basis for understanding how to increase the volume of stormwater managed on-site, through green infrastructure infiltration practices, to maintain or restore a more natural stormwater runoff discharge rate (see chapter 6).

As of 2021, counties and local communities are further improving their stormwater management by using green infrastructure infiltration practices and extended detention for new and redevelopment projects. This work is supported by nonprofit organizations such as Friends of the Rouge, who have expanded the use of green infrastructure through-

Fig. 23. Ford Motor Company interns planting a rain garden at Plymouth Arts and Recreation Complex in Northville with Friends of the Rouge, 2021. (Photograph courtesy Friends of the Rouge.)

out the watershed by working with public and private property owners to create rain gardens and bioswales to reduce runoff volumes (fig. 23). These efforts will decrease peak flows to and within the Rouge River. This will also improve habitat conditions and water quality, help restore the river's beneficial uses, and increase property values and the quality of life throughout the watershed.

The Alliance of Rouge Communities and the Future

Ten years after the beginning of the Rouge Project, key stakeholders had the foresight to establish a locally funded organization to carry out watershed restoration efforts beyond the federally funded Rouge Project, which ended in 2014. After two years of discussion, the Alliance of Rouge Communities formed in August 2003, with a membership of 38 communities and 3 counties. However, the ARC lacked the authority to collect dues from member communities. This led to the passage of

Watershed Alliance legislation as authorized by Public Act 517 of 2004, which amended the Michigan Natural Resources and Environmental Protection Act 451 of 1994. Passage of this act enabled the formation of the ARC in January 2006. Three years later, the ARC was recognized as a 501(c)(3) nonprofit, which opened access to federal grant funds.

The ARC was established to provide an institutional mechanism to encourage watershed-wide cooperation and mutual support to meet water-quality permit requirements for its members while restoring beneficial uses of the river for area residents. The ARC is a voluntary member-based alliance, which in February 2021 consisted of 42 communities, counties, and colleges, and 7 cooperating partners, including the Friends of the Rouge, the Great Lakes Waters Authority, the Rouge River Advisory Council, and the Southeast Michigan Council of Governments.

Standing on the shoulders of the Rouge Project, the ARC has been particularly effective in facilitating communication among watershed stakeholders and developing collaborative approaches to meeting Michigan's municipal stormwater permitting requirements. This has allowed the ARC to focus aggressive stormwater best-management practices on priority areas with the poorest water quality. This is an example of how the operations of the ARC, using a collaborative watershed approach, saves money and yields better results than if communities addressed permit requirements individually.

In 2020, the ARC had an annual core budget of $315,000, which was used to support watershed monitoring, data analysis, public education activities, and illicit discharge investigations. Among other activities, this budget allowed the ARC in 2018 and 2019 to identify 12 illicit connections that were conveying sewage to storm drains (ARC 2020a), and to participate in the regional One Water Public Education Campaign that reached 25 million people in 2019 (ARC 2020b).

The ARC's activities go beyond those required by state permits. As fiduciary for the RRAC, the ARC is responsible for implementing watershed restoration projects that are approved by the RRAC. In this role, the ARC facilitates RRAC meetings, communicates with key state and federal partners, secures grant funding, and oversees the design and construction of many of the restoration projects listed in table 4.

Although its core services are locally funded, the ARC's success has been amplified by state and federal grant funding focused on improving Areas of Concern. The ARC has secured almost $20 million in grant funding (2009–2020), largely to implement restoration projects recommended by RRAC. These grants have resulted in a return of $3.94 in grant funds for every $1.00 of membership dues (ARC 2018). The RRAC estimates that with the expenditure of current and future Great Lakes Restoration Initiative funds, the Rouge River Area of Concern will realize a positive economic impact of $191–$245 million.

The operations of the ARC are critical to continued efforts to restore the Rouge River because they provide local communities with expert technical watershed restoration knowledge, provide services in a more cost-effective manner than if communities were to work individually, allow neighboring communities to share lessons learned, and allow communities to address the worst pollution problems first.

From Cleanup to Restoration to Revitalization

The revival of the Rouge River watershed has been an unqualified success, enabled through pollution prevention and control, contaminated sediment remediation, and habitat restoration. Evidence of improvement in both remedial action and ecological indicators is presented in table 6. Perhaps the best indicator of success is that people are returning to the river and benefiting from living, working, and playing in the watershed.

Concluding Remarks and Lessons Learned

The Rouge Project facilitated the completion of 380 projects by 75 communities and agencies at a cost of over $1 billion (Ridgway et al. 2019). This vastly improved the quality of water, sediment, and biological organisms. After decades of effort and investment, the Rouge River now rarely violates certain water-quality standards. This remarkable recovery was initiated by a small handful of citizens, facilitated by local municipal leaders, and supported by the federal government. The Rouge River is now a model for how a holistic ecosystem approach to water pollution can result in cost-effective, larger-scale, and faster restoration, while meeting local needs (Ridgway et al. 2010).

The success in the Rouge River has shown that a concerted effort from a diverse group of stakeholders can bring a river back to life. The Rouge River cleanup effort evolved with changes in state and federal

Table 6. Examples of Improvements in the Rouge River Watershed since 1985

Remedial Action Indicator	Evidence
Combined sewer overflows (CSOs)	• Ten CSO retention treatment basins and six sanitary and storm sewer separation projects have been constructed. • Approximately 89 of the 126 miles of stream in the Rouge River watershed are now free of the adverse impacts of uncontrolled CSO discharges. • CSO pollutant loads to the river have been reduced by 90% to 100% during most events.
Illicit discharges	• Over 2,000 illicit discharges of wastewater to the Rouge River have been identified and have been or are being corrected. • Over 1,603,000 pounds of polluting materials and 466 million gallons of polluted water are estimated to have been removed from the Rouge River as of 2013, through the elimination of illicit discharge efforts in the watershed.
On-site sewage disposal systems	• 898 failed onsite sewage disposal systems have been found and corrected in the Rouge River areas of Wayne, Washtenaw, and Oakland Counties.
Green infrastructure	• Over 60 acres of native plant grow zones have been installed throughout the watershed. • Over 15,000 native herbaceous plants and 3,500 trees and shrubs have been planted. • Over 8,600 tree seedlings have been distributed. • Over 10,000 cubic yards of invasive plants have been removed.
Streambank stabilization	• Over 17,000 feet of streambank have been stabilized, including restoration of the 2,200 feet oxbow restoration at Greenfield Village to provide natural riverine habitat along the channelized portion of the main Rouge River.
Contaminated sediment remediation	• In a Double Eagle Steel Coating Company project, 40,000 cubic yards of zinc-contaminated sediment was removed from the lower river in 1986 at a cost of $1 million. • In the Evans Ditch project, 9,550 cubic yards of PCB-contaminated sediment was removed and disposed of in 1997 at a cost of $750,000. • In Newburgh Lake, 317,450 tons of PCB-contaminated sediment was removed and placed in a Type II landfill in 1997–1998, at a cost of $11 million. • In the Lower Rouge River Old Channel, 69,975 cubic yards of contaminated sediment were removed in 2019–2020, at a cost of $50 million.
Dam removal	• Two dams were removed from the Rouge River: Danvers Pond Dam along Pebble Creek, a tributary to the Main Rouge River, and the Wayne Road Dam along the Lower Rouge River. Over 122 miles of river and tributary streams have been reconnected to the Great Lakes for fish passage for the first time in over a century. • A fishway around the historic Henry Ford Estate Dam, the first dam on the Main Rouge River, is under construction, effectively reconnecting over 155 miles of river and tributaries to the Great Lakes.

Table 6—*Continued*

Ecological Indicator	Evidence
Dissolved oxygen	• In 1994, the dissolved oxygen was routinely zero. • Today, dissolved oxygen never goes to zero and rarely goes below 5 mg/L. • Dissolved oxygen improved by 0.22 mg/L per year for fifteen years starting in 1994.
Fish kills	• Frequent fish kills, including kills of pollution-tolerant common carp, which occurred in the lower river during the 1960s, 1970s, and early 1980s because of dissolved oxygen depletion, have been eliminated.
Benthos	• There has been overall improvement in benthic macroinvertebrate communities in the downstream sections of all of the major branches, with most sites now considered "fair."
Fish community	• Headwaters' fisheries remain healthy, with species indicative of good water and habitat quality. • In 2017–18, the fishery at stations in the Upper Rouge River had a high diversity with good numbers of pollution-intolerant species. • In the Middle Rouge River in Plymouth Township, fish abundance more than doubled between 2002 and 2018, and fish diversity improved from 6 species historically to 9–11 species in 2018. • However, no improvements have been noted recently in the lower reaches of the Lower Rouge River. • Populations of gamefish have been restored in Newburgh Lake following sediment remediation and habitat rehabilitation. • Anglers have reported that steelhead have returned to the lower river and there are more northern pike in the lower river.
Beaver	• Between the 1940s and 1970s, beaver could not have survived in the lower river because of the significant oil pollution (oiled fur becomes matted and they lose their ability to trap air and water to control body temperature). • Today, they have been found in the river at the University of Michigan–Dearborn and the headwaters, the first time that beaver have been reported in the area since 1877.

programs—from early planning under Section 208 of the 1972 Clean Water Act, to the Rouge River RAP initiated in 1985, to the Rouge Project, started in 1993, that provided millions in federal funding, to the establishment of the ARC in 2006, which continues this restoration work with essential funding from communities and the Great Lakes Restoration Initiative. The cleanup process can best be described as evolving from top-down, command-and-control water-pollution programs to bottom-up, ecosystem-based partnerships to restore impaired beneficial uses. Adaptive management is practiced, in which assessments are made, priorities set, and action taken in an iterative fashion for continuous improvement. Institutional arrangements have been flexible and responsive to local needs.

Urban water quality challenges of the Rouge River watershed are best addressed on a watershed scale. Indeed, Platt (2006) has shown that urban watershed management is part science and part art, and that it depends on creative institutional arrangements, combinations of federal and state mandates, and incentives, regional partnerships, municipal awareness of externalities, and a grassroots sense of community.

Other lessons learned include the following (Ridgway et al. 2019):

- Managing stormwater on-site to prevent pollution and control contaminants at their source is a top priority.
- Urban river restoration is a long-term process—build a record of success and celebrate it frequently.
- Prioritize control programs to maximize environmental improvement as quickly as possible.
- Assess cumulative watershed impacts before fashioning watershed solutions—this discourages treating symptoms and helps focus on cures.
- Tailor action plans and tools to address watershed problems.
- Ensure local ownership of action plans, with financial and technical assistance from state and federal governments.
- Foster community cooperation—innovative solutions arise out of collaboration.
- Ensure flexible institutional arrangements and allow them to evolve over time to meet future needs and build on growing knowledge of problems, causes, and solutions.
- Measure ecosystem responses in a transparent fashion, which builds trust.
- Build the capacity of locally driven institutional structures such as ARC and citizen stewardship efforts such as FOTR, to ensure continuity and sustain partner support.

LITERATURE CITED

Alliance of Rouge Communities (ARC). 2012. "Rouge River Watershed Management Plan." Canton, MI.

Alliance of Rouge Communities. 2018. "Comparing Alternative Methods of Assessing Stormwater Fees for Three Example Communities in the Rouge River Watershed." Canton, MI.

Alliance of Rouge Communities. 2020a. "Rouge River Collaborative Illicit Discharge Elimination Program 2018–2019 Progress Report." Canton, MI.

Alliance of Rouge Communities. 2020b. "Rouge River Collaborative Public Education Program 2018–2019 Progress Report." Canton, MI.

Arnold, C.L., Gibbons, C.J. 1996. "Impervious Surface Coverage: The Emergence of a Key Environmental Indicator." *Journal of the American Planning Association* 62 (2): 243–58.

Beam, J.D., Braunscheidel, J.J., 1998. "Rouge River Assessment." Michigan Department of Natural Resources, Fishery Division, Special Report 22, Lansing, MI.

Bean, C.J., Mullett, N., Hartig, J.H., 2003. "Watershed Planning and Management: The Rouge River Experience." In Hartig, J.H., ed., *Honoring Our Detroit River: Caring for Our Home*, 185–98. Bloomfield Hills, MI: Cranbrook Institute of Science.

Canada and the United States, 1987. "Protocol to the Great Lakes Water Quality Agreement." Windsor, Ontario, Canada.

DeMaria, A., Mullett, N. 2020. "Dissolved Oxygen Levels in the Rouge River." In Hartig, J.H., Francoeur, S.F., Ciborowski, J.J.H., Gannon, J.E., Sanders, C., Galvao-Ferreira, P., Knauss, C.R., Gell, G., Berk, K., eds. "Checkup: Assessing Ecosystem Health of the Detroit River and Western Lake Erie," 207–13. Great Lakes Institute for Environmental Research Occasional Publication No. 11, University of Windsor, Ontario, Canada.

Diebolt, J. 1985. "Bad Rouge Water May Have Killed Novi Man." *Detroit Free Press*. October 5.

Giffels/Black and Veatch. 1980. "Quantity and Quality of Combined Sewer Overflows." Prepared for the Detroit River Water and Sewerage Department, Detroit, MI.

Gnau, T.B. 1975. "Indian Mounds to Dumping Grounds: A History of the Rouge River." *Dearborn Historian* 15 (2): 57–75.

Hartig, J.H. 2010. *Burning Rivers: Revival of Four Urban-Industrial Rivers That Caught on Fire*. Ecovision World Monograph Series, Aquatic Ecosystem Health and Management Society, Burlington, Ontario, Canada. Essex, UK: Multi-Science Publishing Company.

Hartig, J.H., Francoeur, S.F., Ciborowski, J.J.H., Gannon, J.E., Sanders, C., Galvao-Ferreira, P., Knauss, C.R., Gell, G., Berk, K., eds. 2020. "Checkup: Assessing Ecosystem Health of the Detroit River and Western Lake Erie." Great Lakes Institute for Environmental Research Occasional Publication No. 11, University of Windsor, Ontario, Canada.

International Joint Commission Great Lakes Water Quality Board. 1985. "Report on Great Lakes Water Quality." Windsor, Ontario, Canada.

Jackson, G. 1975. "A Biological Investigation of the Rouge River, Wayne and Oakland Counties, May 17 to October 19, 1973." Michigan Department of Natural Resources, Bureau of Water Management, Lansing, MI.

Michigan Department of Natural Resources and Southeast Michigan Council of Governments. 1988. "Rouge River Remedial Action Plan." Lansing and Detroit, MI.

Murray, J. 1994. "Rouge River Watershed Management: Implementing a Remedial Action Plan (RAP)." *Proceedings of the 67th Annual Conference of Water Environment Federation.* Alexandria, VA.

Petrella, S., Maguire, T.J., Thompson, S. 2020. "Benthic Macroinvertebrates in the Rouge River Watershed." In Hartig, J.H., Francoeur, S.F., Ciborowski, J.J.H., Gannon, J.E., Sanders, C., Galvao-Ferreira, P., Knauss, C.R., Gell, G., Berk, K., eds., "Checkup: Assessing Ecosystem Health of the Detroit River and Western Lake Erie," 151–56. Great Lakes Institute for Environmental Research Occasional Publication No. 11, University of Windsor, Ontario, Canada.

Platt, R.H. 2006. "Urban Watershed Management: Sustainability, One Stream at a Time." *Environment: Science and Policy of Sustainable Development* 48 (4): 26–42.

Ridgway, J. 2010. "The Rouge River National Wet Weather Demonstration Project: Eighteen Years of Documented Success." Cities of the Future/Urban River Restoration. Water Environment Federation. Alexandria, VA.

Ridgway, J.W. McCormack, F.M. 1994. "Rouge River Watershed Nonpoint Source Management: Significant Components of Urban Pollutant Loads—Crossing the Final Hurdles for Achieving Water Quality Standards." WEFTEC, Water Environment Federation, Alexandria, VA.

Ridgway, J.W., Tolpa, E.R., Lindquist, E., Schrameck, R.E. 1996. "One Size Does Not Fit All: Storm Water Is a Bigger Issue Since Local Communities Have No Regulatory Requirements Beyond CSO Controls." Watershed 1996, Water Environment Federation. Alexandria, VA.

Ridgway, J., Cave, K., DeMaria, A., O'Meara, J., Hartig, J.H. 2018. "The Rouge River Area of Concern—A Multi-Year, Multi-Level Successful Approach to Restoration of Impaired Beneficial Uses." *Aquatic Ecosystem Health & Management* 21 (4): 398–408.

Rouge RAP Advisory Council. 1994. "Rouge River Remedial Action Plan Update." Lansing, MI.

Rouge RAP Advisory Council. 1999. "Rouge River Report Card." Michigan Department of Environmental Quality, Lansing, MI.

Rouge RAP Advisory Council. 2004. "Rouge River Remedial Action Plan Revision." Michigan Department of Environmental Quality, Lansing, MI.

Schrameck, R., Fields, M., Synk, M. 1992. "Restoring the Rouge." In Hartig, J.H., Zarull, M.A., eds., *Under RAPs: Toward Grassroots Ecological Democracy in the Great Lakes Basin*, 73–91. Ann Arbor: University of Michigan Press.

Vallentyne, J.R., Beeton, A.M. 1988. "The Ecosystem Approach to Managing Human Uses and Abuses of Natural Resources in the Great Lakes Basin." *Environmental Conservation* 15 (1): 58–62.

Vaughan, R.D., Harlow, G.L. 1965. "Report on Pollution of the Detroit River, Michigan Waters of Lake Erie, and Their Tributaries." US Department of Health, Education, and Welfare. Grosse Ile, MI.

World Health Organization. 2003. "A Pocket Guide to Building Partnerships." Geneva, Switzerland.

6   THE NEED FOR GREEN INFRASTRUCTURE

Cyndi Ross

A big goal the US Clean Water Act set for our nation's waters is to restore water quality so that all surface waters are fishable, swimmable, and drinkable. This is a tall order for the Rouge, once one of the most polluted rivers in the country. We're working toward that goal, even if it will take many decades for us to get there.

Friends of the Rouge (FOTR) restoration programs have specific goals to help us track progress and celebrate our successes as we work toward a fully restored Rouge River. Most of these goals focus on telling the public about current threats or impacts to water quality and providing ways for them to reduce these threats or causes of pollution. Engaging the public in restoration helps to develop stewards who will pass on the lessons they've learned at home and in their community. Providing examples they can copy and hands-on experience are critical to reaching our goals, reducing rainwater runoff, and improving water quality.

Point-Source Pollution

Many types and sources of the pollution affect the Rouge River. Historically, industrial and municipal wastes were major sources of pollution. This is known as point-source pollution, which comes from an identifiable pipe or discharge point. This type of pollution has largely been reduced or controlled through the US Environmental Protection Agency's National Pollutant Discharge Elimination System regulatory process implemented by the Michigan Department of Environment, Great Lakes, and Energy.

Detroit and other older communities that have combined sewer systems are working to control sewer overflows that occur during rain or snowstorms. Combined sewers receive wastewater from homes and businesses as well as rainwater from streets and parking lots, and carry it to the Detroit Water Resource Recovery Facility (formerly the wastewater treatment plant) for primary and secondary treatment before the water is returned to the Detroit River near the mouth of the Rouge River near Zug Island. During times of heavy rain and snowmelt, the system fills to capacity. A safety mechanism built into the system to prevent basement backups and street flooding is overflow pipes that discharge directly into the Rouge and Detroit Rivers. These combined sewer overflow (CSO) events send raw sewage, household cleansers, medications, oil, road salt, lawn-care chemicals, and more into our rivers. In addition to the obvious pollution problems, this system has a serious economic drawback—it is very expensive to remediate.

Nonpoint-Source Pollution

Another source of pollution, referred to as nonpoint-source pollution, is more difficult to control. In cities, this pollution is attributed to urbanization. It is the largest threat to the health of the Rouge River today. It is not unique to the Rouge watershed or to Michigan. Nonpoint-source pollution is the leading source of pollution in all of our urban rivers. It is the result of the large amount of land covered by impervious surfaces—roads, parking lots, homes, shopping centers, office buildings, industrial businesses, etc. When rain hits these surfaces it has no place to go, so it runs off the landscape and flows into the nearest storm drain, picking up pollutants along the way. Storm sewers carry trash, lawn fertilizers, herbicides and pesticides from residential and commercial landscapes, bacteria from pet waste and failing septic systems, motor oil, brake dust, road deicers, and many other pollutants to rivers and streams. This happens frequently when it rains heavily in suburban communities with separated sewer systems.

When it doesn't rain and under dry weather conditions, the sanitary sewer system takes the wastewater from our homes and businesses and sends it to the Water Resource Recovery Facility for treatment before discharging it to the Detroit River near the mouth of the Rouge River. When rainfall is light, the storm sewer system collects it from our streets and parking lots and sends it directly into nearby lakes and streams. This seemed like an ideal solution when these communities were newly developed, but it has its own unanticipated issues. The runoff doesn't receive any treatment, and everything it picks up from the landscape is carried to the river every time it rains. The volume of stormwater run-off that quickly flows through the system to the river creates additional problems. The river can rise rapidly during and immediately after rainy weather. These "flashy flows" cause streambank erosion that washes sediment into the river, which can clog the gills of fish and other sensitive animals, leading to fish and water insect die-offs. Sediment also carries phosphorus and heavy metals to the river. During dry summer months, the river often has too little water, in part because we have destroyed the natural process of rain falling on vegetated landscapes and soaking into the ground, where it is cleaned and cooled before slowly making its way to the river.

Green Infrastructure: A Low-Cost Solution

The solution is both simple and incredibly challenging. As mentioned before, nonpoint-source pollution is one of the most difficult to control because it depends on millions of people taking action to reduce this pollution. Just as the problem is the result of nearly a million and a half people living on the 467 square miles of land that make up the Rouge River watershed, so is the solution. It is critical for individuals, governments, and businesses to manage rainwater on their property and along highways and roads.

Work to control CSOs falls to watershed municipalities and the Great Lakes Water Authority, who have constructed expensive human-engineered infrastructure in the form of massive underground storage tanks and screening and treatment facilities. This has improved water quality; the drawback is that it is very expensive to build and maintain, and has limited capacity that is exceeded during large rainfalls or snowmelt. More facilities are currently needed. Weather patterns are changing, and it is predicted the area will experience heavier rainfalls over shorter periods. The facilities will become woefully inadequate with the increased rainfalls associated with climate change.

What Is Green Infrastructure?

A simple, low-cost solution that has transformed urban river restoration work involves mimicking nature and restoring natural processes lost

Fig. 24. Completion of a rain garden by Friends of the Rouge volunteers, Detroit. (Photo credit: Cyndi Ross.)

to urbanization. These nature-based solutions provide storage space for rainwater to pool, soak into the ground, be taken in by plants, and be evaporated by the sun (see fig. 24). The wetlands, which provided these services for thousands of years, are largely gone from the watershed. Rain gardens and bioswales serve in this way on a very small scale. These best practices are part of a growing movement (pun intended) to use a regional system of green infrastructure to improve urban rivers and streams and reduce stormwater runoff. These practices include tree plantings, water harvesting, permeable pavement, green roofs, and amended soils, along with rain gardens and bioswales.

Section 502 of the Clean Water Act defines green infrastructure as "the range of measures that use plant or soil systems, permeable pavement or other permeable surfaces or substrates, stormwater harvest and reuse, or landscaping to store, infiltrate, or promote evaporation [of] stormwater and reduce flows to sewer systems or to surface waters." In the *Journal of Conservation Planning* the definition is expanded to include existing natural ecosystems, farms, parks, wilderness, and open space, and emphasizes the need to conserve these assets (McDonald et al. 2005).

Examples of Green Infrastructure Practices

To understand nature-based solutions better, here are a few examples of common green infrastructure practices that can be implemented to manage rainwater and reduce flooding in urban areas.

Water Harvesting. Water harvesting is an easy first step to reduce run-off from homes and buildings. Water is collected in rain barrels, totes, or cisterns. Rain barrels are most appropriate for residential use. They range in size from 50 to 90 gallons. Generally, one small rain event will fill a rain barrel receiving water from one downspout. The overall impact isn't huge, but, as previously mentioned, every little bit helps. It is important to use the water that has been collected between rain events. This maximizes the impact of your rain barrel. Rainwater can be used to water houseplants, hanging baskets, and flowerpots, perennial beds, lawns, and other landscaping. Due to bacteria from bird droppings on the roof, water should be applied to the soil instead of directly on the plants when watering food crops. The water can also be used to wash outdoor furniture and for other purposes. Rain barrels need to be drained and removed from use during winter months to prevent cracking of the barrels. Larger vessels work in the same way. Totes generally store 275 gallons, and cisterns can hold thousands of gallons. Cisterns can be placed above or below ground. If placed below ground, a pump is needed to make use of the water.

Rain Gardens and Bioswales. Rain gardens are designed to collect and store water and allow it to soak into the ground or evaporate; they are intended to drain within 48 hours so there is no risk of breeding mosquitos. Bioswales are designed to move water (fig. 25). They are usually planted in a straight line and often have a drainage system connected to a storm sewer. Both rain gardens and bioswales are called "bioretention practices." They are planted with deep-rooted native flowers, grasses, and sedges and often accented with shrubs or small trees. Soils are made more porous or removed and replaced with porous soils. Some are designed with gravel below the porous soil to maximize the rainwater storage capacity. Native vegetation in established bioretention areas takes in and releases 10–20% of the rainwater into the atmosphere. Their extensive roots also create pore space in the soil. This provides an ave-

Fig. 25. Construction of a bioswale at Bethany Lutheran Church in Detroit.
(Photo credit: Cyndi Ross.)

nue for rainwater to penetrate deep into the ground, recharging groundwater and stabilizing the river's base flow.

Green Streets. Green streets incorporate green infrastructure practices
such as rain gardens and bioswales in the right-of-way to manage stormwater runoff and filter sediment. These are more challenging to implement, because space is usually limited, and designers have to consider
many modes of transportation (SEMCOG 2013). They often result in
improved space for pedestrians and are a welcomed community asset.
Incorporating green streets in urban areas produces many benefits.

- Native-plant grow zones, streamside buffers, meadows, and prairie
  plantings have very little runoff. These areas restore natural processes similar to what existed before the area was settled. Nearly
  all the rainwater soaks into the ground, is soaked up by the plants,
  or is evaporated by the sun.
- Urban trees can significantly reduce runoff volume and save communities money by minimizing the use of engineered solutions
  to reduce flooding and stormwater pollution. Trees capture or
  intercept rainfall in their canopies where it is temporarily stored

before evaporating or being transferred to the ground via stems, branches, and the trunk for root absorption (Cappiella et al. 2016).

- Green roofs are often used in densely populated areas with limited space for other green infrastructure practices. Layers of membranes and planting media soak up the rain, and it is then used by the plants or evaporated. Green roofs can reduce the peak flow by as much as 65% and increase the time it takes rainwater to flow to the sewer (US General Services Administration 2011). Sedum species are traditionally used, though other species are sometimes used as well (see chapter 4). Buildings and rooftops need to be structurally sound and able to hold the weight of the material.

- Permeable versions of traditionally impervious paving products are available that allow water to soak in rather than run off. This reduces the amount of rainwater runoff while providing the utility of pavement. As driveways, parking lots, walkways, and other impervious surfaces need to be replaced, these can be great alternatives.

Additional Benefits of Green Infrastructure

Green infrastructure produces many other benefits. In addition to managing stormwater, many of these practices help with flood control, filter sediment and pollutants from runoff and floodwaters, provide critical habitat for pollinators and other urban wildlife, beautify neighborhoods and communities, improve human health, and aid in *place-making*—a planning technique that makes a particular place special and that fosters a sense of authentic human attachment. There are economic benefits to green infrastructure as well. According to the Southeast Michigan Council of Governments (SEMCOG), green streets and shopping districts encourage people to stay longer and spend more money (SEMCOG 2014).

Wildlife Benefits. Native plants used in green infrastructure provide food, shelter, and breeding areas for birds, bees, butterflies, and other beneficial insects. Native plants and animals evolved together for tens of thousands of years. They depend on one another for their survival. Plants provide food in the form of nectar, pollen, fruit, nuts, berries, leaves, stalks, and bark. Wildlife supports plants by spreading their seed, pollinating their flowers, fending off predators, and more. Many butterflies are host-specific and must lay their eggs on particular plants. Monarchs are a well-known example of this relationship, as they must lay their eggs on milkweed plants.

Beautification. Native plantings, rain gardens, and bioswales create attractive spaces in the community. Flowering plants provide beautiful color throughout the growing season. Gardens provide structure and interest throughout the year.

Human Health. Research has revealed a wealth of health benefits to "nearby nature." For example, experience with nature can help to reduce stress and improve mental health (Wolf and Brinkley 2016). Nature in cities can help people to be more physically active, which reduces the risk of heart disease and diabetes. According to The Nature Conservancy, 50% of US adults do not engage in the minimum recommendations for aerobic activity and 26% do not engage in any physical activity during their leisure time; they are three times as likely to be physically active when living in areas with more green space (House et al. 2017). Additional benefits of green infrastructure on human health result from improved air quality and reductions in the heat-island effect in urban areas.

What Is Friends of the Rouge Doing to Help?

Restoration

FOTR has been working to inform and involve the public in the restoration of the Rouge River since 1986. It started with thousands of volunteers from across the watershed coming together to clean up trash and manage large woody debris in the river through Rouge Rescue. After decades of organizing Rouge Rescue, river sites improved and public perception of the river changed. People began to value the river as a natural resource in their community. Less dumping occurred, so FOTR shifted its focus from cleanup projects to restoration work which would have a larger impact on improving water quality and the health of the river's ecosystem.

Expanding Volunteer Activities

Early restoration activities engaged Rouge Rescue volunteers in controlling invasive plant species and quickly expanded to streambank stabilization projects and planting native vegetation along streambanks to reduce localized erosion and to filter sediment and other pollutants from rainwater runoff. The work expanded even further and FOTR added a year-round restoration program that offered public-education workshops and hands-on demonstration projects. Between 2002 and 2013, FOTR installed 18 streambank stabilization/riparian buffer projects and organized hundreds of public-education workshops focused on streambank stabilization, creation of riparian buffers, native landscaping, backyard wildlife habitats, pollinator gardens, and healthy lawn care.

Native Plantings

This outreach led to the installation of eight native-plant demonstration projects between 2005 and 2015, coordinated in collaboration with watershed municipalities, county governments, houses of worship, a civic organization, and the University of Michigan–Dearborn. Funding to support the Dearborn project was secured from Ford Motor Company, which also provided a team of employees to help install a 3,000-square-foot native landscape in the side yard of the FOTR's former office on the University of Michigan–Dearborn campus.

Rain Gardens

FOTR first organized a rain-garden planting in 2007 in partnership with the University of Michigan–Dearborn's Environmental Interpretive Center. At the time the FOTR office was located on the university campus, so it was important to support the rain garden. That year, the organization's entire restoration budget was allocated to purchasing native plant plugs for the Environmental Interpretive Center rain gardens. Today, the gardens are a wonderful resource available to the public for learning and observing throughout the season.

Rain gardens were growing in popularity across the country at around that time. FOTR began working with watershed municipalities to create rain gardens in their communities, securing small grants to support the work. The game-changer for FOTR with respect to rain gardens took place in the fall of 2011. FOTR partnered with the Sierra Club Great Lakes, Great Communities program to install a residential rain garden to support the creation of a rain garden how-to guide that would be welcoming to a Detroit audience. This was the first rain garden constructed, at the Detroit home of Valerie Burris, a very active and influential member of the community. Burris spoke about her rain garden with neighbors and others in the community, explaining their value and purpose and generating a lot of interest.

The following year, FOTR and Sierra Club installed six additional rain gardens on her block. Burris continues to speak with others about her rain garden, and often notes that the rain garden has improved her quality of life:

> Having a rain garden has not only taught me about nature, but it has also taught me about life. While cleaning out my rain garden I noticed subtle changes from year to year that made me realize I was changing from year to year too, change is growth. I teach my young family members about the rain garden, it teaches them about nature and about life, it connects them to nature. They get it. I love my rain garden. If you commit to your rain garden, it will always deliver.

Rain Gardens to the Rescue

Out of the rain-garden projects emerged a partnership with Sierra Club to expand this effort. The two organizations came together to craft the Rain Gardens to the Rescue program, which would eventually have a huge impact. This joint program was funded by the Fred A. and Barbara M. Erb Family Foundation. It engages Detroiters in a five-part training course where they learn about rain gardens, native plants, rain-garden design, and maintenance. Participants completing the course receive materials and support to install a rain garden of their own. They also support two of their classmates' rain-garden installations. In addition to managing rainwater, the rain gardens and the program were designed to build community and amplify messaging. Garden recipients recruit friends and family to help with their garden installations, adding another layer of outreach and extending the program's influence in the community. Garden tours shine a light on emerging leaders and celebrate their accomplishments. Since its inception in 2015, 81 rain gardens have been created across Detroit through the Rain Gardens to the Rescue program, with locations that include 73 residences, 5 houses of worship, 2 school sites, and 2 city park gardens. Collectively, these gardens store 60,000 gallons of rainwater per rain event. Over 700 people have been involved with the rain-garden installations.

Land + Water WORKS Coalition

Friends of the Rouge is a member of the Land + Water WORKS Coalition. The coalition formed in 2017 to give Detroit residents the resources needed to become better stewards of their environment. The group, made up of 10 nonprofit organizations and led by Detroit Future City, advocates for sustainable land- and water-use practices to promote healthy and equitable communities and to provide economic benefits by implementing green infrastructure.

Through this work, FOTR and Sierra Club expanded rain-garden programming to the nonresidential audience. Thousands of people participated in rain-garden educational events and installations. Eleven rain gardens totaling nearly 4,000 square feet in size were installed at school sites, public parks, community gardens, and houses of worship. These gardens store up to 26,000 gallons of stormwater per rain event, or just under 560,000 gallons annually.

Experience with the St. Suzanne Cody Rouge Community Resource Center provides an example of the transformative nature of this work. The Resource Center was one of the early participants in the Land + Water Works rain-garden programming with FOTR and Sierra Club. They were hosts to public education workshops and received a small demonstration rain garden on their campus. What happened next was truly amazing. The WAY Academy housed in the Center began to use the garden as an educational tool for their middle-school program, and it was incorporated into multiweek lesson plans. Steve Wasko, director of the Center, fully embraced the rain garden and was eager to do more. He and FOTR had been separately exploring the startup of a social enterprise and workforce development program to provide opportunities to Detroiters and to develop a skilled workforce to maintain green infrastructure. Learning of this shared goal, Wasko offered to host the program at the Center, helping to bring rain-garden education to a new audience. Through this partnership an additional 2,000 square feet of rain gardens were installed at the Center. Eighteen downspouts receiving runoff from 15,000 square feet of rooftop were disconnected from the combined sewer system and directed to flow into the rain gardens, keeping as much as 12,500 gallons of rainwater out of the system every time it rains. Educational programming with middle-school youth continues, and has expanded to include high-school-age summer programs. Wasko also worked with the Land + Water Works Coalition to remove a section of parking lot to further reduce stormwater runoff.

The St. Suzanne Cody Rouge Community Resource Center has been a shining example of what watershed educators dream of, and demonstrates what can happen when you put an idea into motion. "If we were to call a meeting to talk about environmental issues in this Detroit neighborhood, frankly no one would come," said Wasko in a conversation about his experience. "The immediate issues of schools, jobs, and economy are simply too strong. But by coming at the environmental benefits by way of education, employment, and direct economic benefit we have found a way to implement these rain gardens where we otherwise might not have considered doing so. Creating an authentic hands-on educational experience for youth as well as adults created a route to solve overlapping issues of education, employment, economy, environment and, also, empowerment."

Master Rain Gardener Programming

In 2016, FOTR was able to expand rain-garden education to communities in the western portion of the watershed. With funding from the Michigan Nonpoint Source Program, FOTR worked with municipalities, schools, and residents to install 18 demonstration rain gardens in an effort to protect and restore the Tonquish and Johnson Creeks. Projects were installed in Canton, Northville, Salem, Plymouth, and Westland. These two creeks have some of the highest-quality habitat and some of the greatest diversity of "bugs" documented through FOTR's citizen-science programs. Downstream sections of Tonquish Creek also have some of the worst habitat.

A five-part Master Rain Gardener training course, developed by the Washtenaw County Drain Commission, was coordinated through this

grant. The program continues today and has been supported by the cities of Livonia and Southfield and by Oakland County's Pure Oakland
Water.

Looking Ahead

Friends of the Rouge continues to expand and improve restoration programming. A goal and a public call-to-action for "1,000 Rain Gardens
for the Rouge" was recently launched. A green infrastructure mapping
project is being developed to track progress toward this goal. The public
will be invited to report their green infrastructure activities for inclusion on the map. Upcoming collaborative work with the National Wildlife Federation blends Rain Gardens to the Rescue programming with
NWF's Sacred Grounds program to create larger rain gardens that provide habitat for wildlife and space for spiritual reflection among Detroit's
faith community.

What You Can Do

Many things can be done to put green infrastructure into practice. Much
as it takes a village to raise a child, it takes a watershed community to
restore a river. Large buildings, roads, and parking lots generate the
most rainwater runoff. It is critical to manage rainwater runoff from
these areas. However, the largest land use in the Rouge River watershed
is low- to medium-density residential, so homeowners play an important role in improving water quality. Many actions can make an immediate difference:

- Disconnect all downspouts from the sewer and direct the water to
  flow onto the lawn or other vegetated areas. There is one exception, however: residents should not disconnect downspouts where
  water cannot be safely extended to a vegetated area, because this
  can create an ice hazard on paved surfaces.
- Collect rainwater from rooftops in rain barrels. That water is a treasured resource—use it to water houseplants, flower gardens, lawns,
  and more. Installation is easy and takes only a few minutes. Elevat-
  ing the rain barrel is also recommended to easily access the water.
- Add rain gardens to your landscape. Rain gardens are attractive

landscaping features with many benefits. Refer to FOTR website at www.therouge.org for how-to guides, species lists, and other resources.

- Reduce air pollution as well as stormwater runoff by mowing less. Convert more of your lawn to perennial gardens or meadow plantings. You will be rewarded by the winged beauties attracted to your yard.
- Pick up pet waste before it rains. This reduces harmful bacterial flowing into our river through the storm sewer.
- Reduce chemical use in the landscape. Learn to accept a few weeds or spot-treat weeds, rather than treating the entire lawn. Fertilize less, use organic fertilizer, or use only fertilizers that are low in phosphorus and contain water-insoluble nitrogen. Never use whole-yard mosquito killer.

Public Action Will Lead to Positive Outcomes for the Rouge River

According to the US Environmental Protection Agency (2021), nearly 300,000 acres of land use in the watershed is residential, commercial, or industrial. If 5% of this land was converted to rain gardens, that would be 7,500 acres of land dedicated to managing stormwater runoff—roughly the size of Redford Township. The magnitude of impact would be huge, not only for reducing rainwater runoff, but for creating habitat for wildlife and attractive amenities across the region to improve climate resiliency and public health.

LITERATURE CITED

Cappiella, K., Claggett, S., Cline, K., Day, S., Galvin, M., MacDonagh, P., Sanders, J., Whitlow, T., Xiao, Q. 2016. "Recommendations of the Expert Panel to Define BMP Effectiveness for Urban Tree Canopy Expansion." Center for Watershed Protection and Virginia Tech, Blacksburg.

House, E., O'Connor, C., Wolf, K., Israel, J., Reynolds, T. 2017. *Outside Our Doors: The Benefits of Cities Where People and Nature Thrive*. Seattle: The Nature Conservancy, Washington State Chapter.

McDonald, L.A., Allen, W.L., Benedict, M.A., O'Conner, K. 2005. "Green Infrastructure Plan Evaluation Frameworks." *Journal of Conservation Planning* 1:6–25.

Southeast Michigan Council of Governments (SEMCOG). 2013. "Great Lakes Green Streets Guidebook: A Compilation of Road Projects Using Green Infrastructure." Detroit.

Southeast Michigan Council of Governments (SEMCOG). 2014. "Green Infrastructure Vision for Southeast Michigan." Detroit.

US Environmental Protection Agency. 2021. "Rouge River Area of Concern." https://www.epa.gov/great-lakes-aocs/rouge-river-aoc#:~:text=Over%20 50%25%20of%20the%20land,%2C%20suburban%2C%20urbanized%20and %20industrial (accessed 20 April 2021).

US General Services Administration. 2011. "The Benefits and Challenges of Green Roofs on Public and Commercial Buildings: A Report of the United States General Services Administration." Washington, DC.

Wolf, K.L., Brinkley, W., 2016. "Nearby Nature for Human Health Sites to Systems." TKF Foundation, Annapolis, MD.

Sally Petrella

Science may be perceived by some as the domain of eggheads who publish papers, yet much of our understanding of the natural world rests on large data sets collected by the general public. Regular citizens taking and recording careful observations about the world are a critical part of scientific research. Tracking spring bird arrival dates to document the effects of climate change and tagging monarch butterflies to find how they migrate from the United States all the way to Mexico are just a few examples.

Citizen science has grown dramatically in recent years, made easier by the growth of the internet. In 2014, "citizen science" was officially added to the *Oxford English Dictionary*, defined as "scientific work undertaken by members of the general public, often in collaboration with or under the direction of professional scientists and scientific institutions." Major institutions are recognizing its value. In 2016, the US Environmental Protection Agency recommended that citizen science be fully integrated into the agency's work (NACEPT 2016).

For more than twenty years, residents of the Rouge River watershed have volunteered their time to collect data that has unearthed problems, guided restoration work and resource management, led to further research, and helped us to understand the nuances of this abused yet recovering urban river.

Rouge River Watershed Citizen Science—Early Days

Friends of the Rouge (FOTR) began engaging K–12 students in water-quality monitoring in 1987 in collaboration with the University of Michigan, but it was not until 1998 that FOTR started training the general population to participate in citizen science. Rouge River citizen science has its origins in Rouge River Watch, a broad program funded by the Rouge River National Wet Weather Demonstration Project (Rouge Project) to teach residents and organizations such as Cub Scouts and corporate groups to become river stewards through a smorgasbord of activities that included organizing cleanups, stenciling storm drains with the warning "Dump No Waste, Drains to River," and monitoring streams and wetlands.

Two parts of River Watch captivated the attention of residents so strongly that they became programs in their own right. The Rouge Frog and Toad Survey and Rouge Benthic Macroinvertebrate Monitoring both focused on biological indicator species that drew the interest of residents, did not require expensive equipment, and relied on established models of volunteers collecting reliable data. The programs share the dual goals of engaging the public and collecting reliable and useful data about the health of the watershed. Fish surveys were added in 2012.

Rouge River Watershed Frog and Toad Survey

The Rouge River Watershed Frog and Toad Survey was started in 1998 to address a need for habitat monitoring as well as a desire to engage residents with local wildlife. Wetlands are critical to the health of a watershed because they filter pollutants, minimize flooding, and provide critical habitat for wildlife. In the highly urbanized Rouge River watershed, wetland quantity and quality were in question. In the late 1990s, organizations around the country were successfully training volunteers to monitor wetlands through surveying for frogs and toads by listening to their calls.

Amphibians are widely used as wetland "indicator species" because their permeable skin absorbs toxins easily, and their dual life cycle in water and land makes their presence a good indicator of overall habitat quality. Frogs and toads, known as anurans, vocalize in the spring to find mates, and each species is easily identified by its distinctive call. It is simple to monitor anuran's presence by listening, something volunteers can be easily trained to do. The calls not only indicate their presence but also a breeding population. The presence of a diverse array of calling anurans indicates a healthy wetland, because each species has different habitat needs.

The Rouge River Advisory Council (RRAC), a citizens' group that helps the state and the US Environmental Protection Agency implement the Rouge River Remedial Action Plan (RAP), had determined that fish and wildlife habitats were impaired (Michigan Department of Natural Resources 1994), but more data were needed to understand the extent of the impairment. The Rouge Project provided funding for the survey. Partners in the survey included the Rouge Project, FOTR, Applied Science and Technology, Inc., Northville Township, the Michigan Department of Environmental Quality (MDEQ), the Natural Heritage Program of the Michigan Department of Natural Resources, and the Southeast Michigan Council of Governments.

Volunteer Participation

The survey drew an amazing response from the community, with 140 people signing up the first year. Charismatic frogs and toads captured the interest of the local media and the general public. The survey started small because partners had no idea how many people would sign up. The first year of the survey only covered a 60-square-mile section of the watershed, and was limited to the four early-calling species—wood frog, midland chorus frog, spring peeper, and American toad. Yet volunteers signed up to survey 85% of the 57 available blocks, and half of them submitted data.

The success of the 1998 survey led to the expansion of the program to a second area and the inclusion of all eight species. Response remained high, and 261 people signed up for the 1999 survey. In 2000, the survey was expanded to include the entire watershed, potentially covering 2,128 blocks. Participation in the survey grew from the initial 140 participants in 1998 to as high as 708 in 2002. The number of survey blocks for which data were received in one season grew from 208 in 1998 to 259 in 2005. People who signed up one year often came back to survey year after year, and that continues today.

Survey Design

Design of the Rouge River Frog and Toad Survey was contracted out to Applied Science and Technology, led by naturalist Richard Wolinski. He adopted similar protocols to those used by amphibian-monitoring programs in the United States and Canada. One major difference was

Wolinski's choice of survey area. Rather than assign routes with stops, Wolinski assigned quarter sections as the survey block. Measuring 160 acres, a quarter section is one of the smallest survey sizes for any survey of this type. The Rouge is a highly urbanized watershed with small pockets of habitat. It was thought that the focus on quarter sections would allow volunteers to identify small amphibian populations and wetlands that would be overlooked in a broader survey.

To train volunteers for the survey, Applied Science and Technology designed a "Guide for Participants" that is still used today and provides all of the information needed to conduct the survey. A tape of the breeding calls was created, and later transferred to compact disk. A one-page observation log is used to enter date and time, temperature, wind speed, precipitation, and species calling. A one-page map for each survey block allows volunteers to record specific survey locations. All observations for a block are combined on one observation log, but the map is used to mark specific locations.

Potential volunteers were recruited locally through flyers, press releases, the FOTR website, and social media and invited to attend two-hour training workshops held in February and March. At the workshops, a slideshow presentation orients volunteers to the watershed, providing an overview of wetlands, their values and types, the anuran species found in the watershed, their preferred habitat, and breeding calls. Attendees were instructed on how to conduct the survey and given the "Guide for Participants," a compact disc with frog call recordings, observation logs, and a survey block map. Survey blocks were assigned based on where each surveyor lived or preferred to survey. Volunteers are expected to conduct surveys on their own, under the specified conditions and protocol. The training workshops continue today in a similar format.

Survey Management

After the first two years, Applied Science and Technology turned over management of the survey to FOTR, because it was always intended that the data remain in the public domain. The Rouge Project provided the funding and Wayne County assisted with data input and mapping. Wolinski expected the survey to be done every five years, based on the biology. But the communities who drove priorities of the Rouge Project funding were mainly interested in public involvement. Since the survey regularly attracted so many residents who might otherwise not care about the watershed, the Rouge Project funded Friends of the Rouge to continue it annually.

The decision to survey quarter sections has made for an intensive survey that reveals small pockets of amphibians, but translating this design for volunteers has been a challenge. Most people are not familiar with the Township, Range, Section, Quarter Section (TRSQ) system. Initially, Wayne County created a map layer called TRSQ that divided the watershed into 2,128 survey blocks. At workshops, volunteers chose blocks by looking at a large map with the grid overlaid, relying on their knowledge of major mile roads to orient them. Once a block was identified, volunteers were given their survey block map photocopied from an atlas, which showed the boundaries but rarely had any wetland indication. As coverage for the survey grew, the set of maps grew. Six or seven boxes of maps were then required for each workshop, and many had to be mailed out after the workshop. This often meant late nights at the office to get maps out before the frogs started calling.

FOTR recognized the need for more accurate maps for volunteers that included wetlands, but there was no existing GIS wetland layer. In 2005, FOTR obtained funding from the Great Lakes National Program Office to map all wetlands and woodlands in the watershed using 2005 aerial photos and ArcGIS. FOTR staff and interns conducted most of the mapping, with assistance from Michigan State University. The project identified 6,578 wetlands covering 15,937 acres, and categorized each by wetland type. It created a baseline for Rouge wetlands and was distributed to all of the Rouge communities. Ducks Unlimited is in the process of updating wetland maps for the Rouge area.

With the new wetland layer, FOTR worked with Oakland County Planning and Economic Development Services to create PDF maps for all 2,128 potential blocks using Wayne County's TRSQ grid, an aerial view, with the wetland layer overlaid. This made it far easier for volunteers to identify potential wetlands and eliminated the need to carry around boxes of printed maps; most maps are now emailed directly to volunteers.

In 2018, with the assistance of past surveyor and GIS specialist Corrie Fochler, FOTR created an online map using ArcGIS Online. This map allows volunteers to locate a survey block, and anyone interested can view past data for each surveyed block.

Breeding Call Recordings

To teach volunteers the breeding calls, audio recordings were made. In 2019, volunteer Kathy Ableson, who had struggled to learn the calls when she participated with her son, used her coding skills to create an app called "Froggy Voice." This program makes it easy to play each call with simple buttons on one screen. Working with advisors and testers from FOTR and with Michigan State University professor James Harding, she added habitat descriptions and call-time information for each species. Ableson created colorful drawings for each species button that illustrate their distinctive characteristics. Users can play multiple species at one time to learn to distinguish them. Volunteers were enthralled by the app and many now carry it into the field on their smartphones. Professor Harding used it in his herpetology class. Ableson is now working with FOTR on a breeding-call quiz to test the knowledge of participants.

Volunteers are further supported in learning the calls by attending "Group Listens" that are held at a location with many known species. Volunteers can practice their listening skills with staff present to verify calls. It is also a social event where surveyors get to compare notes and show off their frog-themed clothing. Partners such as the Southeast Michigan Land Conservancy, West Bloomfield Parks and Recreation, and the Detroit Audubon Society have collaborated on these popular events, which draw in additional non-surveyors.

Data Management

Data entry and management have grown more complex with the many years of data collection. Wayne County initially assisted with data entry, combining separate observations into a simple "yes" or "no" for each species for each block and mapping the results using ArcGIS. FOTR took over data entry and mapping over time and worked with a consultant to create a database to track all observations, rather than just the compiled data for each block. FOTR volunteer Sandra Hamilton completed data input going all the way back to 1998. While this provides an electronic record for every single observation and allows for easy reporting to the Michigan Herpetological Atlas, synthesizing the data back down to species heard for each block has often been problematic.

In 2018, to allow volunteers to submit their observations online,

FOTR rolled out an ArcGIS Collector app called a "Geoform." Past volunteer and GIS specialist Corrie Fochler helped create this app, which can be used on a smartphone or computer. It records the location of the observer based on GPS, or the surveyor can choose it on a map. The point data submitted must then be translated into the survey block in which the point falls. The Geoform seemed to work for the first two years, but in 2020, a flaw in the system was found when many observers entered data when they were no longer in their block and did not correct the location. FOTR is working with Schoolcraft College's GIS department to find a way for the app to locate the block automatically.

The Pandemic

The 2020 COVID-19 pandemic highlighted the value of the survey to residents. The pandemic forced the last-minute cancellation of the second workshop. Unprepared to immediately hold a virtual training, registrants were asked if they wanted to receive the materials and train themselves; most agreed. With stay-at-home orders in place, going outside in nature was one of the few safe things one could do. Volunteers found solace in listening for frogs and toads, and parents especially appreciated an opportunity to get their children outside. In 2021, the trainings were all held virtually, allowing FOTR to attract an even wider audience. The online format allowed FOTR to open the workshop to more people, and some even attended from out of state.

Funding

In 2014, the Rouge Project ended and funding for the survey ceased. FOTR was aware of this and used it as an opportunity to take a year off from training new surveyors and focus on data analysis. The same body that had called for surveys in 1998—the Rouge River Advisory Council—provided funding for the analysis. RRAC had identified 25 habitat projects to address habitat impairments, and FOTR's analysis was needed to give a broader picture of habitat health and identify gaps.

Despite the lack of workshops in 2015, 102 veteran surveyors still submitted data, for 105 blocks. In 2016, one training workshop was offered to keep the program going and new funding was sought. FOTR secured a grant from Lush Cosmetics in 2017 that supported three workshops, and participation slowly built back up; however, the survey still needed a sustainable funding source. In 2019, Bosch sponsored the survey. FOTR planned to ask Bosch to sponsor again in 2020, but due to the pandemic, the Bosch funding was allocated more generally to the organization. In 2021, FOTR made the decision to continue the program because it brings in so many people who become FOTR members and supporters, but funding and the future of the survey are still uncertain.

Findings

Every year, a report on survey results is distributed to volunteers, local communities, the state, and other stakeholders. Reports are posted online and data are posted to an online ArcGIS map. Data are also submitted to the Michigan Herpetological Atlas.

In 2015, FOTR analyzed 17 years of frog and toad data and the 2005 wetland mapping data (RRAC 2015). The 2015 report confirmed seven frog and one toad species actively breeding in the watershed. The Blanchard's cricket frog (*Acris blanchardi*) and pickerel frog (*Lithobates palustris*), which Michigan has classified as threatened species, were not heard and are assumed not to be present in the watershed. The tolerant American toad (*Bufo americanus*) was by far the most common, heard in 84% of all surveyed blocks. Northern leopard frogs (*Rana pipiens*) and bullfrogs (*Rana catesbiana*) were the rarest.

The 2005 wetland mapping showed that half of all wetlands in the Rouge are small forested areas, mainly floodplain forest. Within the 74 survey blocks that had no species calling, 82% of the wetlands had small forests. Eight wetland-restoration projects are in progress along the Lower and Middle Rouge. The headwaters of the Middle and Lower Branches contain the highest diversity of species but continue to lose green space.

The 2015 assessment proved more difficult than expected due to the uneven and often incomplete coverage, which varies year to year depending on volunteer interest and follow-through. One interesting finding was that increasing the number of volunteers did not correlate with higher block coverage. An average of 200 blocks were covered each year, whether 700 people or only 300 signed up.

Volunteer Stewardship

One goal of the survey is to use the data to protect wetlands. In 2007, FOTR worked with MDEQ to create a program to teach volunteers about wetland regulations and how to advocate for wetlands. Called "Watchfrogs," the idea was to create a better-educated citizenry who could comment on proposed wetland-destruction permits. MDEQ had an interest in having a more-educated citizenry that was able to comment with real data. Armed with this knowledge, participants went on to speak up at public hearings and advocate for the wetland protection.

The Watchfrogs program was held from 2007 to 2008 and volunteers continue today to use their knowledge to speak up for wetlands. One volunteer described her experience: "A year ago, I attended a meeting of the Bloomfield Hills Zoning Committee which met to address neighborhood concerns over the proposed construction of a new housing subdivision on a hillside overlooking 'my' frog pond. When invited with others to step forward to address concerns, I spoke quite passionately about spring without peepers and tree frogs and American toads. After the meeting, a number of those present approached me saying of all the citizen statements, mine had the strongest appeal. While others spoke in terms of cost and traffic concerns and legalities, my comments, they said, spoke to the emotional heart of the matter. Without my involvement in the Frog and Toad Survey, I doubt that I'd have even attended this meeting."

Rouge River Benthic Macroinvertebrate Monitoring

Benthic macroinvertebrates, casually known as "bugs," are used all over the world to assess stream health. Technically, benthic macroinvertebrates are animals without a backbone that live in the streambed and can be seen with the naked eye. They include the aquatic insects, clams, snails, and crayfish that form the basis of the river's food web. As stream residents for part or all their lives, they cannot escape pollution, and they respond to human disturbance in predictable ways. As such, they serve as excellent "indicator species," organisms that can be used to track habitat quality in the river (fig. 26). They are easy to sample and identify and the equipment is inexpensive and reusable.

Fig. 26. Citizens monitoring bottom-dwelling invertebrates in the Rouge River. (Photograph courtesy of Friends of the Rouge.)

Program Origins

FOTR's Benthic Macroinvertebrate Monitoring Program began with a 1998 Volunteer Monitoring Program Grant from MDEQ. The program was designed to support local groups in setting up monitoring programs and provided funding, a monitoring protocol, and MDEQ biologists to train volunteers. After going through training, volunteers were expected to adopt a site and monitor it on their own twice a year. After offering several training workshops, FOTR found that few people followed through. Only two volunteers found a site to adopt, monitored it, and submitted data and specimens.

In 2001, FOTR decided to try a different approach to keep volunteers engaged. The nearby Huron River Watershed Council had a very successful Adopt-a-Stream program that attracted as many as a hundred volunteers. Rather than expecting volunteers to sample on their own, the Council held group sampling days open to anyone and had trained team leaders to take teams of volunteers to sample two sites. The team leaders collected the samples from the river and the additional people picked through trays to find the "bugs." The group sampling format allowed many more people to participate and was safer than sending volunteers out on their own.

In 2001, after offering a training workshop for team leaders, FOTR held its first group sampling event on May 19, calling it the "Spring Bug Hunt." Over 20 people participated in seven teams and sampled 14 sites. Organizing monitoring in this way proved to be successful, and the program grew from there. People volunteer for many reasons, and meeting others is a big driver.

In 2002, a Winter Stonefly Search and a Fall Bug Hunt were added and have been ongoing ever since. The Stonefly Search is similar to the spring and fall Bug Hunts, but focuses solely on one sensitive type of insect that hatches from streams in winter. All three events are held annually and regularly attract 60 to 120 volunteers. Surprisingly, the event in winter often draws the biggest crowd.

Training

Over time, FOTR developed the knowledge and skills to take over the training from MDEQ biologists. Two local biologists became advisors to the program, Canadian fish biologist Bruce McCulloch and Wayne County Department of the Environment's Sue Thompson. Team leader training is held in the spring and fall, prior to the Bug Hunts. The training consists of a half day in the lab to introduce the program and cover benthic macroinvertebrate identification (mainly to the level of taxonomic order), followed by a trip to the river to learn sampling, practice identification, complete forms, and collect specimens. Training in illicit discharge elimination was added to teach leaders how to recognize and report spills, dumping, and other affronts to river health.

Trainees are paired with an experienced leader until they feel comfortable leading on their own. Team leaders are invited to examine the specimens they collected under a microscope and practice identification at Bug Identification events, often called "Bugs 'n' Pizza," held after the Bug Hunts. Additional trainings have been offered, including an identification class on taxonomic family-level identification and a class in freshwater mussels. Both had very good attendance.

In 2019, FOTR started offering a "Stonefly Refresher" prior to the Stonefly Search that was well attended by both leaders and regular volunteers. Team leaders and regular volunteers both seem to have an interest in further training.

Sampling Protocol

FOTR's team leaders are trained to use D-frame nets to collect from all available in-stream habitats (riffles, cobbles, pools, stream margins, overhanging vegetation, undercut banks, aquatic plants, wood, etc.) for half an hour from 100 feet of stream. Samples are dumped into trays and volunteers pick out macroinvertebrates and sort them into ice cube trays. All organisms are identified to taxonomic order and some to family.

MDEQ provided a method to score sites similar to calculating an Index of Biological Integrity, called the Stream Quality Index (SQI). The SQI categorizes organisms (mainly by order) according to their tolerance to water quality and habitat conditions, as sensitive, somewhat sensitive, or tolerant. Organisms are then allocated points based on the category and whether they are common (11+) or rare (10 or fewer). SQI values range from 0 to 62 in the Rouge and translate to Excellent, Good, Fair, or Poor. The majority of Rouge sites are in the Fair range.

In addition to the SQI, teams complete a habitat survey and collect representatives of each type of organism, which are later examined in the lab to check field identifications and to gather more information. FOTR built its identification skills over time, and with the assistance of local biologists has been regularly identifying to taxonomic family and sometimes to genus and species. FOTR uses a form adapted from the Huron River Watershed Council and has identified 69 families of aquatic insects in the river.

The Stonefly Search focuses specifically on stonefly families, and sites with stoneflies are considered healthier than those without. In 2019, in partnership with the Izaak Walton League, FOTR began testing sites for road salt with simple test strips for chloride. Several sites had levels high enough to affect aquatic life, and FOTR now plans to test for chloride in the spring and fall to develop a better baseline.

Partners

Diverse partnerships keep this program strong. Biologists from MDEQ (now Michigan Department of Environment, Great Lakes, and Energy [EGLE]) provide oversight for the program and receive the data. They use it to screen for problems and to guide their site choice for the sampling they do every five years in the watershed. Rouge communities provide free meeting space for trainings, support the program, and receive the data. Local biologists assist in identification, training, and data analysis and advise the program manager. Wayne County monitors a number of sites and provides their staff as team leaders when possible. Schoolcraft College began hosting the Fall Bug Hunt and samples a site on their campus. Wayne State University's "Mussel Lab" regularly sends students, who often become team leaders; they have monitored additional sites, and the Lab supports students who have conducted additional research.

Michigan Clean Water Corps

In 2003, Michigan's then-governor Granholm created the Michigan Clean Water Corps to oversee stream monitoring throughout the state, largely replacing the Volunteer Monitoring Program. This group offers training; facilitates accurate data collecting, reporting, and sharing; and provides a forum for communication for programs around the state. The Clean Water Corps required a Quality Assurance Project Plan and a side-by-side certification of staff, which FOTR completed in 2007. FOTR's Quality Assurance Project Plan has since been certified by the US Environmental Protection Agency, which is the gold standard, and a requirement for most federal grants.

Students and Research

College students have been an excellent source of team leaders and have augmented the program with additional research. Wayne State University's Corey Krabbenhoft, who regularly organized students for the bug hunts, compared volunteer and professional data collection to validate the findings by citizen volunteers (Krabbenhoft and Kashian 2020). Professor Abigail Fusaro and her students from Marygrove College analyzed

caddisfly DNA and tracked the arrival and distribution of a new caddisfly family (Rhyacophilidae) in the watershed through genetic haplotypes
(Fusaro et al. 2019). Two University of Michigan–Dearborn master's
students used FOTR's benthic macroinvertebrate data and specimen
collection—Esma Tuncay examined the effect of the discharge from a
wastewater treatment plant and Andrew Pola tested the macroinvertebrates for heavy metals. In 2016, postdoctoral researcher Tim Maguire,
at the University of Windsor, contacted FOTR seeking data to analyze.
Maguire developed a model to make up for data gaps in the Stonefly
Search data and found a strong connection between summer high temperature and stonefly presence (Maguire and Mundle 2020).

Volunteers

Volunteers are recruited through flyers posted on college campuses and
mailed to FOTR supporters. Flyers and emails are shared through the
Rouge municipalities, to past volunteers and FOTR's large network of
people who care about the Rouge River. Press releases are sent to the
local news outlets and events posted on social media. Over time, paper
flyers have been replaced with PDF flyers, and now most publicity is
done online.

Volunteers sign up as individuals, families, or scout, church, corporate, or school groups and range from college students to seniors to
families with children. One interesting group called themselves CSI—
Critter Science Investigators. Some volunteer for several seasons, then
move on; others continue over decades. Some participate to get credit
for community service or extra credit for their classes. Children have
come up through the program, participating with their families, and
then grow old enough to train as team leaders. Many cite their experience in the program as a reason they chose their careers in the sciences.

Funding

The Benthic Macroinvertebrate Program was fully funded by the Rouge
Project through 2014. Following that, the Alliance of Rouge Communities, an organization that assists Rouge communities with stormwater
permits, funded the program. The Alliance funding came to an abrupt
end in December 2018 due to budget cuts and lack of use of the data by

the state for the permits. FOTR struggled to find a sustainable source of funding for several years. Volunteer donations and small corporate and foundation grants barely keep the program going.

In late 2018, RRAC helped secure funding for both the benthic monitoring and fish surveys through a Public Advisory Council grant. RRAC has always been interested in this long-term data collection to guide restoration efforts. This funding was expected to continue, but was held up in 2019 as Michigan's new governor reorganized MDEQ into the Department of Environment, Great Lakes, and Energy. Frustrated, FOTR sought a more sustainable source and approached the communities in which the data is collected. After calculating the cost of sampling a single site, FOTR solicited each community in which they sample to sponsor their sites. More than half of the communities and one of the three counties agreed. Following that, Department of Environment, Great Lakes, and Energy allocated funding for the Public Advisory Council grant, and the Alliance of Rouge Communities offered to sponsor the annual Stonefly Search. This hybrid model of Rouge communities and the state sharing the funding with additional support from individuals could be sustainable, but is subject to political climate.

Findings

Benthic macroinvertebrate communities in the Rouge average Fair SQIs, with higher scores (Good to Excellent) in the headwaters of all four major branches and their tributaries. Scores decline in a downstream direction (a predictable phenomenon). Evans Creek in Southfield and the downstream portion of the Middle Rouge have Poor scores. Trend analysis shows improving scores in the Johnson Creek and Middle Rouge and declining scores in the other branches. The documentation of a Poor benthic community at a site on the Tonquish Creek led to the state investigating further and setting goals for its restoration (MDEQ 2007).

New species have been identified by FOTR volunteers, including a caddisfly (*Rhyacophila lobifera*) that was not only new to the watershed, but also the first record of it in the state of Michigan. However, new species are far more likely to be exotic invasive species. FOTR has been at the forefront, documenting the appearance and movement of organisms not native to the watershed. Zebra mussels (*Dreissena polymorpha*) were first documented in Minnow Pond in 2003, the Middle Rouge in

2004, and Johnson Creek in 2005, followed by Asian clams (*Corbicula fluminea*) in the Middle Rouge in 2009. Red swamp crayfish (*Procambarus clarkii*) were discovered in a Novi retention pond in 2018 by FOTR volunteer Philip Kukulski, leading the Michigan Department of Natural Resources to mount eradication efforts that have been continuing since. FOTR volunteers continue to check nearby streams for red swamp crayfish and alert residents to be on the lookout for them.

In 2019, Ford Motor Company's Ford Fund and Global Data Insight and Analytics Team volunteered their data experts to analyze FOTR's data. This turned into a one-day data "Hackathon" held in 2019, and repeated in 2020 as a virtual event. With the assistance of Tim Maguire, the Ford teams crunched large amounts of data and found correlations between SQI scores and land-cover variables, including impervious surfaces, contaminated areas, and wetlands. Maguire worked with FOTR to hire a 2021 summer fellow from the Cooperative Institute for Great Lakes Research where Maguire now works to continue to expand on the models and explore the correlations.

In the process of collecting the data, FOTR citizen scientists have unearthed problems that needed immediate attention. Trained to recognize illicit discharges, volunteers have found raw sewage discharges, a hydraulic fluid spill in progress, a diesel oil spill, a collapsed bridge, sediment discharges, and more. All of these issues were reported, and FOTR worked to get them addressed. Many of these problems would have continued for years if volunteers had not visited the site. These trained volunteers report similar problems any time they see them. In 2020, when volunteer Bill Eisenman woke up one morning and noticed that the creek in his backyard had turned fluorescent green, he knew who to call.

Rouge River Fish Surveys

In 2012, an undergraduate student from the University of Michigan–Dearborn contacted FOTR about doing an internship focused on sampling fish. The student, Robert Muller, was already a citizen scientist, having taught himself to identify and collect native fishes while in his teens. His knowledge and skill, combined with FOTR's organizational skills, access to volunteers, and partnerships with state and local agencies, created the perfect opportunity. To determine a focus for the surveys, FOTR met with MDEQ, RRAC, and the Michigan Department of Natural Resources, and asked what FOTR could do to fill in gaps in fish data. Two projects arose from the meeting: searching for the redside dace (*Clinostomus elongatus*), an endangered minnow last found in the Rouge's Johnson Creek in 2004 and Seeley Creek in 2005, and tracking fish response to an upcoming dam removal on the Lower Branch.

The internship focused on the status of the endangered redside dace and brought in a second intern, Kristina Blott. Muller's friend Philip Kukulski, a fellow native-fish enthusiast, brought years of experience in fish sampling to the team. FOTR was able to easily recruit volunteers from their large audience of citizen scientists already volunteering for Bug Hunts.

Sampling Protocol

Fish surveys were done using seine nets and dip nets. Muller and Kukulski's extensive experience with seine nets made this the better choice for sampling than electroshocking (a typical survey method that uses electricity to temporarily "stun" fish so they are easy to catch). Seining is also more likely to catch benthic fish (those that occupy habitats near the streambed), since species without swim bladders remain on the substrate when shocked. Nets are stretched across the stream and volunteers chase fish into nets or nets are pulled up to the shoreline. Various techniques are used to sample riffles, pools, wood, and other in-stream habitats. Kukulski directed the sampling and the volunteers and Muller oversaw the measuring and identification of the fish. All fish were returned to the stream, with the exception of any unknown fish, which were photographed and/or sent to University of Michigan biologist Gerald Smith.

Funding

Muller and Kukulski agreed to continue to oversee Rouge fish surveys if funding could be found. In a collaboration between FOTR and University of Michigan–Dearborn, the new University of Michigan Water Center funded a proposal to track benthic macroinvertebrate and fish response to the opening of the Wayne Road Dam in 2012. The grant provided stipends for Muller and Kukulski and support for FOTR staff time to oversee surveys. Muller joked that he went from paying the university (his tuition) to do fish surveys to getting paid to do them. The study lasted through 2015. In subsequent years, funding for surveys was provided by a Healthy Urban Waters Grant through Wayne State University and by RRAC through a Public Advisory Council grant.

Findings

During the first year, 11 sites were sampled on Johnson Creek and 12 on the Upper Branch and its two tributaries (Minnow Pond and Seeley Creeks), and 4,329 individual fish were found. A total of 18 redside dace were found: 10 at 3 Upper Branch sites and 8 at one Johnson Creek site. In Johnson Creek, minnows declined in a downstream direction as stocked brown trout increased in size. This report led the DNR to discontinue stocking of this nonnative species. In Farmington Hills, a population of nonnative mummichog was found and reported to the Department of Natural Resources, which responded by eliminating them. No redside dace have been found since 2012 despite the repeated sampling.

In the second year of surveys, FOTR focused on the Lower Branch and the response of the fish community to the opening of a dam. Muller had been the first to identify the presence of the invasive round goby (*Neogobius melanostomus*) in the Rouge when he found them just below the Fair Lane Estate Dam in 2011. He realized that gobies could access the Lower Branch since its confluence was downstream. The Wayne Road Dam had been opened in August of 2012, and FOTR worked with Muller to sample the Lower Branch in November 2012. A large number of gobies were at the Inkster Road site downstream of the dam, but none were found upstream. This provided the perfect opportunity to observe the impact of an invasive species.

Round goby moved quickly upstream from the dam, 5.2 miles in the first year after dam removal and an additional 3.4 miles over the next three years. Native johnny darter (*Etheostoma nigrum*), the only type of darter remaining in this branch, declined quickly at the invasion front, and the decline has persisted. With the planned fishway around the Fair Lane Estate Dam, there was concern that it would allow the goby to move upstream. Unfortunately, round goby were found upstream on the Middle Branch in 2014, probably due to bait bucket release in one of the impoundments frequented by anglers.

Over time, FOTR has sampled every branch and tributary in the watershed, and even many of the impoundments. Muller is also a skilled photographer, using V-shaped aquariums and lighting to take beautiful close-up photos of fish. He created a booklet of photos, distribution maps, and information about each species for RRAC, which he eventually published as a book (Muller 2019).

FOTR now has the most current data on Rouge River fish, comparable to but more extensive than the last thorough study of Rouge River fish in 1998 (Beam and Braunscheidel 1998). The fish community has vastly improved since the 1998 survey. Sixty-five species have been identified, 70% of them pollution-tolerant and 4% intolerant or sensitive. New native species found include northern logperch (*Percina caprodes*) and the state-endangered pugnose shiner (*Notropis anogenus*), found in one Oakland County lake. New invasive species include round goby, western mosquitofish (*Gambusia affinis*), a small population of mummichog (*Fundulus heteroclitus*) that was subsequently eradicated, and one three-spine stickleback (*Gasterosteus aculeatus*). The river has a surprising diversity of species and has made a remarkable comeback from a time when even common carp (*Cyprinus carpio*) struggled to survive. In 2019, FOTR noted that channel catfish (*Ictalurus punctatus*), absent in the 1998 survey except in a small part of the Middle Branch, had now become a regular catch along the concrete channel, which once ran thick with sewage. The fish community still remains poor in the areas where combined sewer overflows are not yet controlled, and in Evans Creek.

Challenges

Sustainable, long-term funding is currently the biggest challenge for Rouge River citizen science. Good-quality programs need dedicated full-time staff. FOTR was lucky to have a consistent source of funding in the beginning that enabled it to establish protocols, design training programs, recruit volunteers, and set up systems to manage data. Federal, state, and local agencies funded the monitoring because they all supported the goal of training volunteers to collect these data. But over time, priorities changed. The Frog and Toad Survey became more difficult to fund because wetland status is not as directly connected to stream health as other indicators that are now prioritized. The Benthic Macroinvertebrate Monitoring Program lost funding in 2018, in part because the state moved from requiring in-stream monitoring to outfall monitoring for stormwater permits.

Diversifying funding sources by asking for a small amount from all stakeholders may be the key to the stability of citizen-science programs. Stakeholders interested in the data, as well as those interested in public education and engagement, are two separate audiences to solicit. The US Environmental Protection Agency's 2016 embrace of citizen science may also open more doors for funding.

Data management and analysis are also a huge challenge. FOTR has collected a large amount of data for many sites over many years. Data sets like those now held by FOTR are extremely valuable for a variety of environmental and monitoring needs, and the consistency and long-term nature of the FOTR data are practically unparalleled. As the data set has grown, the analysis is more complex. Reaching out to partners such as colleges and universities or even Ford data analysts can increase the use and understanding of the data set. Making the data more accessible online increases its use. FOTR is currently working with Schoolcraft College's GIS department to improve both input and display of the data.

Contributions to Understanding the River and Stewardship

Rouge citizen scientists have contributed to a deeper understanding of the Rouge River watershed, helping to clean it up and guide restoration work. We now know what species of frogs and toads are found in Rouge wetlands and where, and what types of benthic macroinvertebrates live in Rouge streams. We have a good understanding of the fish community, having identified new native species and watched new invasive species invade. One nonnative invasive species was eradicated after we reported it. Our findings have led to changes in how fish are managed. In the process of collecting, we have found and addressed sewage, hydraulic fluid, and other substances going into the river. Our data have guided habitat projects and led to new ones. Sensitive areas have been identified, and recently one community has been looking for special protection for the river as it flows through their community due to the endangered minnow and the other sensitive fish and bugs found there. The Rouge River is much healthier due to the dedication of Rouge citizen scientists.

Rouge citizen-science programs have influenced thousands of people who now understand the value of wetlands and streams and the animals that inhabit them. Residents who might not otherwise care about watershed issues are drawn in because they can learn and make a difference (or because their kids like frogs and bugs). They are not passive learners but must learn the calls, find the wetlands, and learn about the frogs and toads, the bugs and the fish, and this experience changes them. Participants become aware of and use this knowledge to educate others and to advocate for the watershed.

Rouge citizen scientists are some of the best stewards of the watershed because they see firsthand the impact of stormwater and other urban development on our wetlands and streams. They understand the life in the stream and can speak knowledgeably about its value and vulnerability. They look at a wetland and see a home for frogs and toads rather than a useless swamp. These citizen scientists become long-term members and go on to participate in other FOTR programs. They become lifelong advocates and caretakers of the watershed. Many carry this through a career choice and a lifetime.

The Future

Rouge citizen-science programs have a critical role in the restoration of the Rouge River because they engage the public and provide data to evaluate and guide restoration work. To continue to succeed, the programs need to stay relevant, engage new partners, and attract new participants. The partnership with the Izaak Walton League to test sites for chloride will improve understanding of the impact of road salt on benthic macroinvertebrate communities. A partnership started in 2020 with Oakland County and two local watershed councils to survey for European frogbit (*Hydrocharis morsus-ranae*) is engaging FOTR in understanding the extent of a new "watchlist" invasive species in the Rouge. FOTR is working to understand the extent of per- and polyfluoroalkyl substances, or PFAS (a group of emergent chemical contaminants) in the watershed as the state begins testing for them. Partnerships like these will help keep the programs strong and diversify funding.

The two life-altering events of 2020—the global pandemic and the racial justice movement—have led to changes in Rouge citizen science. Virtual training and a broader offering of online resources begun in response to the pandemic will continue long after the pandemic is over because they opened up the program to more people. Working to ensure that Rouge citizen-science programs reach a more diverse audience is a goal that FOTR has embraced. In 2021, FOTR partnered with Trout Unlimited to offer two sessions of "STREAM Girls." This day-long program targets middle-school girls, who often turn away from science at that age, and engages them in bug-sampling, fly-fishing, and fly-tying. FOTR will use the partnership to engage a new audience of girls in becoming future citizen scientists.

LITERATURE CITED

Note: All websites accessed for this essay during May 2021.

Beam, J.D., Braunscheidel, J.J. 1998. "Rouge River Assessment." Michigan Department of Natural Resources, Fisheries Division Special Report No. 22. Lansing.

Cooper, C. 2016. *Citizen Science: How Ordinary People Are Changing the Face of Discovery.* New York: Overlook Press.

Fusaro, A.J., McCulloch, B.R., Petrella, S., Willis, V. 2019. "Discovery, Dispersal, and Genetic Diversity of *Rhyacophila lobifera* Betten, 1934 (Trichoptera: Rhyacophilidae) in Southeast Michigan, USA." *Zoosymposia* 14:177–88.

Krabbenhoft, C.A., Kashian, D.R. 2020. "Citizen Science Data Are a Reliable Complement to Quantitative Ecological Assessments in Urban Rivers." *Ecological Indicators* 16:1–9.

Maguire, T., Mundle, S.O.C. 2020. "Citizen Science Data Show Temperature-Driven Declines in Riverine Sentinel Invertebrates." *Environmental Science and Technology Letters* 7 (5): 303–7.

Michigan Department of Environmental Quality Water Bureau. "Total Maximum Daily Load for Biota for the Rouge River Watershed, Including Bishop and Tonquish Creeks. Washtenaw, Wayne, and Oakland Counties." August 2007. https://www.michigan.gov/documents/deq/wrd-swas-tmdl-biota-riv er-rouge_577534_7.pdf

Michigan Department of Natural Resources and Southeast Michigan Council of Governments (SEMCOG). 1994. "Rouge River Remedial Action Plan Update." https://www.epa.gov/sites/production/files/2015-04/documents /1994_rouge-river-rap-update.pdf

National Advisory Council for Environmental Policy and Technology (NACEPT). 2018. "2018 Information to Action. Strengthening EPA Citizen Science Partnerships for Environmental Protection." April. EPA 220-R-18-001. https://www.epa.gov/sites/production/files/2020-04/documents/nace pt_2018_citizen_science_publication_eng_final_v3_508.pdf

Oxford English Dictionary. "New Words List June 2014." Archived from the original on 9 May 2016. Retrieved 3 June 2016.

Ridgway, J.A. 2010. "The Rouge River National Wet Weather Demonstration Project, Eighteen Years of Documented Success." *Proceedings of the Water Environment Federation* 2:337–54.

Realizing Bill Stapp's Vision

Sally Cole-Misch

Few people have the ability to shape the trajectory of another person's life. Even fewer can do so with humor, boundless enthusiasm, and quiet persistence to help that person seize opportunities that propel their trajectory forward, while holding true to their own vision of themselves and the world.

For everyone who knew Dr. William B. "Bill" Stapp, he was *that* person. His life's guiding mission was devoted to kindness toward every person he met and to the philosophy and spirit of environmental education, which he first defined in the 1960s and further refined while chief of the United Nations Educational, Scientific and Cultural Organization's (UNESCO's) first Environmental Education Section. He transformed what had previously been considered "conservation/outdoor education" into an interdisciplinary, action-based approach to learning about the natural world that empowers citizens to understand that world and to act to restore and protect it through problem solving and personal and collective action (Crowfoot 2001). The Rouge River was one of the "laboratories" where he realized his vision.

The approach provides opportunities to understand the urban, rural, and natural environment through direct experiences and observations; to identify the root causes of its destruction by individual and community behaviors through collaborative investigations using the natural, social, and political sciences; and to act to change damaging behaviors to restore and protect local, regional, national, and international ecosystems. Dr. Stapp's creative perspective about action-based teaching helped provide the groundwork for the first Earth Day in 1970 and led to the creation of the North American Association for Environmental

Education (which he served as its first president). His pioneering work in the 1980s to identify how particular sectors of society were affected by environmental degradation began decades before the term "environmental justice" had even been coined.

The Evolution of Environmental Education

Dr. Stapp first penned the definition of environmental education in 1969 (Stapp et al. 1969) with fellow professors and his students at the University of Michigan.

> *Environmental education is aimed at producing a citizenry that is knowledgeable concerning the biophysical environment and its associated problems, aware of how to help solve these problems, and motivated to work toward their solution.*

In 1975, as the first International Director of Environmental Education for UNESCO, Dr. Stapp worked with educators from every continent to expand and clarify this definition.

> *Environmental education should be an integral part of the educational process, aimed at practical problems of an interdisciplinary character, build a sense of values, and contribute to public well-being. Its focus should reside mainly in the initiative of the learners and their involvement in action and guided by both the immediate and future subjects of concern.* (Belgrade Working Conference on Environmental Education 1975)

At the Tbilisi Intergovernmental Conference on Environmental Education in 1977, Dr. Stapp's expanded definition of environmental education was unanimously accepted by all 135 countries:

> *Environmental education is a process aimed at developing a world population that is aware of and concerned about the total environment and its associated problems, and has the attitudes, motivations, knowledge, commitment and skills to work individually and collectively towards solutions of current problems and the prevention of new ones.*

This definition includes core principles of:

- *Awareness: to help individuals and social groups acquire an awareness of and sensitivity to the total environment and its allied problems;*
- *Knowledge: to help individuals and social groups gain a variety of experiences with the total environment and to acquire a basic understanding of the environment, its associated problems and humanity's critical responsible presence and role in it;*
- *Attitudes: to help individuals and social groups acquire social values, strong feelings of concern for the environment and the motivation for actively participating in its protection and improvement;*
- *Skills: to help individuals and social groups acquire the skills for working toward the solution of environmental problems and to foster a dialogue between these two groups; and*
- *Participation: to help individuals and social groups develop a sense of responsibility and urgency regarding environmental problems to ensure appropriate action to help solve these problems and avoid future problems.*

Dr. Stapp's legacy of professional and personal accomplishment, including enduring environmental education curricula and programs and engaged citizens around the world who are committed to restoring and protecting their watersheds, was achieved with the highest of personal grace. It is fair to say that the lives and attitudes of teachers, students, and citizens—from the Rouge River watershed to the more than 120 countries where he taught and mentored environmental awareness and civic action—have been forever changed by their connection with Bill. His students at Michigan, known as "Stapplings," continue to spread his model of thoughtful, interdisciplinary, and cooperative learning and action through curricula and organizational programs around the globe.

Think Globally, Act Locally: Precursors to the Rouge Education Project

As much as Bill considered global environmental issues and effective educational responses in his teaching and while at UNESCO, he lived the environmental motto, "Think globally, act locally." After earning his

BS, MS, and PhD from the University of Michigan by the late 1950s, he created the outdoor/environmental education program for Ann Arbor public schools that remains a vital part of the curriculum today. He contributed to developing and preserving nature centers and natural areas throughout Washtenaw County as laboratories for learning and places to enjoy nature's beauty, complexity, and fragility. When the city decided to build a second high school, Huron High, he volunteered to work with the architect to protect as many trees as possible, establish an on-site nature center, and ensure that the science classrooms had visual access to the property's woods and stream. It's this "act locally" perspective that brought Dr. Stapp's vision for effective environmental education and action first to the Huron River, then to the Rouge River watershed, and ultimately to river watersheds throughout the world.

On his return to UofM from UNESCO, Dr. Stapp focused on concrete ways he and his students could actualize the definitions of environmental education he and others had worked so hard to create and to gain acceptance for from the world community. While many of his students were just learning about and becoming comfortable with an entirely new approach to teaching about the environment, Bill was already years ahead in conceptualizing a local project for research and action that could provide valuable linkages throughout the world.

His first chance to actualize his ideas came in 1983–84, when cases of hepatitis were contracted from the Huron River—only steps from the Huron High School he had helped to design. His vision to respond to this issue through education quickly became the primary focus for several of his graduate students: how to teach students about the nine parameters of water quality (i.e., dissolved oxygen, temperature, pH, total phosphorus, nitrates, total suspended solids, biochemical oxygen demand, fecal coliform bacteria, turbidity) in the classroom setting, including practicing each test; travel to the Huron River to obtain samples for testing and search for on-site parameters of water quality such as benthic organisms; complete the tests and analyze results, including comparing results among class groups within and among schools via an interactive computer program; consider how their results could be used to help the local government find a solution; present their findings to each other and to elected officials; and participate in the final resolution of the problem. And do it all within a finite time period and in the parameters of a well-defined, thoughtful model.

By 1985, Dr. Stapp and Mark Mitchell, a graduate student on the Huron River team who would become Bill's partner to further develop the model's watershed projects nationally and internationally, had written and published the first edition of the *Field Manual for Water Quality Monitoring* (Mitchell et al. 1988). The guide was an outgrowth of the intensive work with Huron High and other high schools in the Huron River watershed that provided the initial model for student-based water-quality monitoring and civic action.

At the core, the initial model allowed teachers and students to learn how to assess water quality and the environmental and social practices that influenced it. It integrated direct experience with the river, reflection on test results and personal experiences, and multidisciplinary scientific and local information to inform students. Teachers served as coaches and facilitators for collaboration within and between classes to help students reach conclusions about factors affecting water quality and the actions that could help to change or ameliorate those factors.

The Second Watershed: The Rouge River

As news of the success of the Huron River program spread throughout southeast Michigan, energy and momentum developed for a similar program for the Rouge River watershed. Identified in 1985 as one of the most severely degraded rivers in the US–Canadian Great Lakes Basin and a key source of pollution flowing into the international waters of the Detroit River, local and state governments were joining forces to consider how to reverse many decades of treating the Rouge River as a garbage and sewage dump. Jim Murray, at the time Washtenaw County Drain Commissioner and Chairman of the Michigan Water Resources Commission, founded the nonprofit environmental organization Friends of the Rouge in 1986 to help the community become involved in the cleanup and restoration process. Its mission was "to restore, protect, and enhance the Rouge River watershed through stewardship, education, and collaboration."

Murray learned about the success of the Huron River program in bringing together teachers, students, and community leaders to identify the river's water quality throughout its watershed and develop stewardship plans, and he invited Dr. Stapp to bring the program to the Rouge River watershed. Friends of the Rouge sponsored the project to educate and involve the watershed's residents in evaluating and understanding the problem and mobilizing media attention to the river and its issues. It obtained project funding from the Ford Motor Company, the Michigan Department of Natural Resources, the Kellogg Foundation, and the Sussman Fund.

Creating the Rouge River Water-Monitoring Project

Thirty-two middle and high schools were interested in participating in the project's first year. To ensure that the program's specifics were designed to meet the schools' interests and needs, an advisory committee was formed with science and social studies curriculum coordinators, science teachers, water resource professionals, and a Friends of the Rouge representative. The committee identified teachers in 16 schools to participate to reflect the economic, social, and cultural diversity among the watershed's upper, middle, and lower sections, and ensured that one resource person from UofM would be assigned to each classroom throughout the project. Teachers, principals, curriculum coordinators, Friends of the Rouge, and the project's UofM resource people all signed a letter of agreement, so roles and responsibilities were clear.

Key to the project's success was Dr. Stapp's ability to involve UofM graduate and undergraduate students as resource people for each classroom. Students from the then–School of Natural Resources (now called the School for Environment and Sustainability) were eager to participate, and with Bill's encouragement students from the Schools of Education, Public Health, Engineering, and Literature, Science, and the Arts joined in the training and implementation. Seven intensive training sessions ensured that each person understood the water-quality problems facing the Rouge River, the action-research and civic-action education model, how and why to test for nine water-quality parameters, and how to operate the interactive computer-conferencing program among schools to share results, discuss insights and conclusions, and develop action plans.

While some UofM students organized and led a spring workshop for one teacher and two students from each school to prepare for the program's implementation, others created dynamic historical, economic, cultural, and environmental materials to share once the 15-day program began. As in the Huron River model, students first learned about each water-quality parameter's importance and practiced the tests before travelling to their respective portion of the Rouge River to complete the tests and experience the river firsthand (fig. 27).

Fig. 27. Students sampling macrobenthic invertebrates in the Rouge River. (Photograph courtesy Friends of the Rouge.)

Many students had lived in the Rouge watershed their entire lives, and yet didn't know the river even existed. At the time, a major portion of the lower 126-mile route was little more than a concrete-lined open sewer into which multiple contaminants were released from nearby municipalities and industries. Even though it may have smelled, and students found little life in their search for benthic organisms, seeing and experiencing the river firsthand resulted in a collective emotional attachment and commitment to action. This was reflected in the subsequent cross-school conversations about test results and their recommendations for actions to restore the Rouge River, which dominated the rest of the program's time in the schools. Students were able to connect broader environmental issues such as the effects of industrial pollution, sewage overflows, and inadequate garbage disposal to their own community, consider how their own lifestyles were affecting the watershed, and experience the differences in higher water quality in the Upper suburban stretches compared to the lower levels found in urban Detroit sections with a heavy industrial presence and lower socioeconomic populations.

While we may take online interactions for granted today, in 1985 the ability to communicate with students throughout the Rouge watershed was state-of-the-art. Clancy Wolf, then a UofM School of Education doctoral student, designed the program first used in the Huron and Rouge projects, and later in river watersheds across the country and internationally. In the Rouge River watershed, the technology helped to eliminate normal barriers between vastly different socioeconomic, racial, and ethnic communities as students shared results and considered future actions. It was the first time that many students had ever talked to a student from a different part of the Rouge River watershed.

If teachers hadn't bought into the Rouge education project before it started, they were convinced of the program's value when they saw the high level of energy and enthusiasm their students brought to class each day. Once students graphed and shared their data, they could compare and contrast issues facing different parts of the watershed. Through samples with fecal coliform bacteria counts as high as 15,000–25,000 colonies/100 ml sample—versus the state standard of 200 colonies/100 ml sample—they identified combined sewer overflows releasing human wastes, as well as a leaking pumping station in a tributary to the main branch of the river. Higher levels of biochemical oxygen demand, turbidity, and total solids in the river's lower stretches also showed the cumulative impact of human and industrial pollution on the watershed's health.

During brainstorming sessions, the students had the opportunity to talk with the region's water-resource professionals to confirm possible pollution sources and consider effective personal and community responses. These conversations helped them to feel they were a valued part of their broader community, and that decision-makers were listening to their findings and ideas.

Everyone's efforts to create positive change for their watershed erupted at the project's final event, a day-long student-run congress that brought 270 students, teachers, water-resource professionals, and the UofM resource people together at Martin Luther King Jr. High School in Detroit. Representatives from each middle or high school shared their water-quality data and the issues identified in their community's stretch of the river, then generated recommendations for actions to address those issues in smaller groups for each branch (fig. 28). Examples of specific recommendations included:

Fig. 28. Rouge River watershed students participate in student-led symposium to share monitoring results and develop recommendations for action. (Photograph courtesy Friends of the Rouge.)

- Incorporate the Friends of the Rouge's annual river cleanup as a school project—encourage responsible consumer behaviors such as avoiding plastics, nonrecyclables, and aerosols throughout their communities.
- Educate younger students through presentations in lower-level schools to reflect on their personal behaviors affecting the watershed.
- Conduct community surveys to identify residents' knowledge and attitudes about the river and encourage awareness.
- Convince local governments to restrict development in sensitive areas such as wetlands and floodplains.
- Continue the Rouge project in future years to develop long-term trends in data as communities and their governments acted to restore the Rouge River.

The students attending the congress had previously identified several topics for skill-building workshops for the afternoon, which ranged from river cleanup, to community/school organizing, to learning how to write public service announcements, editorials, and letters to elected officials, to creating videos, posters, and street theater. Students and teachers presented a summary of the congress's events to everyone at their schools and finished the project with individual assessments of how they and their families could change or eliminate behaviors that might be contributing to the Rouge River's poor health.

Anyone in the educational community or who has organized an event of any size, will understand the extensive preparation, design, time, and energy required to pull off the Rouge project in 16 schools in its first year and 31 schools in the second. Dr. Stapp's vision and guidance permeated every school; he freely offered his energy and enthusiasm to every teacher, resource person, and student to then share with others. His focus on the original goals of environmental education—to help students develop the listening, communication, and problem-solving skills needed to become knowledgeable about the biophysical environment and its associated problems, and to help them learn how to solve these problems and become motivated to work on them—drove the project's goals and design, and ultimately its success.

In just 15 days, every person involved in the first Rouge water-monitoring project gained an awareness and deep understanding of the Rouge River and its problems. Students and teachers had the freedom to explore problems directly related to their communities, which gave them a sense of accomplishment and empowerment that they can affect change. It demonstrated the potential for education to create citizens who are aware of and motivated to contribute to their community's environmental health by focusing on a problem that directly affects their lives.

Continuing Dr. Stapp's Vision in the Rouge Watershed and Beyond

By 1989, students in all 40 Detroit metropolitan-area school systems in the Rouge River watershed, from its northernmost stretches to where it empties into the Detroit River, were participating in the Rouge River Education Project. Each year, the project further refined the initial water-monitoring and civic-action project in the Huron River into four cornerstones: watershed education and analysis, school-community-university partnerships, telecommunications among and between students in each participating school, and educational advancements that lead to personal and collective stewardship.

By the time the Huron and Rouge River watershed programs were firmly established, Dr. Stapp had already shared the model with teachers across the US, Canada, and Mexico, as well as in several European, African, and Asian countries. In 1989, Bill created the Global Rivers Environmental Education Network, or GREEN, a nonprofit organization to support and provide materials to educators using the model and to create valuable linkages between countries with similar and different water-quality issues. It provided an opportunity for cross-cultural sharing and collaboration in spite of each watershed's differing cultures, economics, and politics. Through GREEN, Dr. Stapp provided the leadership to create a model for peacemaking through the watershed monitoring and civic action model. Schools in Israel and Palestine, for example, collaborated to establish a joint GREEN program focused on the Jordan River watershed, as did disparate communities in watersheds in South Africa, Australia, and Southeast Asia. In 1993, Dr. Stapp was nominated for the Nobel Peace Prize for this work.

GREEN provided an innovative, action-oriented approach to education, based on an interdisciplinary watershed education model, and sought to improve education through a global network that promotes watershed sustainability (Cole-Misch et al. 1996). GREEN staff worked closely with educational and environmental organizations, community groups, businesses, and governments across the United States, Canada, and Mexico, and in over 130 countries around the world to support local efforts in watershed education, stewardship, and sustainability. Its creation also marked the beginning of an explosion of such programs in the three North American countries through the financial support and active participation of the General Motors Corporation. Many programs continue today throughout the world and have evolved to suit each watershed's needs.

In 1999, Dr. Stapp recognized the obvious synergy between GREEN's work and that of Earth Force, another nonprofit educational organization that focuses on helping young people develop their sense of civic efficacy to improve their environment and communities through knowledge and action (Power et al. 2000). Students complete community environmental inventories; decide on an issue to research; develop goals, strategies, and a plan to take civic action; and then review and share their results. GREEN's model follows the same steps, only with a focused topic: water.

The melding of GREEN into Earth Force has allowed the water-monitoring and civic action program to continue to evolve to suit each watershed, and over time Earth Force's focus on policy and civic action and providing the support and direction necessary for teachers to develop their own programs has shown great success (Earth Force 2017). Earth Force's efforts have resulted in a 77% increase in students' interest in science, an 84% increase in their understanding of environmental issues, and a 94% increase in what curriculum designers term "21st-century skills" (Earth Force 2021).

"We've learned many valuable lessons from Bill and the GREEN model," said Vince Meldrum, Earth Force's president and CEO. "Most important is sharing: our models and information, to create a broad network that wants to develop programs to expand environmental awareness and civic action, and also sharing how to enhance the capacity for teachers to work with local organizations to develop their own programs, with our assistance. Bill created a wonderful model, and our staff are still proud to be connected with him and his work."

The Rouge Education Project Today

Thanks to Friends of the Rouge, which incorporated the Rouge education project into its programs and mission, teachers who participated in the program's first year, and who are still teaching, include it in their classroom curriculum. At its height in the late 1990s and with funding from the Rouge River National Wet Weather Demonstration Project, 92 schools participated in the GREEN model in the Rouge watershed (Friends of the Rouge 1999). Teacher retirements and turnover, reduced school funding for experiential learning opportunities, and changing curriculum standards have forced the model to adjust and realign with its original goals, but the organization's commitment to the program as an essential and valuable component of its mission continues.

Today, around 30 schools participate every year. Education manager Erin Cassady provides hands-on training for educators using materials from the Project Wet program as well as components of the original GREEN–Earth Force models: how to test for water quality via the nine water-quality parameters, a protocol on searching for and identifying benthic organisms and surveying physical conditions at the river such as land use and habitat, and river field trip organization tips, along with curricula and action-planning assistance (Project Wet International Foundation 2003, 2006). The organization's office was recently renovated to become fully equipped for these training purposes. "We strongly encourage teacher recertification at least once every three years," said Cassady. "We've found that some of the best parts of these sessions are the experienced teachers talking with each other and with the new teachers about how they do the program in their classrooms. There's as much diversity in the schools as there is in the communities in the watershed, so it's important to let teachers lead the design and implementation of the education component to best suit their own schools."

When funding is available, Friends of the Rouge also gives each teacher additional support through money for buses, substitute-teacher stipends, and monitoring equipment, as well as trained volunteers who help with river monitoring. It also maintains an extensive, active online catalog of resource materials, activities, and historical monitoring data, so teachers and water-resource professionals can easily find direction, ideas, and connections. Cassady hopes to bring back a student congress–type symposium as a regular part of programming. An education committee helps provide an excellent historical perspective and shapes the project's evolution.

Earth Force's chief program officer, Grace Edinger, has worked with Friends of the Rouge over the past four years to reinvigorate the teacher's civic-action component and support Cassady's efforts to connect students with adults who can help them enact change or provide more information. "When experts want to meet with students to help them and are interested in their testing results, it always reinforces that their work is important," Edinger said. "And it leads to the civic-action component that is so vital to the success of the GREEN and Earth Force models."

What reminds Cassady most of the value of Rouge Education Project over the past 34 years are the adults who live in the Rouge watershed and who eagerly recount their experiences monitoring the river as students. "I will meet people in my daily life who can tell me that they did the Rouge monitoring program when they were in school," she said. "They all light up when they talk about it. The program has reached almost 100,000 students to date, so it shouldn't come as much of a surprise anymore, but I'm still in awe when they hear what I do and vividly remember their own experience—sometimes decades later. It is truly unforgettable. We reach young folks who aren't often given opportunities to feel like they are a part of nature. Some have even gone on to environmentally focused careers because of their participation, but even the ones who don't never forget seeing the bugs and learning about the local ecosystem by studying their hometown river."

Bill's vision—to create a learning opportunity involving a broad spectrum of people, talents, and resources on a meaningful issue, identify a shared set of values to address discordant beliefs and attitudes, and work toward mutually respected goals and actions—lives on in the Rouge River watershed and in hundreds of other watersheds around the world. So too does his kindness, enthusiasm for discovery, and persistence, through the many people he taught and touched through the GREEN model.

LITERATURE CITED

Cole-Misch, S., Price, L., Schmidt, D. 1996. "Sourcebook for Watershed Education." Global Rivers Environmental Education Network, and Dubuque, IA: Kendall/Hunt.

Crowfoot, J. 2001. "Bill Stapp's Life and Legacy: A Gift from Which to Learn." *From the Ground Up*, official publication of the Ecology Center, 33 (3): 4–7.

Earth Force. 2017. "Community Action and Problem Solving Process: Educator's Guide." Denver: Earth Force.

Earth Force. 2021. "Impact of Earth Force Programs." https://earthforce.org/impact/

Friends of the Rouge. 2000. "Final Report 1998–1999 Rouge Education Project." Presented to Wayne County Department of Environment. Dearborn Heights, MI.

Mitchell, M., Stapp, W.B. 1988, 1995, 1997, 2000, 2008. "Field Manual for Water Quality Monitoring." Dubuque, IA: Kendall/Hunt.

Power, D.L., Richardson, S. 2000. "The Watershed Protection Guide, An Earth Force GREEN Civic Action Publication." Alexandria, VA: Earth Force.

Project WET International Foundation. 2003, 2006. "Healthy Water, Healthy People: Water Quality Educators Guide." Bozeman, MT: Project WET.

Project WET International Foundation. 2003, 2006. "Healthy Water, Healthy People: Field Monitoring Guide." Bozeman, MT: Project WET.

Stapp, W.B., Bennett, D., Bryan, W., Fulton, J., Havlick, S., MacGregor, J., Nowak, P., Swan, J., Wall, R. 1969. "The Concept of Environmental Education." *Journal of Environmental Education* 1 (1): 30–31 (amended in 1980 by W. Stapp).

9 THE ROUGE RIVER REBORN

From Wen to Wonder

Orin G. Gelderloos, Dorothy F. McLeer,
and Richard A. Simek

Awe and Wonder are Being Human

The Rouge River—a Wen

Rainwater, snowmelt, groundwater, and gravity from about 466 square miles of southeast Michigan made and maintain our Rouge River and send it to the Detroit River. The Rouge River and the land from which its water flows constitute the Rouge River watershed.

The Rouge River, born from glaciers (chapter 1), was essential as a major travel route for the First Peoples (Ricks 2020; see also chapter 2) and for early French farmers. As hunting and agriculture diminished, industrialization and urbanization became the "coin of the realm" for those seeking their fortunes during westward expansion. The prologue describes the stealthy and insidious, intentional and unintentional, decisions by which the Rouge River became the one of the most polluted rivers in our country. It justifiably earned the appellation of a "wen." By definition, a "wen" is an abnormal or a pustulous growth protruding from the skin. Fifty years ago, adjectives such as "unsightly," "repulsive," and "nauseating," as well as "abused," "avoided," and "forgotten" would have applied to the Rouge River, a true "wen."

A little-known practice that contributed to making this waterway a wen was revealed in a conversation with a resident (now deceased) who lived on the banks of the Rouge River just north of Ford Road. We learned that many residents living on the river's banks had their outhouses located on a dock above the river. That image may seem disgusting, but outhouses were common throughout the area before sanitary sewers. When sewers were installed after 1940 (Johnson 2011) to carry sewage to large underground sewers called interceptors, they were still not large enough to carry all the wastewater and stormwater during heavy rainstorms. Consequently, sewers backed up into basements. The solution devised was combined sewer overflows (CSOs) that carried the excess flow of stormwater and sanitary wastes directly to the Rouge River. Over time, 168 CSOs (Beam and Braunscheidel 1995) were installed, and all the substances that could float flowed into the Rouge River. Thus, in actuality, thousands of houses and businesses once again had their "outhouses" on the river. Today, more than half of the CSOs have been closed. This sequence of actions and decisions illustrates the axiom that today's solution can be tomorrow's problem.

An Unforgettable Experience on a Wen

A memorable example of the Rouge River as a wen was a several-mile canoe trip downstream on the Rouge River from Henry and Clara Ford's Fair Lane Estate in 1971, before the concrete channel was installed. The paddlers in the canoe flotilla consisted of middle-school and high-school teachers of science and social studies in an eight-week summer program sponsored by the National Science Foundation at the University of Michigan–Dearborn.

Launching from the below the dam at the Fair Lane Estate, we traveled downstream in the roiling, murky, muddy water coming over the waterfall. Within a mile downstream and south of Michigan Avenue, we encountered floating mats of blue-green algae about one foot in diameter, grayish in color. This species of algae thrives in the human sewage that came from the CSOs along miles of the river. Despite the significant pollution, paddling a canoe down a stretch of an urban and abused river produced a sense of awe and wonder. The decimated, dead elm trees on the banks, killed by Dutch elm disease a decade before, provided resting limbs for Red-tailed Hawks, Eastern Kingbirds, and Belted Kingfishers. Even a couple of Spotted Sandpipers skittered along the shore looking for morsels of food.

Due to changes in the sewer system of the Rouge River and major improvements in wastewater treatment, initiated by the Clean Water Act and implemented by the Rouge River National Wet Weather Demonstration Project championed by the late Congressman John D. Dingell, the mats of blue-green algae are no longer a common sight.

The Rouge River as a Watershed Wonder

Look at the map of our Rouge River watershed in the prologue. We recognize the landmarks throughout the 466 square miles and along the four tributaries. Our watershed is a "good fit" for us. We can get our arms around it (figuratively speaking), and we feel at home in it. After visiting any one of the trickles of water at the headwaters of four tributaries, one can drive to the junction of the Rouge River with the Detroit River at Zug Island within an hour. One can easily visit numerous natural areas or well-known cultural features without overnight travel. Whether visiting museums or attending sporting events, food festivals, or volunteer opportunities, we are participating with our "watershed neighbors." A "right-sized" watershed that "fits" us has the power to bring people together physically and digitally—we have shared experiences.

Examining the land and water together opens our eyes to amazing features and processes in our watershed. Let's continue to wear our "awe and wonder" spectacles while we explore and awaken our sense of time, sense of place, and sense of quality in our Rouge River watershed.

With selected vignettes, we will reacquaint ourselves with our watershed, its meanders and floodplains, our lessons learned while trying to "control" it, its success with partnerships, its gifts of experiences and knowledge, and our expression of apology and commitment to its future for generations to come. We will learn that "wonders never cease," and the rebirth of the Rouge River has been happening in small increments even while it was being abused, and it continues through efforts to provide experiences of wonder for thousands of inhabitants and visitors.

Floodplain Wonders, or the Wonder of Meanders

The floodplains of rivers are overlooked and underappreciated. Historically, we have seen floodplains as unused and undeveloped land. Nevertheless, they are ecologically complex, and "useful" to their watershed because they absorb the overload of water during heavy rains and snowmelts. Unfortunately, floodplains are flooded so infrequently that we tend to think something is wrong with the river or that the river "needs to be fixed" when it floods our roadways and property. For example, Hines Drive is built on a floodplain and may flood a dozen or more times per year. When we are rerouted due to closure, do we utter a word of thanks for this wonder of our watershed for absorbing the extra rain, or are we aggravated and grumpy?

We suspect that very few of us ever "wonder" how floodplains are formed. A knee-jerk reaction would be that floodplains are formed from flooding—right? Sorry, that's wrong! Floodplains are formed by erosion, deposition, and time.

Take a look at the path of the Rouge River in figure 1 in the prologue. It seldom flows in a straight channel. It may twist and turn due to a number of factors, such as soil composition, bedrock, and other physical features. Yet these twists and turns are the result of a dynamic process that causes the path the river to meander over time despite the topography. Raindrops flowing down our windshields also meander.

When a river flows over flat or low-gradient land, it develops beautifully shaped meanders. An excellent example of the meandering Rouge River is its Lower Branch as it flows from Brady Street in west Dearborn to join the other three branches just north of Michigan Avenue. It is obvious that it meanders in U-shaped patterns (fig. 29).

In 1971, one of us (OGG), with his colleague and predecessor Calvin De Witt and all the students in the inaugural freshmen class of Matter, Energy and Life for non-science students at the University of Michigan–Dearborn, examined the relationships within this series of meanders. Throughout a week in each of our 10 laboratory sessions, with a sextant, survey rod, and tape, students measured a portion of the meanders in 10-foot intervals from a fence along Michigan Avenue to the riverbank. From the collective results, we determined that we would travel nearly twice as far, if we canoed downstream over the two meanders, than a crow would fly in a straight line. This ratio of 2:1 distance-traveled-downstream to distance-over-land is within the ratio of meandering rivers throughout the world.

The next question is, "What is the result of the meandering pattern"? The velocity of a river depends on the slope of the land. If it flowed straight down the land, it would flow faster. On the other hand, if a river meanders as it flows downstream, its velocity is slower, just as coasting down a series of switchbacks on a mountain road is slower than traveling

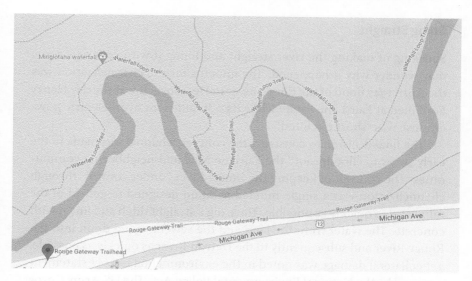

Fig. 29. The meanders of the Lower Rouge River between Brady Street and the junction with the three other branches near Michigan Avenue, Dearborn, Michigan. (Credit: Google Maps.)

straight down the slope. Of interest to some of us, but important to all of us, is that the water in a meandering river has the most uniform pattern of energy loss of all the possible flow patterns. As a result of the steady flow of the water, the river steadily erodes from one side and gradually deposits the eroded material on the opposite side downstream. Over time, the river forms a flat floodplain capable of serving as a reservoir and absorbing thousands of gallons of water during rain events. The meandering patterns of our Rouge River over time are a remarkable phenomenon. Stand on its bank and say "Amazing, I didn't know that!" Straightening a river would not be a kindly way to treat this feature of our community.

Let's rest our paddles for a moment and take an anecdotal interlude. Recently, a former student, now an esteemed 68-year-old highly distinguished epidemiologist who participated in the analysis of the Rouge River, recounted the "awe and wonder" she experienced when measuring and monitoring the Rouge as a student. Educational experiences on the ground and in the water can have a lifetime impact.

Going Straight

Speaking of making the river straight and lining it with concrete, some may wonder why it happened. The impetus for the channelization was the April 1947 flood of the Rouge River in Dearborn. It was the day Henry Ford died at Fair Lane Estate while its self-sufficient hydroelectric powerhouse was "short circuited."

The final decision to construct the concrete channel was made in the early 1970s to "floodproof" the Fairlane Mall and neighboring communities. The concept of keeping the Rouge River "under control" through channelization was a single-minded solution designed to get rid of the rainwater as quickly as possible. Thus, dig a straight ditch and line it with concrete. The water from the land and the sewers would drain into the Rouge River and subsequently to the Detroit River as quickly as possible. Yet collateral damage was noted in the environmental impact statement required by the National Environmental Policy Act. The US Army Corps of Engineers, the agency in charge of flood control, stated forthrightly that the natural habitats adjacent to the river would be removed.

Considerable comment in opposition to the channelization came from the citizens of Dearborn and the region. One proposal suggested that we keep the original 5.8-mile meandering channel and use it as overflow capacity to collect and hold the floodwater until it could be reintroduced to the river. The proposal was rejected with criticisms of the proposer (not the proposal), who did not live in Dearborn. Why did he think he could solve Dearborn's problems better than the officials of Dearborn? Thus, only after the natural river was destroyed did we realize that we had missed observing the complexity of a river, its habitats, biodiversity, and aesthetics, which contributed to quality of life. As a result, the attraction of the Rouge River, a water body in an urban area, was fenced off, and rightly so, because hazards were abundant. As water trickled from drains over the concrete channel, algae grew on the concrete and any pedestrian risked sliding into the channel.

Today, decades later, the four-mile concrete channel has been called an "insult" to the Rouge River. In addition, looking back to the original purpose of the channel to control flooding, the US Army Corp of Engineers could only guarantee that the channel would hold the flood waters of historic magnitude until 1985, because there were no data about the future magnitude of impervious surfaces to be installed upstream in the watershed.

Concrete and Irony

An ironic twist in the rebirth of the Rouge River took place on Rotunda Drive in Dearborn. When the river was channelized with concrete, the former river was filled in from the beginning at Michigan Avenue and beyond Rotunda Drive to the location where it had previously connected to the natural channel.

North of Rotunda Drive the filled-in channel became part of the Tournament Players Golf Course. Eventually, the land south of Rotunda Drive became part of Oakwood Commons, a senior citizens residence and assisted-living facility. To provide a visually peaceful and aesthetically pleasing environment for the residents to enjoy the outdoors and nature, the landscape plan included *restoring* the section of the original channel, complete with water features. We canoed this portion of the channel in 1971, and this idea was included in the suggestions to maintain the original channel for overflows. After the original channel was rechanneled, restored, and replanted, the landscape designers received an award for habitat improvement.

Yet the real heroine of this restoration project was Ms. Betty Welch, a resident of Oakwood Commons, now Beaumont Commons. A retired sociology professor at Wayne State University, she championed the value of the natural features of the reborn channel. She initiated the placement of interpretive signage along the bank, designed by University of Michigan–Dearborn Environmental Education students who Betty recruited.

To increase awareness of this resource right outside their windows, Betty spearheaded the Oakwood Commons' Wildlife Committee. The committee leads regular bird walks on Thursday evenings in spring, summer, and early autumn along the paved trail that hugs the wetland. A journal of wildlife sightings and related climate conditions is placed in an accessible common area to encourage residents to observe and document seasonal changes throughout the year(s). The committee also wrote a booklet describing the formation of the wetland and its surrounding habitat.

The reborn river habitat provided the free-of-charge gifts of wonder once again, with Red-tailed Hawks perching in the trees, woodpeckers nesting in dead tree trunks, herons stabbing fish from the water, insect-eating birds feeding in the shrubbery, and the nectar-sipping insects pollinating the native species of flowering plants. When the residents observe the snapping turtles emerge from the water and the map turtles bask on the fallen logs in the water, they can reflect on the fact that these turtles' ancestors showed this behavior 100,000 years ago without design or training by humans.

Partnerships and Lessons Learned

The rebirthing initiative of the Rouge River by the senior citizens at Oakwood Commons was the first of several community restoration projects.

In the fall of 1998, a series of hands-on workshops called the Ford Field Streambank Buffer Project provided training for erosion control by rebuilding and stabilizing streambanks with live native plants. It was led by Swiss soil bioengineer Beat Sheuter in partnership with the US Department of Agriculture–Natural Resource Conservation Service and eight other organizations. Participants from municipalities across the nation worked on the riverbanks along the Ford Field stretch of the Rouge River, which had been eroded by flash flooding. The use of materials such as live fascines, coconut fiber logs, and brush mattresses provided alternatives to hard-surface controls like the 1975 concrete channel. In a few years these plants not only stabilized the banks, but established wildlife habitat for foraging songbirds along the river and sandy nesting areas for turtles.

Two decades after the installation of the concrete channel, University of Michigan–Dearborn vice chancellor and visionary Edward Bagale gathered ten organizations into a "Gateway Partnership" to highlight the assets of the Rouge River. The plan would remove the concrete channel and provide suitable habitat for rest and food for fish and other aquatic creatures navigating the river during both low- and high-flow times. This plan was interrupted after 2001 because the US Army Corp of Engineers had to take responsibilities for projects in New York City and Washington, DC following the 9/11 tragedy. Currently, the Gateway project is still underway with plans to extend the pedestrian/bicycle pathway south beyond Michigan Avenue and to connect to the Fort Street Park on the Rouge River at Oakwood Street. This project includes the already-completed oxbow restoration at the Henry Ford, which is a partnership with the Gateway project, the Alliance of Rouge Communities, Wayne County, and many others. This rebirth has been successful. The recently restored feeding and breeding habitats have attracted many species of fish not previously found in the concrete channel.

These regional partnerships represent the communities' revived and restored relationship to the river and present a stark contrast to the four-mile concrete channel. Again, the lesson we can learn from these events is that "Today's solution may be tomorrow's problem."

The Gift in Spring

In late winter, many of us in the Rouge River watershed look for the first American robin of spring. Truth is that many robins stay over winter in our southeast Michigan habitats due to suitable weather and food supply. Although overwintering robins are not a sign of spring, many other lesser-known birds return from their wintering grounds in our southern states and South America. Throughout March and April, red-winged blackbirds, killdeer, and common grackles arrive as harbingers of spring, signaling that we are in for a treat as tens of thousands of birds migrate to and through our area.

The Environmental Study Area at the University Michigan–Dearborn is a favorite stopover location for birds to refuel for one or more days following their overnight flight on southerly winds. Documenting the abundance and diversity of birds in our watershed, the dedicated ornithologist Julie Craves, who observed and banded birds at the university's Rouge River Bird Observatory for the nearly three decades, has recorded 250 species (Craves 2007). This number is nearly half of all the species of birds documented in the state of Michigan, and is especially significant because no large body of water is present, nor are the resident birds of the northern Lower Peninsula or boreal forests of the Upper Peninsula.

An abundance of birds is also present throughout neighborhoods with suitable habitat, especially during the peaks of migration in May and September. A resident of Dearborn recorded 95 species over time in his back yard.

During the rich migration seasons, we marvel at the ability of these birds to travel hundreds to thousands of miles each spring and fall. Consider this: a Grey Catbird was banded at the Rouge River Bird Observatory on August 23, 1983, and recaptured in the same location on May 10, 1991 (Craves 2007). Thus, it made 16 flights between our watershed and the Gulf Coast. How do they do it?

Much of migration is still a mystery. Yet ornithologists' research shows that many species use stars to travel at night, and keep in contact with each other with species-specific vocalizations. Those that travel by day use the sun. In addition, we know that birds can use magnetic fields, landmarks such as the Rouge River valley, polarized light, leadership by experienced birds, and infrasounds such as waves crashing onto shorelines. When you see the flashing orange and black of a male Baltimore Oriole and the more muted female, pause and marvel at the incredible guidance system it used as it flew to Central America and back to the Rouge River watershed in less than a year.

Enhancing Wonder and Awe through Education

Because of the the generous gift of the Fair Lane Estate by the Ford Motor Company, the Regents of the University of Michigan in 1971 designated the property west of Fair Lane Drive to be used for educational purposes in its natural state, as developed by Jens Jensen (Jensen 1990) with his insistence of planting native species. This designation enhanced the University of Michigan–Dearborn's field-study opportunities, not only in the natural sciences, but in anthropology, music, art, literature, and writing. Equally important, the action of the Board of Regents stimulated a vibrant community-outreach program of education about the watershed's natural world for school children, families, and inquisitive individuals.

As students and community members learn about the watershed's numerous creatures and ecological principles, they have been guided by the advice of Rachel Carson in her classic volume, *A Sense of Wonder*. She fervently wrote:

> If a child is to keep alive his [*sic*] inborn *sense of wonder*, he needs the companionship of at least one adult who can share it, rediscovering with him the joy, excitement, and mystery of the world we live in.

In 2001, William Clay Ford Jr. gave the keynote address at the dedication of the Environmental Interpretive Center at UM–Dearborn. He stood in front of the entrance wall, with the 1080 tiles donated by Ford Motor Company, each tile designed and painted by community school students. The title of the wall states our task: "Encouraging a Sense of Wonder."

Over the past 50 years, university students have engaged students of all ages in programs on the diversity and adaptations of species well suited to life in the Rouge River watershed. In recent decades, a signature learning experience at the Center has been the "Trip of a Drip," in which students, using topographic maps, analyze the path of a drop of rain, from the cloud to falling on a walking trail or rooftop or sidewalk, to the roadway, the sewer, and the Rouge River via an underground pipe. As a result of their calculations about the amount of water that runs off an area of land or impervious surface into a storm sewer, they appreciate the value of a rain garden, which collects hundreds of gallons of water in a modest rainfall and recycles the water through plants.

A pond built in the rose garden established by Mrs. Ford became a treasure trove of aquatic life. From its rock-sided edge, students easily netted and studied dozens of species of aquatic plants, frogs, toads, turtles, dragonflies, damselflies, water striders, and water scorpions. It's hard to stop naming all the WONDER-ful adaptations to aquatic life of these creatures. Over the last several decades, we estimated that 60,000 students of all ages "ooohed" and "aaahed" over these aquatic plants and animals.

In recent decades the wonders of the Rouge River watershed have been enhanced by the myriad activities that the Friends of the Rouge (see chapters 6 and 7) initiated with their signature programs of School Water-Quality Monitoring, Rouge Rescue, and Invertebrate Analysis. Grants to the University of Michigan–Dearborn for teacher-education programs from the National Science Foundation and the US Environmental Protection Agency not only provided information about the natural and social sciences, but conveyed a sense of awe, wonder, and enthusiasm for teachers and their students. To again quote Rachel Carson, "It is not half so important to know as to feel."

Looking for Wonders

Enlightened experiences of awe and wonder are available as no-cost benefits of living in the Rouge River watershed.

Let's take a walk in a wooded area such as the forested part of Rouge Park at the Stone Bridge Trail next to Tireman Avenue and Outer Drive, the Environmental Study Area at the University of Michigan–Dearborn, or the woodlot in your neighborhood. You should see the forest floor covered with leaves. When did these leaves fall to the ground? Of course, they fell in the autumn of the most recent year. Slowly pick up some of the leaves and see if you can find the leaves that fell during in the autumn before last. You may be able to see a distinct difference between the leaves of the current year and the year before. How many leaf layers can you find? These trees have been producing leaves for many years, sometimes for many decades. Why don't you see at least 20 layers of leaves, perhaps more than a foot thick? Who came with a leaf blower and blew the leaves onto trucks and hauled them away?

You probably have heard that a variety of creatures live in the soil. They decompose and digest the leaves of previous years and leave recycled nutrients and rich organic materials. You may be standing on thousands of living creatures. Some of them are the size of a millipede or a snail, others are microscopic. Without the adaptions of these myriad of creatures chewing the leaves each year, we would have soil devoid of nutrients and just sandy and rocky.

Leaves are not the only plant organs that decompose. You do not have to look far to see fallen tree trunks and branches. How long will they lie there? Here is an example of the time spans in a forest. On a windy and cold March 15, 1972, a group of teachers walked in the floodplain forest at the University of Michigan–Dearborn and saw for the first time a large American Beech tree lying across the trail. It had fallen in a wind and ice storm during the night. The tree was still lying there the next day, and the next. It appeared to be a permanent fixture. In fact, from day to day we could not observe any changes. Yet if we looked at the fallen giant once each year, we would see that the tree slowly decomposed, until 35 years later only the long, slightly rounded mound of its trunk was barely visible. Again, a host of animals, fungi, and mosses received their nourishment from it over the course of the forest's time scale.

When we speak about the places with the most species of plants and animals, we are talking about biodiversity, and our thoughts usually go to the plants and animals in the tropical rainforests. Contrary to common perceptions, the biodiversity of microscopic species in the soil of our Rouge River watershed forests is many times greater than that of all the mammals, birds, and trees found there. The difficulty is that we cannot see them; the old saying 'out of sight, out of mind,' conveys the limits of our understanding of the wonders of our watershed and challenges us to explore the leaf layers and soil under our feet.

Another impressive example of the time scales of events in our watershed is the demise of a white oak tree that was nearly 6 feet in diameter and 18 feet in circumference. Estimates are that it was over 300 years old—older than the Constitution of the United States. The year 2000 was the last year it produced leaves. A section of the trunk split off in 2013, and in January 2021, the large still-standing trunk of the tree toppled to the ground to begin the cycle of decomposing and recycling its nutrients into the soil and roots of its younger neighbors. We may have difficulty considering that the atoms of carbon in an acorn from more than 300 years ago are part of the decomposing wood of the white oak and may become part of another tree that will be a giant in year 2400. A watershed may change over a time scale of centuries, which should help us appreciate the perspective of the First Peoples, who thought about the future for the seventh generation.

Personal Experiences of Awe and Wonder

Perhaps our most memorable experiences with the Rouge come from paddling in canoes or kayaks or walking its banks; sights and sensations from these experiences come readily to mind. We recall the ambience first; peering into dark bowers in the forests reminds us of fairytales. One neighbor took his son in a canoe to a wooded stretch of the Lower Rouge River and reported a sensation of being transported to a different, isolated world. We could not wait to tell our families about hearing the *frahnk, frahnk* of a startled Great Blue Heron as we disrupted its fishing expedition, and the *quark* of a Black-crowned Night-Heron as it stalked a fish.

The flight of a Bald Eagle just over the treetops made one septuagenarian express gratitude for the foresight of those who championed and legislated the Endangered Species Act. Another commented on the behavior of the Belted Kingfisher, which flew from its perch on an overhanging limb to a similar limb nearly 500 feet upstream, repeating this behavior twice before flying back overhead to reclaim its territory. We remarked on the role of the male Spotted Sandpiper in its reproductive cycle. It puts its "best nest forward" for review and inspection by a prospective female, which compares it to the offerings of competing nest-building males before choosing a mate. In addition to the pressures of building the best nest, the male is responsible for sitting on the eggs and feeding the young. How did that system develop?

Welcome Home: Beaver Come Back to Dearborn

Some comebacks that signal the Rouge River's rebirth happen quietly, unaccompanied by any fanfare. I (RAS) was fortunate enough to be at the right place at the right time to witness such an event from a bankside seat along the Rouge River in Dearborn. It was May 13, 2012. I was enjoying an evening walk in the University of Michigan–Dearborn Environmental Study Area. About an hour before sunset, while pausing along the edge of the river where two foot trails meet, I paused to watch a flight of Common Nighthawks heading north, the first I had seen that year. As I was looking up, my eye caught a movement in the river, at close to eye level and very close by. A furry head sticking out of the water and the V-shaped trail behind it indicated a swimming mammal. My first thought was "muskrat." But something about the head was different. It was large and robust, and it jutted almost completely out of the water. I thought to myself "If I were up north that would be a beaver." After just a few moments the animal turned toward the bank of the river. I held by breath as it reached the river's edge and began to crawl up onto the bank. It was a big animal, and if it were a muskrat it would have been the biggest I had ever seen. Then came the tail. A large, flat, broad tail. I was not up north, but it was indeed a beaver!

A few months later, around the same time of the evening, while pausing on the bike-path bridge over the Rouge River south of the Henry Ford Estate, I had my second beaver sighting. I was surprised and delighted to see two beavers this time. One large and one much smaller, they were nibbling on the twigs and branches of a large Silver Maple that had recently fallen into the river, very close to the bridge. Perhaps because I was looking at them from overhead they were not alarmed by my presence or that of the other pedestrians who were walking or biking across the bridge. I spent a good half-hour enjoying calling the attention of passers-by to the beaver, and all paused for a look. A few days later, I was able to get a photo of the smaller of the two beavers at the same spot. This was the first documented evidence of beavers in Dearborn in well over a century. They had come back home!

And they've stayed. In the years since, a small but seemingly stable population of beavers has become established in Dearborn. Sightings with photos from the Rouge River all through Dearborn are fairly regular. As this continues, it remains to be seen as to how effectively we can welcome this animal back to our part of the watershed. There are some challenges: beavers like to cut down trees, of course, and those may include trees in the home landscapes that border the river.

To me, the return of the beaver to the Rouge River in Dearborn is cause for celebration. It is also a sign that the water quality of the river has improved to the extent that beavers can thrive. Their presence also gives us a chance to enjoy observing these fascinating animals, which are so much a part of the rebirth of the natural heritage of the Rouge River watershed.

A Personal Letter to Our Rouge River Watershed

In summary, the three of us have lived for total of more than a century and a half, and we wish to write a letter of respect and admiration to our Rouge River watershed, in accord with the convention of the First People, as portrayed by Robin Wall Kimmerer (2013).

Dear Rouge River Watershed,

We hope our informal salutation is not disrespectful but rather an honor that recognizes our status of familiarity with each other. We send you our greetings with hesitancy and recognition of the abuse we have heaped on you in the past, and we extend our commitments to honor you in the tradition of the First Peoples whom you supported with food, fuel, and fiber. We admit that those of us who arrived on your shores in the past three centuries accepted your gifts without reciprocity, contrary to the practice of our First Peoples sisters and brothers. We hope that you will accept our efforts to reestablish our relationship with sincerity and the best of intentions.

We apologize that we have been numb to the centuries-long vitality you provided for our generations of First Peoples. In recent decades, we used you as an open sewer for tons of carelessly discarded objects and lethal substances. Consequently, your ability to provide for the reproduction of scores of creatures in your water and on your landscape was diminished or destroyed. We covered you with bridges and sped across you with thousands of vehicles per day as we attended to our every-day activities with an "out of sight and out of mind" mentality, failing to acknowledge for a nanosecond your contributions to our health and well-being. Contrary to our First People predecessors, we assumed you were an *it*—a watershed composed of many objects distinct from us humans, rather than a multitude of beings with their own personhood, kinship, and animacy. By seeing you as an *it*, we separated ourselves from you and saw you only as *natural resources*. We took our self-imposed rift as license to abuse and exploit, because you were beyond our world of moral consideration. Even now we euphemistically call our misdeeds "legacy" actions rather than violations against your integrity and wholeness.

Over the past 50 years we have painstakingly come through a rebirth canal. With this volume, we pledge consideration for your water and landscape, which comprise a dynamic, vibrant, and highly interactive ecosystem of integrated beings, forces, and functions. We accept responsibility for your continued rebirth and restored vitality. As such, we not only give you our respect and appreciation, we recognize that we have a moral responsibility for making decisions for those yet unborn and without agency. Thus, we pledge to do our best to develop practices of reciprocity for your health as you continue to provide prosperity for us as we work to achieve the transition from wen to wonder with awe.

Sincerely,

[Dear reader, your signature is kindly requested.]

LITERATURE CITED

Beam, J.D., Braunscheidel, J.J. 1998. "Rouge River Assessment." State of Michigan, Department of Natural Resources. Report 22, Lansing.

Carson, R. 1965. *A Sense of Wonder*. New York: Harper and Row.

Craves, J.A. 2007. "The Birds of Dearborn: An Annotated Checklist." Rouge River Bird Observatory. Dearborn, MI.

Jensen, J. 1990. *Siftings*. Baltimore: Johns Hopkins University Press.

Johnson, B.N. 2011. "Wastewater Treatment Comes to Detroit: Law, Politics, Technology and Funding." Dissertation, Wayne State University, Detroit.

Kimmerer, R.W. 2103. *Braiding Sweetgrass: Indigenous Wisdom, Scientific Knowledge, and the Teachings of Plants*. Minneapolis: Milkweed Editions.

Ricks, T.E. 2020. *First Principles: What America's Founders Learned from the Greeks and Romans and How That Shaped Our Country*. New York: Harper Collins.

10 RECONNECTING WITH OUR HOME WATERS

Rouge River Offers Growing Number of Recreational Opportunities

Kurt Kuban

When I grew up in the 1970s, Wayne County's Hines Park was quite a popular hangout. I remember many picnics and afternoon family outings in Hines. My dad and his friends would play softball, while us kids would explore the park. It was an idyllic setting for a kid. In the fields and meadows, we'd chase butterflies, frogs, and whatever other critters caught our attention. This would sometimes get us in trouble if we wandered off too far, however.

"Don't go near that river!"

Those stern warnings from my parents to stay away from the Rouge River, which weaves its way through Hines Park, were my first introduction to the Rouge. I quickly learned that the Rouge River was polluted and dangerous, something to be feared and avoided, unless you wanted to grow a third leg, turn into some kind of toxic creature, or even die. At least that's what people would say if you made contact with the water—a pretty compelling reason to stay away. And, for years, that's exactly what I did—stayed away from the Rouge River. Just like my parents warned me to do.

Given those origins, it seems unlikely that I'd one day be writing about the recreational opportunities the Rouge River has to offer, and actually encouraging people to not only go "near" the river, but connect with it.

The fact is, the Rouge River is a much different river today than it was in the 1970s and early 1980s. These days it's not uncommon to see people floating in a canoe or kayak, fishing from the shore, or biking and walking along the various tributaries that cut though a large portion of metro Detroit.

I began to learn this in the late 1990s, when I used to walk my dog in the city of Wayne, which has a nice trail system that straddles the Lower Branch of the Rouge River. On our walks, I was surprised by how much wildlife lived in and around the river, and I began to realize what an oasis the Rouge really was. Those walks changed my perception of the Rouge. It didn't really look like the toxic mess people had been warning me about since I was a child. There was plenty of trash in the river from years of neglect, but I could see the potential.

About that same time, I landed a job as a newspaper reporter for the *Observer & Eccentric* newspapers. As fate would have it, one of my first assignments was covering Rouge Rescue, the annual cleanup organized by Friends of the Rouge. I was very much impressed by the group's passion and all the hard-working volunteers who pulled shopping carts, old tires, and just about anything else you can imagine from various sections of the river. I'd never seen a dirtier bunch of individuals with smiles on their faces. It must have been contagious, because a year later, I was organizing Rouge Rescue in the city of Wayne and cleaning up the section of the Lower Rouge where I walked with my dog. As I was hip deep in the river pulling apart a logjam that first year, I remember thinking, what would my parents say if they could see me?

Little did I know then, but my relationship with the river had just begun. From that day forward, I've been an advocate for the Rouge River. I've spent hundreds of hours in various sections of the Rouge, removing trash, opening logjams, and exploring one of the most accessible and underappreciated waterways in Michigan.

As a reporter, I've written many articles about the efforts to restore the Rouge, by local governments, organizations such as Friends of the Rouge, and just everyday volunteers who want to see their local streams cleaned up so they don't have to worry about the safety of their own children who may wander down to the water. During my time as a reporter and volunteer, I've discovered some of the best places for recreation along the Rouge River, whether for canoeing and kayaking, fishing, or just taking a nice hike and enjoying nature. Here are some of the best places and opportunities I know.

Lower Rouge Water Trail

For me, if you want to talk about recreational possibilities on the Rouge River, you start with what has become known as the Lower Rouge Water

Trail, which encompasses about 27 river miles of the Lower Branch, from Canton Township on the west to the river's confluence with the Detroit River near Zug Island. Some twenty years ago, the idea of a recreation trail with canoeing and kayaking along the Lower Rouge was almost unthinkable. This stream goes through some of the most built-up and industrial areas of the entire watershed.

I still remember the looks people gave me and my buddy Mike Gotts the first time we launched my canoe on the Lower Rouge River at Goudy Park in Wayne. Kind of like, "Are you guys crazy?" Yet as we glided along the water through the forested corridor slicing through downtown Wayne, I realized we were onto something. Not only was it satisfying to be able to canoe along areas we had cleaned up, they were also our home waters, literally traversing through the neighborhood where we lived.

As our group of volunteers grew and we opened more logjams (during various Rouge Rescue events and on other workdays), we began to develop a nice paddling course in Wayne. Soon, Friends of the Rouge saw what we were doing as a great opportunity to showcase the river; they organized a group paddle in the fall of 2003 that attracted a group of curious canoeists and kayakers from outside of Wayne. It was a great success, and we have done the fall trip almost every year since.

By 2011, Friends of the Rouge had concluded that the Lower Branch of the Rouge River offered the only viable opportunity in the watershed to have an extended paddling route. That October, I was among a group of about a dozen or so volunteers who set out on a three-day expedition to explore 27 miles of the Lower Rouge, from Canton Township all the way to the confluence of the Main Branch in Dearborn. The point was to draw attention to the possibility of canoeing on the Rouge, which at that time many still saw as a far-fetched idea.

The trip itself was a struggle. The first day was spent entirely in Canton, where the river is scenic, but narrow and clogged with woody debris. It seems like we did more climbing over logjams than paddling through open water, and we didn't make much progress. That would be a common theme over the three days. By the time we made it to Fair Lane, Henry Ford's beautiful estate on the Main Branch in Dearborn, we were exhausted. Over the three days, we climbed over, walked around, or ducked under nearly 200 logjams between Canton and Dearborn. And a couple of us had major cases of poison ivy, to add insult to the soreness of our muscles.

As physically draining as the trip was, we also saw the potential.

We went through many sections of the river where we felt like we were floating through a forest in northern Michigan. We saw plenty of wildlife, including deer, kingfishers, turtles, hawks, mink, and even evidence of beavers. Most of the land along the Lower Rouge River is owned by Wayne County Parks and is still relatively undeveloped. We floated past wetlands, and mature forests with towering cottonwoods, sycamores, oaks, and maples. You really get a sense of what this region must have felt like when the first European settlers moved into the area (see chapters 2 and 3). We also paddled through some historic neighborhoods in Wayne and Dearborn, where people watched us float by, somewhat amazed. That novelty added to the excitement.

Since that time, Friends of the Rouge has brought many stakeholders to the table to create the Lower Rouge River Water Trail Committee, which meets monthly. Members include representatives from the 11 communities the trail passes through, including Canton Township, the city of Wayne, Westland, Inkster, Dearborn Heights, Dearborn, and Detroit, as well as representatives from Wayne County Parks and even the National Park Service, which has provided some technical advice on how to get recognition as a designated water trail. Currently Michigan has eight state-designated water trails, including the nearby Huron River. The committee has created maps of the trail, and it is designing signage and developing a management plan. Slowly but steadily the water trail is becoming a reality (fig. 30). The Lower Rouge Water Trail also connects to the Detroit Heritage River Water Trail that has been identified as one of the top 11 water trails in Michigan by the Michigan Department of Natural Resources.

Some of the communities along the trail see the recreational potential and are starting to put in the infrastructure to make it a reality. The city of Wayne, using a grant from Wayne County, was the first to construct a canoe launch at Goudy Park (where I put my canoe in for the first time). Wayne County is constructing two launches at Venoy-Dorsey Park, a county-owned park located in Wayne and Westland. Further downstream, the city of Dearborn received a grant through the Michigan Department of Natural Resources Trust Fund to build two kayak and canoe launches—at Dearborn Hills Golf Course and Ford Field Park, both owned by the city. They hope to have the launches built sometime in 2022.

Even in the most industrial area of the watershed, near the hulking

Fig. 30. A group of canoeists make their way along the Lower Rouge River through Dynamite Park in the city of Wayne. (Photograph credit: Kenneth Gregones.)

Ford Rouge plant, a green oasis has been created as a result of the Fort Rouge Gateway Project (FRoG for short). In 2016, the Michigan Department of Transportation reconstructed the Fort Street Bridge, a historic drawbridge that spans the Rouge River, where Ford's security men once attacked union members. As part of the project, the land adjacent to the bridge has become a pocket park featuring a kayak launch and environmental exhibits to educate the public.

Adjacent to this new park, Marathon Oil Company has bought up most of the homes in the Oakwood Heights neighborhood to create a green buffer around its refinery. And the city of Dearborn has partnered with the Michigan Department of Natural Resources, the US Environmental Protection Agency, and Marathon in hopes of purchasing all of Fordson Island, a man-made island near the park, which the city wants to maintain as greenspace. The goal for Fordson Island is to remove the motorized vehicle bridge and restore natural habitat on the island. The long-term plan is to install pedestrian and bicycling bridges at each end of the island and incorporate the island into the Rouge Gateway Trail.

Dearborn is taking a leading role with the Lower Rouge Water Trail and making it more accessible for its residents. The city is in the early planning stages of installing another launch at the Dearborn Historical Museum site at Brady and Morley Streets. This launch would be in recognition of a historical river launch site that supported the Dearborn Arsenal.

David Norwood, Dearborn's sustainability coordinator, said the Rouge River offers an incredible opportunity for the community, even though many residents don't realize it. "It has generally been my experience that most Dearborn residents don't have a true idea about the river and what it really is," Norwood said. "Once anyone—I mean 100%—gets a chance to paddle the river, they are blown away how beautiful it truly is."

Norwood is exactly right. Connecting people to the river is really what the entire Lower Rouge Water Trail effort is all about. It's one of the main reasons that fellow volunteer Mathew Mulholland and I staged a canoe race over a three-mile stretch in Wayne. We held the race, called the Logjam Classic, for three years (2013–15), as part of an event we organized called Rouge-a-Palooza, a celebration of all that was going on with the Rouge River.

We had about 20 teams enter the race each year. It was a great feeling to see so many people paddling on a river that people once told me was dead and a waste of time trying to save. My hope is to someday be part of a canoe race that traverses the entire Lower Rouge Water Trail— from Canton to the Detroit River. Of course, the main obstacle preventing that from happening, and the biggest impediment to the water trail itself, are the logjams.

Because the Lower Branch is very "flashy" due to all the impervious surfaces (roads, parking lots, buildings, etc.) in this section of the watershed, the banks of the river are constantly being eroded, so downed trees and other woody debris accumulate in the river. That causes jams. For even the most experienced paddlers, getting over or around a logjam is a difficult proposition. For amateurs, it can be very dangerous. Right now, the effort to open the logjams is largely the work of volunteers wielding their own chainsaws, and it's a constant struggle. Just in the stretch in Wayne, which is only about seven river miles total from end to end, we've struggled to keep even short sections open and free of logjams. We'll open a logjam, and then it rains, which moves the woody debris around and leads to more jams, most of the time containing wood we've already cut up. There was a reason we called our race the Logjam Classic.

For the water trail to ever be viable, the water trail committee must find the resources to pay for woody debris management. It's hoped that the various communities and Wayne County Parks, which owns most of the land along the water trail, will dedicate funding to seeing this ambitious water trail concept come to fruition. Relying on volunteers to do the work is not a viable option, in my opinion. It is difficult, time-consuming work. Fortunately, communities such as Dearborn are leading the way. The city applied for and received grants for woody debris management work between the two canoe launches they are in the process of constructing. We hope that is a model that will work in other communities in the future.

Other Places to Paddle

I've canoed through other sections of the Rouge watershed, and some areas are really scenic. Two of the nicest are the Main Branch through Southfield and the Middle Branch through Hines Park. Unfortunately, both of these stretches, pretty as they are, don't hold enough water for paddling for most of the year. You will scrape the bottom, and end up walking your canoe through long, shallow stretches—not something most paddlers want to do. Kayakers might find it an easier go, but they will still be dealing with woody debris and logjams that will prevent longer, unimpeded trips.

There are two other paddling options. The first is Newburgh Lake, a 105-acre impoundment of the Middle Branch located in Hines Park and the city of Livonia. Created by a historic dam built by Henry Ford to power one of his "Village Industries" plants (see chapter 3), the lake provides plenty of recreational opportunities, and is popular with canoeists and kayakers. It has a nice launch, but is not open to motorboats. Newburgh Lake is surrounded by a mostly forested shoreline, with several recreation areas. The eastern end of the lake is deeper as it leads to the dam, while the western portion of the lake is narrower and less busy. You can also paddle a little way up the Middle Rouge near the I-275 overpass until logjams become an issue.

The other paddling opportunity worth mentioning is through the industrial section of the Rouge River, from a boat launch behind the Melvindale Civic Arena down to Belanger Park in River Rouge, which is nestled along a heavily industrialized section of the Detroit River just downstream of the confluence with the Rouge. Friends of the Rouge has been leading an annual kayaking trip through this section for a number of years. It can be done in a canoe, but kayaks are better vessels for the larger open water. I can tell you, it's quite a sight to see a brigade of kayakers floating through one of the most industrial landscapes in the world. Massive factories tower above the banks of the Rouge River, including the Ford Rouge complex, the former Rouge Steel factory (now owned and operated by Russian-based Severstal), and the Marathon Oil refinery.

This is the stretch that includes the Fort Street Bridge Park and drawbridge, Fordson Island, and Zug Island. While this is technically part of the Lower Rouge Water Trail, it is a much different experience than the rest of the trail upriver. Let's just say logjams are not an issue in this section of the watershed, though you might encounter an occasional submerged abandoned boat or a passing freighter once you get into the Detroit River.

Despite being in the buckle of the Rust Belt, you are bound to encounter wildlife. Turtles are common, as are waterfowl, birds of prey, blue herons, and kingfishers. During one of the group trips the paddlers encountered a bald eagle standing atop a slag pile on Zug Island. It was quite a contrast, and a sign of hope for everyone who paddled that day.

While not for everyone, this really is a unique float, which offers incredible views of our area's industrial underbelly and some of the places that put Detroit on the map. It is also an area where there is a concerted effort to repair the landscape, including efforts at the Fort Street Bridge Park and Fordson Island. Communities such as Dearborn have made and continue to make huge investments in the Rouge corridor here, turning it into a viable recreational resource. It's exciting to think what the future holds.

Please remember to follow safety protocols whenever and wherever you decide to paddle on the river. Always wear a floatation device, and try to paddle with others if possible. If it rains, or if the water is running high, it's not a bad idea to stay away from the river. It can be dangerous.

Wet a Line

My second favorite form of recreation on the Rouge is fishing. With more than 400 lakes and nearly 600 miles of rivers, streams, and creeks in the Rouge watershed, there are almost limitless opportunities to wet a line and catch some fish. Fish communities are rebounding throughout the watershed, largely because of cleanup efforts and improved dissolved oxygen levels and habitat. For a fisherman like myself, this is welcome news. And I've seen the results on the end of my line.

Depending on where you try your luck, the fishing experience differs from place to place and stream to stream. While most anglers are reluctant to reveal their favorite fishing holes, I'm happy to do so when it comes to the Rouge. The more people who discover the Rouge River, the more pressure there will be to continue cleanup efforts. Here are a couple of my favorite places for fishing in the river.

Hines Park (including Newburgh Lake). Hines Park is still one of the treasures of the Wayne County parks system, and Newburgh Lake is its crown jewel. In addition to being a great place to paddle, it's home to plenty of fish. A good friend of mine and my first newspaper editor, the late Jeff Counts of Livonia, used to fly-fish for panfish here with great success. Using lightweight gear, he got a thrill when the little fish would hit his flies on the surface of the water. Personally, I like to go after the larger fish, such as bass, pike, and channel catfish, and the lake holds plenty of structure and holes where they can be found.

In 1998, Newburgh Lake was dredged and cleaned up as part of the Rouge River National Wet Weather Demonstration Project. More than 500,000 tons of polluted sediment, much of which contained PCBs and other toxic chemicals, was removed from the lake. At the completion of the project, which included reestablishing aquatic vegetation and fish habitat, the lake was stocked with bass, bluegill and other panfish, walleye, and other game fish (see also chapter 5). By 2003, due to improved sediment and water quality, the Michigan Department of Natural Resources lifted the fish-consumption advisory ban for some of the fish species in the lake. Today, you will see anglers at the lake year-round.

Newburgh Lake isn't the only impoundment of the Middle Branch in Hines Park. Anglers also target Phoenix Lake (Northville), Wilcox Lake (Plymouth), and Nankin Lake (Westland). Boat access is a little more limited in these impoundments, but certainly not impossible. Many people just fish from shore. Wilcox Lake does have a fishing dock.

Personally, I like to fish in the Middle Branch in the sections between the lakes throughout Hines Park, particularly in the upper stretches in Northville, Plymouth, and Livonia. The river is loaded with smallmouth bass, giant rock bass, catfish, panfish, and pike. I've even caught an occasional walleye in and around Newburgh Lake, as well as brown trout that have migrated into the river from Johnson Creek in Northville. Without a doubt, some of my best days fishing have taken place in this stream. You can fish from shore, but I like to don some waders and get into the river, which allows you access to some really good fishing holes.

Johnson Creek. Yes, you read that right in the last paragraph. There are trout in the Rouge River, mostly in Johnson Creek. This clear, cold-water tributary has its origins in rural Washtenaw County and makes its way through Northville before dumping into the Middle Rouge in Hines Park near Seven Mile Road. Johnson Creek is one of the few coldwater streams in southeast Michigan, and is home to a healthy, naturally reproducing population of brown trout. For fly fishermen, this means, of course, that you don't have to travel to northern Michigan to find a trout stream. One of the main problems trying to fish Johnson Creek, however, is getting access. Much of it traverses through private property. I've found one of the best places to access it is in Northville's Fish Hatchery Park on Seven Mile Road west of Sheldon Road. Trails along the stream provide relatively easy access for anglers. The park is the former location of a historic trout hatchery that shipped the fish it reared all over the world. There still is a spring-fed pond just yards from Johnson Creek. In fact, the park just underwent a million-dollar habitat-improvement project. The pond was dredged and the riverbanks along Johnson Creek were reconstructed and stabilized with plenty of native vegetation. Fish will now be able to move easily between the river and pond.

Carpenter Lake Nature Preserve. I wanted to mention this five-acre impoundment located on 10 Mile Road just east of Inkster Road in Southfield. It is part of a larger 42-acre nature preserve that came about after members of the public pressured the city of Southfield to preserve the small lake, which is an impoundment of the Ravines Branch of the Rouge River.

The city was able to secure a grant through the Michigan Natural Resources Trust Fund and purchase the property, improve the dam that creates the lake, and preserve a natural slice of Oakland County. The park is home to woodlands, forested wetlands, and native meadows. A nice trail system ties it all together. Anglers can find a number of fish in Carpenter Lake, including largemouth bass, channel catfish, bluegill, and sunfish. There are accessible fishing and viewing platforms along the lake, helping make it a popular place to fish. The Southfield Parks and Recreation Department has even hosted its annual Fishing Derby at Carpenter Lake.

Lower Branch. I wanted to briefly mention the lower Rouge, which has traditionally been the most impaired portion of the watershed because it traverses through some of the older communities where there are a lot of impervious surfaces. Fish communities in the Lower Branch have really rebounded since the mid-1980s, when environmental laws began to be enforced. For example, in 1986, the Michigan Department of Natural Resources sampled for fish in Dearborn's Ford Field. They found only 6 species, and a total of 33 fish. Most were carp or goldfish, including many with fin rot or tumors. When Friends of the Rouge surveyed the river in 2015, they found 15 species, a total of 353 fish—and only one carp.

The Lower Branch also is the only branch unimpeded by dams, meaning fish can come up from the Detroit River and Great Lakes and travel all the way to the headwaters region in western Wayne County and even neighboring Washtenaw County. The Wayne Road dam in the city of Wayne was the last real impediment, but it was removed in 2012–2013 thanks to a federal grant. The removal of that dam was the impetus for us to organize our Rouge-a-Palooza events in Wayne. It was definitely something to celebrate, and I still own a piece of that dam, which sits on a shelf in my office.

Salmon and steelhead can be found in the upper regions each year, as they migrate up from the Detroit River (fig. 31). In the fall, I often find salmon in the area of the old Wayne Road dam. Those fish now can migrate further upstream into Canton. The river gets sucker runs in the spring, too. In Canton, there is also a resident population of rainbow trout. When I was a reporter for the *Canton Observer*, a local man tipped me off. I didn't believe him, so I headed to the spot on the river he mentioned. I was shocked when I caught a nice steelhead with my first cast. I still keep the exact location a secret, which was his only request when telling me about his honey hole. Friends of the Rouge have confirmed their existence during recent fish surveys.

I've also fished down in the industrial part of the river, not far from Fordson Island and the big industrial factories. I never had much success,

Fig. 31. Wayne resident Mathew Mulholland helps a group of middle-school students release salmon they grew in their classroom into the Lower Rouge River in Wayne's Goudy Park. (Photograph by Kurt Kuban, used by permission.)

but it was an interesting experience nonetheless. With all the improvements going on in this area, I can see a day down the road where it could be a productive fishing area, especially considering its proximity to the Detroit River.

Find a Trail

One of the greatest assets of the Rouge River system is its riparian corridor, which has largely been left in a natural state. Some of the best places to find nature in southeast Michigan are along the Rouge River and its many tributaries. Fortunately, communities in the watershed have taken advantage of this fact and built trails along the waterways. Many towns I've covered over the years have sent out surveys to their residents, asking them what kind of recreational priorities they would like to have. Time and again, building recreational trails for walking, jogging, and biking is near the top of the list.

Canton, Southfield, and Dearborn are just some of the towns that have built excellent trail systems. Canton and Dearborn are among the towns working with Wayne County Parks to develop a new greenway trail along the Lower Rouge River that would coincide with the water trail. Both communities already have sections of trail along the river, so this would connect the dots as more sections are built. The goal is to offer convenient and safe access to the Lower Rouge River for all users.

Of course, this ambitious plan is just that at this point—an ambitious plan, much like the water trail. It may take years to build the entire thing—if Wayne County is able to get the funding. However, there are still many great places to hike or bike along the Rouge River. Here are some of my favorites.

The Holliday Forest and Wildlife Preserve. This 550-acre nature preserve owned by Wayne County Parks straddles Tonquish Creek in northwest Wayne County, mostly in Canton Township and Westland. There are more than 10 miles of hiking trails through various natural terrains, including upland and wetland sections. There are towering beeches, maples, and oaks, and it's a great place to see wildlife including a great blue heron rookery, and even beavers. According to Wayne County, the foot trails that follow the Tonquish Creek streambed date back to the days of the Potawatomi Indians (see chapter 2). Legend has it that Chief Tonquish of the Potawatomi was killed by European settlers and buried within what is now the preserve.

Rouge River Gateway Trail. This roughly three-mile mixed-use trail in the City of Dearborn is popular with both walkers and cyclists. It passes by cultural sites such as the Henry Ford Estate, the campuses of University of Michigan–Dearborn and Henry Ford College, as well as beautiful natural areas, including the 300-acre UM-Dearborn Environmental Study Area, home to a rare climax beech-maple forest. More than 250 species of birds have been identified here, as well as lots of other wildlife.

In 2012, Rick Simek of UM–Dearborn spotted and took a photo of a beaver in this section of the river (see chapter 9). It was the first time in well over a hundred years that a beaver had been seen in the Rouge watershed. Since that time, the aquatic rodents have expanded their range in the watershed and are not uncommon anymore. I've personally seen them far upstream in the city of Wayne. There are two bridges that cross the Rouge River along the Gateway Trail, which are nice places to stop and check out the river corridor. To get access to the trail, there are trailheads on campus and across the street from Greenfield Village and The Henry Ford museum. The trail also connects to the bike path in Hines Park, which travels 19 miles to Northville.

Rouge Park. At nearly 1,200 acres, Rouge Park is the largest park in the city of Detroit, which owns and operates the park. It is home to ball-fields, model airplane fields, the famous Brennan Pool complex designed by Albert Kahn, and a stable area for the city's mounted-police horses. But the park, which straddles Outer Drive south of 1-96, also contains plenty of nature, including woodlands and restored meadows featuring native wildflowers and grasses planted by volunteers with the Friends of Rouge Park.

There are also a number of trails, including a mountain-biking trail north of Tireman, the appropriately named Stone Bridge Nature Trail (that features a historic stone bridge, of course), Sorensen Nature Trail, and Scout Hollow Nature Trail. Most of the trails in the park provide easy access to the Main Branch of the Rouge River, which flows through the sprawling park. If you ever want to see the wild side of Detroit, this is the place to do it.

Dynamite Park. Okay, I'm including this 37-acre park in the city of Wayne because I've been so involved in helping restore it to its natural state. Located just east of downtown Wayne and north of Michigan Avenue, the park includes a section of the Lower Branch of the Rouge River (and is part of the water trail).

The city of Wayne built a large underground stormwater retention basin in the park, which prevents sewer overflow into the river, something that used to be a common occurrence after rains. As a result, the city leases the parkland from Wayne County. Historically, a large section of the park was mowed, but in around 2001, local volunteers like myself convinced the city to allow us to restore it to a more natural state. Many of our Rouge Rescue events have taken place here, as we planted native plants in areas that had been mowed, and we built a trail system that traverses through woodlands, wetlands, and the native prairie that we restored. A local Boy Scout troop also built footbridges over wetland areas and a small creek that feeds into the Rouge River. Our efforts were recognized when the city received a habitat-restoration award from the Rouge River Advisory Council.

Dynamite Park, so named because Wayne County once stored dynamite for road-building on the location (at least that's what I've been told by the old-timers), is home to an array of wildlife, including deer, foxes, hawks, blue herons, wood ducks, and coyotes. I've been in the park and heard a group of coyotes howling, which was a cool experience. With the bustling traffic of Michigan Avenue and downtown Wayne so close, Dynamite Park really is a green oasis in an urban jungle. It also includes a bluff that rises more than 50 feet above the Rouge that is one of my favorite spots in the entire watershed.

Wonderful Resource

"No man ever steps in the same river twice," or so says the Greek philosopher Heraclitus. That is probably true for the Rouge River, which can be moody and flashy when there is rainfall or snowmelt. But don't overlook this wonderful resource, which previous generations took for granted and treated with such disregard.

In the last 25 years, I've seen a lot of determined people, both volunteers and government employees, do the hard work to reverse the actions of generations past and help turn the tide for the Rouge River. The Rouge has come so far. It really is a success story—one that continues to be told. I urge you to get out and explore "our" river. As one of the most accessible rivers in the state, this river has so much to offer, especially for those of us who are able to take advantage of its recreational opportunities.

I've told you about my relationship with the Rouge River. I think I can speak for most of the volunteers who have made saving this river one of their passions. For every minute I've given to the cause—all the hard work and sweat equity—the Rouge River always gives back more in return. It has provided me with a place to fish and canoe, and my kids with a place to explore. It is full of surprises if you just take the time to look. Nothing would make me happier than for you to connect to this river and make your own story.

John H. Hartig

"I would argue no river has shown more dramatic improvement than the Rouge River, and there is no one person more responsible for that success than Jim Murray," says Jim Ridgway, former executive director of the Alliance of Rouge Communities and vice president of Environmental Consulting & Technology, who worked closely with Murray for more than 30 years.

"Murray had the audacity to think big, the vision to address ALL the environmental and institutional challenges, the wisdom to listen to the experts, the skill to build the political coalition, the charm to develop the public support, and most importantly, the patience to build the consensus required to attract federal funds and convince the local elected officials to provide the funds required to finish the job," Ridgway added.

Water pollution of the Rouge River has long been an enormous problem, one that would eventually require cooperation on a scale never before seen in southeast Michigan. Twenty-three percent of its 466-square-mile drainage area is covered by rooftops, parking lots, roads, and other hard surfaces, so stormwater cannot infiltrate into soils, but runs off that land and pollutes creeks, drains, and eventually the Rouge River. At the outset of the cleanup effort in 1985, there were 168 combined sewer overflows, discharging nearly eight billion gallons of stormwater and sewage into the river during wet weather periods each year.

A Career Defined by Water

Some people's passion for a particular cause is so strong that their vocation and avocation become one. Murray is one of those individuals. He has sustained his passion for water for the majority of his 40-year career, and at the center has been the Rouge River.

In 1980, Murray was elected as the Washtenaw County drain commissioner to protect surface waters and the environment, including a small portion of the Rouge River watershed in Washtenaw County. In 1983, he was appointed by then-governor James Blanchard to the Michigan Water Resources Commission charged with protecting the waters of the state.

Under Murray's chairmanship, the Rouge River was identified as a top priority because of its grossly polluted condition. He led the charge to develop an action plan in 1985 to spur cleanup of the river. Knowing that for such an action plan to succeed it would have to be built from the ground up, he helped establish the Rouge River Basin Committee, made up of all the mayors from the 48 communities in the watershed.

Murray fostered regional thinking by chairing the Areawide Water Quality Board of the Southeast Michigan Council of Governments. He also advocated local ownership and involvement by helping establish Friends of the Rouge. He served as the organization's first president for five years.

In the 1990s, Murray moved on to become the director of the Wayne County Department of Environment, where he helped establish the Rouge River National Wet Weather Demonstration Project, which is now heralded by the US Environmental Protection Agency as a national model and a "blueprint for success" on a watershed scale. In 2006, he helped establish the Alliance of Rouge Communities, which encourages watershed-wide cooperation and mutual support for meeting federal and state water-quality standards and restoring beneficial uses.

From the beginning, Murray recognized that the technical solutions were less of a challenge than convincing the general public (and the elected officials who served them) that they were a big part of the problem. Early surveys showed that most Rouge River watershed residents believed that the problems in the Rouge River were caused by industry. Residents with a little more awareness added Detroit's combined sewer overflows to the list of polluters. Of course, the list of pollutant sources was far longer than that.

So, armed with the available technology of the time—a AAA road map of the region mounted to a foam board with known and unknown pollution sources pasted on it—Murray spent the early years meeting throughout the region with city councils, advocacy groups, business groups, and any others who would hear him out. Once citizens realized that they were contributing sewage, contaminated stormwater, and toxic materials to the river, they accepted that they could do better.

This groundswell of support drove the process, but as we all know, it takes money to make progress. Ridgway continues:

> Murray worked with Congressman John Dingell and others in the con-gressional delegation to access $350 million of federal funds. He shared those funds with the individual communities within the watershed. To encourage sustainability, he required these communities to match the federal funds with local funds—dollar for dollar. The federal dol-lars acted as a sweetener and encouraged the communities to proceed in the restoration in a timely manner. Stated simply, communities had the choice between accepting federal funds and help in moving forward toward compliance with the Clean Water Act or face reprisal from Fed-eral Judge John Feikens and/or the regulators. For many of these com-munities, the cost of compliance—even given the federal support—was the single largest expense they had ever authorized.

So, with the prodding of the federal courts, all the communities joined the watershed-wide cleanup effort. Ridgway adds,

> Murray required rigid procurement procedures to assure that the fed-eral support—and local contributions—would continue for years. Con-gressman Dingell insisted that the federal funds be "squeaky clean." Thus, Murray chose to require all funds comply with the requirements established in the no-longer-applicable, federal "Construction Grants Program." This self-imposed requirement was far more restrictive than required by the congressional directed funds, but it also made the entire process transparent to the federal government, the local units of govern-ment, and the citizens of the watershed.

In the end, all 48 communities, all three counties, all industries and busi-nesses, and all stakeholders had to do their part.

Formative Years

Murray grew up in the 1950s and 1960s in what is now Westland, Mich-igan, which is located along one of four branches of the Rouge River.

Even back then, the waters of the Rouge were polluted. Mothers always know best, and his mother regularly told him to stay away from the river because of the pollution. Despite his mother's plea, Murray was drawn to the river, and he fell in love with it. He has fond memories of playing "Tarzan in the jungle" in the Rouge River behind his elementary school. He recalls what fun he and his friends had swinging on a rope from a large willow tree hanging over the water's edge, and just as he reached the peak of his swing, letting go and free-falling into the river. He obviously did not share those stories with his mother. However, those early childhood experiences stayed with him and he vowed to one day clean up his river.

Uncanny Ability to Evoke Outrage and Compel Action

One story worth telling concerns Murray's communication skills and unique ability bring about change. As noted earlier, Murray served as the Washtenaw County drain commissioner and on the Michigan Water Resources Commission in the 1980s. In 1984, Jim came to me—I was an aquatic biologist working for Michigan Department of Natural Resources—over concern about the grossly polluted waters of the Rouge River. He asked if I would prepare a scientific report for the Michigan Water Resources Commission on the pollution of the Rouge River. All available scientific studies and monitoring data were reviewed, documenting that the Rouge River was severely polluted with raw sewage and stormwater entering from combined sewer overflows, decomposing algae, lack of oxygen causing fish kills, sludge mats, litter and debris, elevated turbidity, and toxic substances (Hartig 1986).

After the findings were presented to the Michigan Water Resources Commission, Murray organized a meeting on the banks of the Rouge River in Melvindale with Congressman Dingell and Wayne County Executive Ed McNamara—two prominent elected officials with responsibility for the watershed. We met in the parking lot of the Melvindale ice arena and the four of us walked behind the arena and down the floodplain to the banks of the Rouge River. However, the river at this point was no normal river. In the 1960s, the US Army Corps of Engineers constructed a straightened 4.2-mile concrete channel in this section of the lower Rouge River to move stormwater out of the area as fast as possible. During storms both stormwater and raw sewage were backing up into basements, causing a health hazard; the solution was to move it out of sight and hopefully out of mind. This did help alleviate some basement flooding, but the Rouge River continued to deteriorate. So much raw sewage and stormwater were entering the river that this entire section had gone anaerobic—that means the river had no oxygen. When there is no oxygen in a river, hydrogen sulfide, which smells like rotten eggs, forms through decomposition of waste and plant material. Even the most pollution-tolerant fish, like carp, were dying.

Here you have one of the longest-serving and most respected members of the United States House of Representatives (Congressman Dingell) and Wayne County Executive Ed McNamara standing on the concrete banks of the Rouge River, with Murray and me smelling the rotten-egg odor of hydrogen sulfide and watching dead carp float by. What a surreal experience! However, believe it or not, that is not the worst part of the story. Also floating down the river was raw sewage. Murray pointed down and exclaimed, "Look at that raw sewage and the albino eels." Congressman Dingell and County Executive McNamara, looking puzzled, squinted down to get a better look. It was condoms floating in with the raw sewage. Murray's goal was to shock these two elected officials with the gross state of pollution of the Rouge River and provide them with such an unforgettable experience that they would help bring about change. And it worked! Congressman Dingell eventually delivered $350 million in federal funding for the cleanup effort and McNamara helped bring along all the communities in the Wayne County portion of the watershed, along with local money, to ensure a comprehensive solution to the water pollution.

Insights into Leadership Style

Flora McCormack spent over a decade working with Murray as his deputy director. The first time she met him was when she was asked to come down to Wayne County to be considered for a position to oversee the county's solid waste program. At the time McCormack was working at the Michigan Department of Environmental Quality (today called the Michigan Department of Environment, Great Lakes, and Energy) in the Solid Waste Division. Her counterpart at the county was leaving for another position in the private sector, and he recommended her as a potential replacement. McCormack was more curious than interested in what Wayne County was offering, so she agreed to meet with Murray.

"My first impression of Murray was quite good," noted McCormack. "This was a man who knew what he was looking for and how to find it. He asked probing questions about my knowledge of solid waste laws, as well as questions about the potential issues facing the county as it prepared and implemented a solid waste management plan. They were anything but the usual canned questions typical of most job interviews. His knowledge was extensive and practical. It was far beyond the typical understanding of the issues I encountered in other officials from county governments around the state."

McCormack continues: "Our discussion was lively and at times heated, especially when I disagreed with him on some points. I even had the brass to tell him he was wrong on some things. Little did I know at the time that this was exactly what he was looking for. As I came to know while working for him, it was vitally important for Murray to know that he could trust his employee to tell him the truth without fear of repercussions."

"I thoroughly enjoyed my 'interview' with him," noted McCormack. "I came to admire him more and more as I worked for him. I was able to learn so much from him and for that I am eternally grateful."

Murray is a "bottom line" guy—he wants to see results and will not suffer fools gladly. McCormack recalls:

We had 7 AM Friday morning staff meetings covering all the areas Murray was responsible for. They started at 7 AM because by 8 AM you should be back at your office getting your work done just as he was. He expected a concise but informative report from each of his managers on the issues of the day. He had zero tolerance for someone being unprepared, especially if they tried to bluff their way through with a made-up response. While this led to sweaty palms at times, it made all of us better employees and ensured we weren't wasting his time or ours by not staying on top of issues. Murray applied the same work ethic to us that he applied to himself. Many of the issues we dealt with were complicated and with no easy answers. Murray pushed us to be creative and refused to let us pick the easy "same old" solutions. I believe that in many instances he had already formulated a possible strategy to solve a problem, but he wanted his team to either confirm it by coming up with the same solution or to refute it by devising a better one. We were "a team" and Murray expected a lot from us, but none of us ever doubted for a moment that he made the final decision on how to proceed.

When it comes to "suffering no fools," one story has stuck to McCormack and makes her smile to this day. She explains:

> Murray and I had a meeting with the director of one of the state departments in Lansing. Having worked at the state, I was familiar with this director and how not to approach topics with him. Murray and I met for coffee before the meeting so I could go over some last-minute strategies with him. This director was a very principled religious man who was offended by off-color language. Now, anyone who knows Murray knows that his language is often peppered with some level of profanity. I knew that if Murray lost his temper and slipped in a few of his favorite phrases we'd severely jeopardize our case. So, even in the ride up in the elevator to the director's office my whispered mantra to him was "Remember: don't swear, don't swear, don't swear." The meeting with the director was "chilly" to say the least and, while the director had agreed to meet with us, it became clear that this was an exercise in futility from the start. As we got close to the end of this waste of time, Murray could hold back no longer and, even though it was quite restrained for him, he let fly what he thought of the department's position on the issue with a few of his favorite adjectives for emphasis. It was all I could do to stop from bursting out in laughter watching two men with very red faces for two entirely different reasons. Working for Murray was never boring!

McCormack continues:

> Some of my favorite times while working for Murray were when he would come into my office, sit down across from my desk, and he'd start the conversation using one of his colorful phrases about how certain parts of a cow's anatomy were useless on a bull. That was my cue that he was not going to "suffer some fool." It was during those conversations that I got to fully appreciate how passionate and committed Murray was to solving the problems he cared about. He was a visionary, unafraid to be the leader and to imagine what could be achieved if we all worked together. Little did I know on that first day in his office that the door that was opening for me would let me be part of so many important things,

not least of which were efforts to restore the Rouge River ecosystem. I was honored to be a part of it and to say that I had the pleasure (and challenge) of working for Jim Murray. He is an amazing guy.

Proudest Achievement

Nearly everyone concerned would agree that Murray has had a huge impact on the revival of the Rouge River. But there is one project that he is most proud of—the Rouge River monitoring program for students in elementary through high school, which is covered in greater detail in chapter 8. While working as Washtenaw County drain commissioner, Murray recruited Professor Bill Stapp of the University of Michigan, a pioneer in the field of environmental education, to bring his innovative student-led water-quality-monitoring program to the Rouge River watershed. As an incentive, Murray awarded a $10,000 grant from Washtenaw County to the University of Michigan to get Stapp's program off the ground. It became an enormous success, and Murray convinced Professor Stapp to bring his program over to the Rouge River watershed. The goal was to empower high school students to inform community leaders and affect change.

Murray remembers vividly one Water Quality Congress where the high school students brought water samples in glass jars from each of their sampling stations and lined them up from downstream to upstream for the audience. It was a dramatic moment—the color of the water ranged from chocolate brown in the lower end of the watershed to much clearer in the upper watershed. It was a powerful moment and received considerable media attention. But most importantly, the program helped reconnect young people to the river, raise awareness of water pollution, increase environmental literacy, and expand civic-mindedness. Murray has always felt that an uninformed, unaware public is one of the greatest environmental threats in the Rouge River watershed.

Key Lessons Learned

Murray feels strongly that public involvement is critical to watershed protection and river revival (Schrameck et al. 1994). Indeed, it has been shown that urban watershed management is part science and part art, and it depends on creative institutional arrangements, combinations of federal and state mandates and incentives, regional partnerships, municipal awareness of externalities, and a grassroots sense of community (Platt 2006). After 36 years of cleaning up the Rouge River, the public is engaged, the Rouge River is incorporated in many of the curricula of local schools, and there is a new spirit of collaboration that has, in Murray's language, "replaced top-down, 'throw money at the problem' and 'Big Brother will save us' syndrome."

Murray notes: "People support having clean water and a healthy watershed—give them a workable program and they will support it. If you have the public engaged and speaking out, you will get the attention of politicians and the necessary political support."

Concluding Thoughts

The Rouge River has become a leader in use of an ecosystem approach on a watershed scale. In fact, it is the first watershed in the United States to have all 48 watershed communities with a stormwater permit (Ridgway et al. 2018).

It is indeed amazing to think that the Rouge River was once the most polluted river in Michigan and one of the most polluted in the United States. Today, the Rouge River has risen like a phoenix from the ashes; a burning river overcame enormous obstacles and achieved surprising environmental improvement and ecological revival (Hartig 2010).

For over four decades Murray has worked tirelessly on the cleanup of the Rouge River (fig. 32). Thanks to Murray's leadership and the partnerships he forged, the US Environmental Protection Agency is now heralding the Rouge River cleanup effort as a national model of watershed management and a blueprint for success. Murray is particularly proud of the "friends" organization he helped to establish—Friends of the Rouge—and how it has continued to grow in influence and impact 36 years after its creation.

Murray's legacy is:

- A cleaner river.
- A more educated and engaged citizenry in all 48 watershed communities.
- A changed attitude about the Rouge River—it is no longer just a working river in the Rust Belt, but a river that provides many ecosystem services and benefits that enhance quality of life.

Fig. 32. Jim Murray on the banks of the Rouge River at the Henry Ford Estate in Dearborn, Michigan. (Photo credit: Associated Press/Carlos Osorio.)

- A spirit of collaboration that extends from the headwaters to the mouth of the Rouge River.
- A growing sense of community pride in the watershed.

LITERATURE CITED

Hartig, J.H. 1986. "Toxic Substances Contamination of the Rouge River." Michigan Water Resources Commission, Lansing.

Hartig, J.H. 2010. *Burning Rivers: Revival of Four Urban-Industrial Rivers That Caught on Fire.* Ecovision World Monograph Series, Aquatic Ecosystem Health and Management Society, Burlington, Ontario, Canada; and Essex, UK: Multi-Science Publishing Company.

Murray, J. 1994. "Rouge River Watershed Management: Implementing a Remedial Action Plan (RAP)." Proceedings of 67th Annual Conference of Water Environment Federation. Alexandria, VA.

Platt, R.H. 2006. "Urban Watershed Management: Sustainability, One Stream at a Time." *Environment: Science and Policy of Sustainable Development* 48 (4): 26–42.

Ridgway, J., Cave, K., DeMaria, A., O'Meara, J., Hartig, J.H. 2018. "The Rouge River Area of Concern—A Multi-Year, Multi-Level Successful Approach to Restoration of Impaired Beneficial Uses." *Aquatic Ecosystem Health & Management* 21 (4): 398–408.

Schrameck, R., Fields, M., Synk, M. 1992. "Restoring the Rouge." In Hartig, J.H., Zarull, M.A., eds, *Under RAPs: Toward Grassroots Ecological Democracy in the Great Lakes Basin*, 73–91. Ann Arbor: University of Michigan Press.

12 REFLECTIONS

John H. Hartig and Jim Graham

In this final chapter, we reflect on human history and its impacts in the Rouge River watershed. Our goal is to think about these changes in a way that will inspire readers to reconsider their relationship with the watershed they call home. This brings to mind Danish theologian and philosopher Søren Kierkegaard's statement, "Life can only be understood backwards; but it must be lived forwards."

The story of reviving the Rouge River is a very human story. It spans centuries, beginning with the First Peoples who built their villages near the river's edge and revered it as a source of life.

First Peoples

The First Peoples to live in the watershed of the Rouge River viewed themselves as the inheritors of a bounty provided for them as part of creation (Cornell 2003). They believed they were responsible for stewardship of the animals, plants, and water that sustained them. First Peoples routinely gave thanks for food—animals and plants—so that their families might survive. They often shared stories of how "we are all related"—acknowledging the integrity of animate earth and creation and their personal and spiritual relationship to these elements. This perception of spiritual relatedness dictated First Peoples' behaviors as they interacted with their ecosystem. Early First Peoples lived as hunters and gatherers, and no evidence exists of major negative environmental impacts because land, water, and all life were sacred and revered, and First Peoples' population density was relatively low. Today, we must teach and manifest that we all live in a watershed and depend on these waters to sustain life, and all must show reverence for it and care for it as their home.

Changing Perception of the Rouge River

During the fur trading era, beginning in the 1600s, trappers viewed the Rouge River watershed as an exploitable resource providing an inexhaustible supply of beavers to help meet European fashion demand for hats made of beaver pelts (Johnson 1919). In less than two centuries, however, beavers had been trapped to local extinction. Commerce, agriculture, and lumbering became the basis of the next economy. Once again the watershed was perceived as an inexhaustible resource.

Soon, demand for more efficient transportation led to development of railroads. By the 1850s, railroads linked Detroit to the emerging national market, and tracks were laid alongside the Rouge River. With the development of railroads, the shores of the lower Rouge River were considered a promising industrial zone and the lower river a navigational channel to transport raw materials.

Creation of a shipping channel increased the depth and width of the river, created a new river mouth south of the original one, and dramatically altered the hydrology of the lower river (Coles 1980). With the completion of a shipping channel in the late 1800s, the perception of the lower Rouge River as a working river that supported commerce and industry was sealed.

From 1910 to 1920, Henry Ford dammed the Rouge River to supply power to his Fair Lane mansion in Dearborn on the lower river, and to supply hydroelectric power to small Ford factories producing parts for his auto assembly plants. Then, in 1915, Ford bought 2,000 acres along the lower Rouge River to build the largest integrated automobile manufacturing facility in the world—the Rouge Plant (Hartig 2010). In 1918, the "turning basin" on the lower Rouge River was dredged to a depth of approximately 20 feet to support freighters bringing in raw materials to the massive Rouge Plant. During this time, the Rouge River was subordinated to industrial production, and the lower river essentially became an artificial waterway.

Following the Japanese attack on Pearl Harbor in 1941, the United States plunged into World War II. President Roosevelt quickly recognized the need to help supply Europe with the implements of war and implored Americans to stand up as the "Arsenal of Democracy" as though it were their own war. The president called on the nation to swiftly unite to produce vast shipments of weaponry to aid Europe. Metropolitan Detroit became the leading US supplier of the military goods that ultimately led to victory in World War II. Ford Motor Company's Rouge Plant was converted into a tank arsenal. In total, metropolitan Detroit companies produced about $29 billion of military output during 1942–1945 (Hartig 2019).

But World War II would also have unintended consequences. The country's sole focus was winning the war. There were no major environmental regulations—the Clean Water Act was not passed until 1972. Water pollution was rampant during these war years.

For over 150 years, the lower Rouge River had been considered a working river that supported industry, commerce, and technological progress. Pollution was considered just part of the cost of doing business. But that is now changing thanks to the efforts of industries, watershed residents, and all levels of government. Today, it is perceived as a river that provides many beneficial uses and quality-of-life benefits.

Ecosystem Approach

From the fur trading era through logging, agriculture, industrialization, and urbanization, there was a sequence of human impacts on the Rouge River. This climaxed in a 1985 "tipping point," when putrid odor problems in the lower Rouge River and the loss of a man's life due to leptospirosis caused by raw sewage in the river led to widespread recognition of severe water pollution (see Prologue). These two pollution incidents led to the realization that everyone must begin to work together to restore the Rouge River.

But 1985 was a watershed moment not just for the Rouge River, but for the entire Great Lakes. It was in that year that the Rouge River became part of a network of grassroots efforts to clean up the most polluted areas of the Great Lakes—43 Great Lakes Areas of Concern (AOCs). Before we proceed, however, we need to understand the difference between an "environment" and an "ecosystem." Most people think of an "environment" as a system external to humans, detached. With an ecosystem approach, however, we talk about humans as elements of a system; thus, what humans do to their ecosystem, they do to themselves. An ecosystem approach accounts for the interrelationships among air, water, land, and all living things, including humans, and involves all user groups in management.

In 1985, the eight Great Lakes states and the Province of Ontario committed to working with the federal government and local stakeholders to develop remedial action plans (RAPs) to clean up each AOC within their political boundaries and restore impaired beneficial uses, using an ecosystem approach. At the outset, the use of an ecosystem approach in RAPs was an earth-shaking development for state, provincial, and federal governments. They were accustomed to implementing water-quality programs in a top-down, command-and-control fashion—telling local communities and industries what they had to do. For example, one of the primary programs of state, provincial, and federal governments was to issue discharge permits to municipal wastewater treatment plants and industries that prescribed the level of wastewater treatment required and the quality of effluent. But because this commitment to RAPs was made under the auspices of the US-Canada Great Lakes Water Quality Agreement, it had the legitimacy of the International Joint Commission and the 1909 Boundary Waters Treaty.

The use of an ecosystem approach in RAPs charged all stakeholder groups to work in a collaborative effort. Think of an ecosystem approach, then, as a grassroots ecological democracy designed to clean up polluted areas of the Great Lakes. An ecosystem approach brings all stakeholders who influence or are impacted by a natural resource together to reach agreement on what needs to be done to clean up and care for their ecosystem, their home. You can imagine the difficulty in bringing factory managers, fishing groups, conservation and hunting clubs, port authorities, sewage treatment plant operators, governments, and others together to reach agreement on what needs to be done to clean up their shared waters. Another way of thinking about an ecosystem approach is as a more holistic way of undertaking integrated planning, research, and management of specific places such as the Great Lakes AOCs. If there were an ecosystem approach to drivers' training for four students, the driver-training car would have four steering wheels to show how all need to work together—navigation would require cooperation and coordination (fig. 33).

It is fair to say, then, that there were 43 locally designed ecosystem approaches in AOCs that helped involve stakeholders in a meaningful way, foster cooperative learning, share decision-making, and ensure local ownership. Structuring the process to create a sense of local ownership of the RAP by stakeholders, who were the very businesses, state

Fig. 33. An ecosystem approach to driving school. (Credit: Scott Raft.)

and local agencies, and citizens responsible for carrying out the recommendations, was a critical factor in RAP acceptance by all involved. It cannot be emphasized enough how important this was. Use of an ecosystem approach in the cleanup of Great Lakes AOCs empowered local stakeholders to become leaders in cleaning up their local watersheds and provided a laser focus for all levels of government to work with local stakeholders to make it happen.

Because of the 1985 "tipping point" mentioned above and in the Prologue, Rouge River watershed stakeholders had a clear sense of urgency for working together to clean up their river. Working together was not always easy, and the 48 watershed communities even had to be ordered to cooperate by federal judge John Feikens. Since 1985, however, the Rouge River has gone on to become a Great Lakes and North American leader in using an ecosystem approach in restoring a polluted watershed.

The Rouge River's story hasn't always been a happy or pretty one. Over the centuries, the river was exploited by a wide variety of people—hunters and anglers, farmers, industrialists, urban and suburban residents, and governments. As mentioned in earlier chapters, it was so utterly degraded that in the late 1960s it actually caught fire. It became so toxic that people were warned to not touch its waters. People literally turned the river into a dump, a convenient place to discard things like trash, broken furniture, appliances, tires, and even cars.

Today, it's very heartening to be able to say things are different. More and more people recognize the Rouge River as the positive resource it has become. Local residents, visitors to the watershed, and government regulators can see how the river is being revived, thanks to the work of many, many people.

Institutional Arrangements for Ecosystem-Based Watershed Management

In ecosystem-based management, effective institutional arrangements are essential to restoring and protecting the watershed. These are the organizational structures and mechanisms to achieve cooperative planning and action among different organizations whose missions influence or are influenced by elements of a watershed. Such institutional arrangements evolve over time. In the early days of the RAP, the Rouge River Basin Committee was an important mechanism for coordinated planning among the 48 watershed communities. When federal money was provided to the Wayne County Department of the Environment for the Rouge River National Wet Weather Demonstration Project, the Rouge Program Office became an important player in planning and action. Today, institutional arrangements can best be described as a constellation of stakeholders working together to restore and protect the watershed, including communities, counties, state and federal governments, nongovernmental organizations, regional planning organizations, universities, businesses, and many other stakeholders. However, three organizations stand out and warrant special discussion.

First, for over 35 years, Friends of the Rouge has been on the front lines of public participation, citizen involvement in science and restoration, reconnecting people to the Rouge River, and developing a stewardship ethic. From a fledgling organization in 1986, it has grown into a vibrant, watershed-based entity with 15 staff and a $2.3 million annual budget. It has become part of the community fabric, the place where people go with questions and concerns about the Rouge River. This organization is viewed as the trusted and accepted caretaker of the Rouge River.

Today, the Friends of the Rouge is not only restoring, protecting, and enhancing the Rouge River watershed through stewardship, education, and collaboration, it is also the storyteller of the river. It works at the grassroots level to share the perspectives of people who are passionate about the river. The goal is to create a sense of belonging to the watershed and a sense of place so that it becomes an anchor of peoples' identities. Experience has shown that over the long term, having a sense of belonging and place helps develop an ethic of stewardship and civic-mindedness.

Friends of the Rouge is a Great Lakes leader in citizen science and has strong programs in green infrastructure such as rain gardens, bioswales to manage stormwater, buffer zones along the river and its tributaries, and more. Considerable effort is now being made to reconnect people to the Rouge River through a water trail and greenways. This can help people see that they are part of their ecosystem, not separate from it, and that what they do to their ecosystem, they do to themselves. This helps create a psychological connection that brings people to see that water is part of their lives and culture. This connection also supports the development of a stewardship ethic that builds the political base for watershed preservation and sustainability.

Second, during the heyday of the Rouge River National Wet Weather Demonstration Project, key stakeholders came together to form the Assembly of Rouge Communities in 2003. Membership included 38 communities and three counties. However, the Assembly lacked the authority to collect dues from member communities. This led to the passage of the Watershed Alliance legislation (Public Act 517 of 2004) that enabled the formation of the Alliance of Rouge Communities (ARC) in 2006. Three years later, it was recognized as a 501(c)(3) nonprofit, which opened access to federal grant funds.

Today, ARC is a voluntary member-based alliance of 42 communities, counties, and colleges, and seven cooperating partners, including the Friends of the Rouge, the Great Lakes Water Authority, the Rouge River Advisory Council, and the Southeast Michigan Council of Governments. The ARC provides the institutional mechanism to encourage watershed cooperation and mutual support to meet water-quality permit requirements for its members while restoring beneficial uses of the river for area residents. Standing on the shoulders of the Rouge River National Wet Weather Demonstration Project, the ARC has been particularly effective in facilitating communication among watershed stakeholders and in developing collaborative approaches to meet Michigan's municipal stormwater permitting requirements. This has allowed the ARC to focus aggressive stormwater best-management practices on priority areas to address the worst water-quality problems. ARC has broken the Rouge River watershed down into sub-watersheds, undertaken essential sub-watershed planning, and brought about necessary restoration actions, while ensuring that communities have "skin in the game."

As noted in chapter 5, the Rouge River RAP is the long-term cleanup plan for restoring impaired uses in the river. In 1993, after completion of the initial RAP and the disbandment of the Rouge River Basin Committee, the Michigan Department of Natural Resources established the Rouge RAP Advisory Council, now called the Rouge River Advisory Council—the RRAC, the third group. Its purpose is to ensure public participation in the RAP process and advise the State of Michigan. It provides advice to both Michigan Department of the Environment, Great Lakes, and Energy, and the Michigan Department of Natural Resources on implementing and updating the RAP. It has fulfilled that mission ever since. With the enactment of the Great Lakes Legacy Act and the establishment of the Great Lakes Restoration Initiative in 2002 and 2010, respectively, major funding became available to implement RAPs throughout the US portion of the Great Lakes.

Today, RRAC continues to fulfil its mission of ensuring public participation in the RAP and providing advice on RAP updates. It is also the facilitator of the Great Lakes Legacy Act and Great Lakes Restoration Initiative funding for restoring beneficial uses. RRAC works with partners such as ARC, FOTR, and others to undertake major habitat restoration projects such as the Henry Ford Estate Dam Fishway and the completion of the Rouge River Oxbow on the lower river. RRAC is also a key player in remediating contaminated sediment in the lower river, as took place in the Rouge River Old Channel at a cost of $50 million. RRAC will continue to be a critical player in continued efforts to restore impaired beneficial uses and to eventually delist the Rouge River as a Great Lakes AOC.

The Rouge River Has Become an Asset and Gained Respect

In 1969, when the Rouge River caught fire, oil spills and releases were still common, and even pollution-tolerant carp were dying in the lower river through lack of oxygen. Today, oxygen conditions have substantially improved, fish are returning to the river, the invertebrate community living in river sediments is improving, beavers have come back after more than a 100-year absence, and peregrine falcons have returned at the river mouth.

As a result, people now view the river as an asset. The Lower Rouge River Water Trail welcomes kayakers, greenway trails are popular with walkers and joggers, and fishing is on the rise. For over a century, businesses and communities faced away from the river, treating it as an afterthought outside their back door. Today, they are embracing the Rouge River and working to create a new river "front porch." As Aldo Leopold, considered by many the "father of wildlife ecology," noted, "When we see land as a community to which we belong, we may begin to use it with love and respect." The Rouge River is now seen by an ever-growing number of people as a valued community asset that provides many ecosystem benefits and services.

Strong and Effective Leadership

Jim Murray, as noted in chapter 11, played a key role in providing regional leadership and making cleanup programs work. He has been an effective problem-solver and coalition-builder on a watershed scale. Two of Murray's accomplishments stand out: (1) helping establish Friends of the Rouge as a nonprofit organization, and (2) helping establish the Rouge River National Wet Weather Demonstration Project, which the US Environmental Protection Agency (EPA) heralds as a "blueprint for success" on a watershed scale.

Other leaders warrant recognition as well. For 33 years, US District Court judge John Feikens used the federal court and his influence to address the water-pollution problems in southeast Michigan and the Rouge River watershed. It started in 1977 when the EPA filed a lawsuit to stop pollution from the Detroit Wastewater Treatment Plant—the largest single-site facility in the United States. The case addressed discharges from the Detroit Water and Sewerage Department, which included stormwater runoff, sewer overflows, illicit sewer connections, failed septic tanks, and a whole host of sources from all 48 watershed communities. Through this case, Feikens came to be known as the "Sludge Judge."

Judge Feikens had his critics over the years as he presided over this case. His watershed approach to resolving water-pollution issues took into account all the sources that contributed to degraded water quality. In part due to Feikens's judicial leadership, the EPA now promotes using a watershed approach to regulating and restoring waterways; he used the EPA's 1977 lawsuit to begin a series of formal orders and regular hearings to bring together three counties and 48 communities to cooperate on a plan to restore the entire Rouge River watershed. Judge Feikens made all watershed communities understand their role in the pollution problems, accept responsibility, and face the pollution control costs collectively. He made them understand that to be a world-class metropolitan area requires a clean environment.

Congressman John D. Dingell, a national conservation hero for authoring many environmental laws, such as the National Environmental Policy Act (considered the Magna Carta of environmental laws), the Clean Water Act, the Endangered Species Act, and more, championed the Rouge River at the federal level and helped bring in $350 million to showcase watershed cleanup through the Rouge River National Wet Weather Demonstration Project. This federal money in turn leveraged another $650 million over a 15-year period. This federal money, often called "Dingell dollars," was essential to the river revival we see today.

Together, Murray, Feinkens, and Dingell provided strong leadership for managing a watershed in a complex urban area. They used a "carrot and stick" approach—a combination of reward and punishment to induce desired behavior through financial incentives and public accountability.

As in a relay race where one runner passes the baton to the next, leadership changes over time. In the Rouge watershed, the leadership baton was passed from these three early champions to leaders such as Kelly Cave, who became the director of watershed management for the Wayne County Department of the Environment, and the Rev. Hurley Coleman, who was the director of Wayne County Parks and Recreation and later an assistant county executive, while also serving as board president of Friends of the Rouge. Another leader is Marie McCormick, who now serves as FOTR's executive director. It is critically important that mentoring and inspiring the next generation of Rouge River watershed leaders be a priority to sustain our efforts and achieve our long-term goals.

The Goal of Making the Rouge Fishable and Swimmable

We must never lose sight of the Clean Water Act goals of making waters fishable and swimmable. These noble long-term goals must be ingrained in our schools, houses of worship, communities, and businesses. In 1985, when the 23-year-old man died of rat fever caused by exposure to raw sewage in the river, local health departments had no choice but to issue a health advisory warning against human contact with the river. In those days, no one would have considered canoeing or kayaking in the lower Rouge River because of raw sewage. Today, Friends of the Rouge sponsors kayak events and has created a 27-mile Lower Rouge River Water Trail to connect people to the river, celebrate history, and connect communities.

In the mid-1990s, high levels of PCBs were discovered in the Newburgh Lake impoundment of the Rouge River in Livonia, resulting in a ban on human consumption of fish. Following cleanup of 30,000 pounds of PCB-contaminated sediments in Evans Products Ditch—the primary source of PCBs—and Newburgh Lake in 1997 and 1998, PCBs in fish declined by approximately 90%, resulting in the lifting of the fish-consumption advisory on certain species of fish from Newburgh Lake. This was the first time in over two decades that some of the fish caught in Newburgh Lake were safe to eat.

Looking to the future, we must make sure that watershed denizens embrace the goals of making the Rouge River fishable and swimmable. There are people who want to hold a triathlon on Newburgh Lake; our collective goal should be to make sure that that is possible in the future.

Anticipate and Prevent

It is important to anticipate problems and prevent them from occurring. As the old adage says, an ounce of prevention is worth a pound of cure. A good example in the Rouge River watershed is climate change. In 2014, a storm swept through the lower watershed and drenched communities with 5.8 inches of rain, flooding highways, streets, and basements. In 2021, an even larger storm ravaged the area, causing even greater damage to properties and disruption of the economy. Climate change is the root cause of these problems, and scientists worry that it is increasingly making more commonplace events that were once considered extraordinary. Warmer, wetter, and wilder weather is coming, and this will be one of the greatest environmental challenges of the 21st century. Climate change is a serious issue and a good example of the need to anticipate problems and prevent them from occurring. We need to reduce carbon emissions and adapt to changing climate by protecting floodplains, building green infrastructure, and reducing to 10% the amount of impervious surface in the watershed from its current level of 23%.

Concluding Thoughts and a Call to Action

For three centuries the Rouge River watershed was perceived merely as a source of raw materials that produced goods for or provided services to society. During the fur trading era, beavers were trapped; during the lumbering era, forests were cut down to build houses, ships, and railroad ties. During the 20th century, it increasingly became the receptacle of human waste from homes and industrial waste from factories. Sixty-two dams were added to the Rouge River, which substantially altered stream flow and hydrology. The lower river was straightened and converted into a shipping channel to bring in materials to support industry, and a 4.2-mile section of the lower river was lined with concrete to quickly move stormwater out the area.

This human use and abuse of the Rouge River watershed substantially reduced ecosystem benefits to all its residents. The mid-1980s tipping point began an awakening that would grow into a "watershed spring" of citizen action to bring their river back to life. This story of the revival of the Rouge River provides hope to all who are working to care for their watersheds. If the Rouge River can be revived from its incendiary past, it can be done elsewhere. Clearly, there is much to be proud of in the revival of the Rouge River, but this pride must be tempered by the knowledge that much remains to be done to restore the physical, chemical, and biological integrity of the river and reap the full spectrum of benefits it can provide.

We must remember that we are part of the ecosystem we live in. What we do to our ecosystem, we do to ourselves. The fish, birds, and plants are also part of our ecosystem. First Peoples have long viewed fish, birds, and plants as their relatives. Through traditional knowledge, First Peoples taught us how to be better relatives to all members of an ecosystem and better stewards of creation, and we have much to learn from them.

As a society, our next great challenge is to learn to live sustainably. We need a balance among people, nature, and growth. Arthur Golding (1998), an architect and urban designer who was a leading voice in the restoration of the Los Angeles River, captured the spirit required to meet this sustainability challenge in the Rouge River and other urban watersheds: "To deny the river is to deny the origin of the city. To rethink the river is to discover a unique opportunity to define urban places, join neighborhoods and communities together, and reconnect us to our landscape and our history."

In 1917, Henry Ford began construction of his famous Rouge Plant on the banks of the lower Rouge River, and it became the largest integrated factory in the world at that time and a 20th-century model of the industrial revolution. When Ford Motor Company rebuilt its Rouge Plant in 2000, it recruited William McDonough, a renowned architect and industrial designer, to ensure that the plant would be a 21st-century model of sustainability. McDonough's philosophy is particularly poignant, and it expresses a perspective that is worth striving for in both the Rouge River watershed and globally:

There are millions of difficult challenges and delightful opportunities ahead. I think the only constraint is the willingness to dream, to create and to hope and feel undefended enough to face the tough questions and ideas that must be fiercely engaged at this moment of human history. If design is the signal of human intention then we must continuously ask ourselves—What are our intentions for our children, for the children of all species, for all time! How do we profitably and boldly manifest the best of those intentions?

In 1992, more than 100 heads of state from throughout the world attended the Earth Summit in Rio de Janeiro, Brazil. It concluded that the concept of sustainable development—development that meets the needs of the present generation without compromising the ability of future generations to meet their own needs—was an attainable goal for all the people of the world, at the local, national, regional, and international levels. This Earth Summit noted that humanity now stands at a defining moment in history (Global Environment Facility 2002). One choice in life is to follow a path toward stewardship of our natural resources and sustainable development. Another choice is to continue to deplete natural capital, degrade environments, and thereby limit the choices that will be available to our children and grandchildren. The legacy is ours to shape.

Although much has been accomplished in reviving the Rouge River, much remains to be done to restore it to full ecosystem health. It is no time to be complacent—climate change is already affecting the Rouge River watershed with increased flooding caused by a greater frequency and intensity of storms. Scientists and policymakers now recognize climate change as a "threat multiplier" in which warmer, wetter, and wilder climatic conditions amplify other threats such as stormwater runoff, combined sewer overflow events, species changes, the effects of poor air quality on vulnerable residents, and more. The time to act is now, and all must get involved in watershed stewardship.

We urge you to follow the lead of Bill Ford, the great-grandson of Henry Ford and executive chair of Ford Motor Company, who in the foreword to this book, writes, "I encourage you to get involved in caring for the watershed you call home."

Your actions and voice matter. Personal things that you can do include:

- Value all life and take care of all species, as First Peoples did before us.
- Make the Rouge River your river, and teach your children and other family members that we are part of the Rouge River ecosystem, and that what we do to our ecosystem we do to ourselves.
- Go out to the Rouge River on a regular basis and experience its beauty.
- Tell stories about the river to your neighbors and friends that show you have a personal relationship with it and have a deep respect for it, a reverence.
- Get involved in caring for the river. Don't sit on the sidelines— volunteer with Friends of the Rouge, the Alliance of Rouge Communities, or a local school, church, or community group working to protect and restore the river.
- Advocate for the ecosystem approach, and make sure all schools are teaching that humans are part of nature and ecosystems and practice citizen science as described in chapters 7 and 8.
- Sign the personal letter to the Rouge River watershed presented at the end of chapter 9, making a pledge to better care for the river for both present and future generations.
- Start or continue your journey to live more sustainably through

your personal choices—recycle, practice energy conservation, carpool, install a rain barrel, build a rain garden or pollinator garden, stop using single-use plastics, become a watershed ambassador and steward.

Clearly, much work still needs to be done to make the Rouge River fishable and swimmable. But when we look back at how far we've come, and how many people continue to strive to revive the river, it's gratifying to know that the goal is achievable, within our grasp.

LITERATURE CITED

Coles. 1980. *The Saga of the Great Lakes*. Toronto: Coles Publishing.

Cornell, G.L. 2003. "American Indians at Wawiiatanong: An Early American History of Indigenous Peoples at Detroit." In Hartig, J.H, ed., *Honoring Our Detroit River, Caring for Our Home*, 9–22. Bloomfield Hills, MI: Cranbrook Institute of Science.

Global Environment Facility. 2002. *The Sustainability Challenge: An Action Agenda for the Global Environment*. Washington, DC.

Golding, A. 1998. *The Los Angeles River: Reshaping Our Urban Landscape*. Los Angeles: Target Science.

Hartig, J.H. 2010. *Burning Rivers: Revival of Four Urban-Industrial Rivers that Caught on Fire*. Ecovision World Monograph Series, Aquatic Ecosystem Health and Management Society, and Essex, UK: Multi-Science Publishing.

Hartig, J.H. 2019. *Waterfront Porch: Reclaiming Detroit's Industrial Waterfront as a Gathering Place for All*. East Lansing: Michigan State University Press.

Johnson, I.A. 1919. *The Michigan Fur Trade*. Lansing: Michigan Historical Commission.

CONTRIBUTORS

Sally Cole-Misch is a proud Stappling and knew Bill Stapp as her graduate chair, mentor, and friend. She contributed to designing the initial GREEN model tested in the Huron River watershed and later served as Assistant Director at GREEN to ensure its smooth transition to Earth Force. Throughout her career in environmental communications and education, she's focused on our essential connections with nature—particularly the Great Lakes through her work at the International Joint Commission—and the role each of us can play to restore, protect, and enjoy all that nature gives to us. She holds a bachelor's degree in journalism from the University of Missouri, a master's degree in environmental education and international water policy from the University of Michigan, and a master's certificate in fiction writing from Stanford University. Her debut novel released in 2020, *The Best Part of Us*, explores the essential roles that nature, family, and place hold in our lives. The story has been called the "*Where the Crawdads Sing* for the Great Lakes region" and has received six national and international literary awards. For more information, please visit sallycole-misch.com.

Nancy Darga serves as the chair of the Northville River Restoration Task Force. In 2019, she retired as the Executive Director from the historic Ford Piquette Plant, where the Ford Model T was created and first produced, after helping to build the National Historic Landmark into an international destination. Previously, she was the managing director of Motor Cities National Heritage Area, dedicated by Congress in 1998. A licensed landscape architect, she served as Chief of Design for Wayne County Parks during 1978–2003, spearheading many large regional park and trail development projects. During her tenure with Wayne County, she was one of the founding members of the Friends of the Rouge. For her efforts she was awarded the Best Friend of the Rouge Award in 1997.

Other awards she has received include the Michigan Public Servant of the Year Award (1999) from the Public Administration Foundation, Inc.; the Governor Swanson State of Michigan Historic Preservation Award (2005) from the Michigan Department of Interior for her work in historic preservation and heritage trail development; and the Henry Ford Heritage Association's individual Friend of Ford Award in 2017 for her work in establishing Ford Heritage Trails and saving the Ford Village Industry Plants.

Annette DeMaria is a registered Professional Engineer in Michigan and a certified Project Management Professional with 25 years of experience at Environmental Consulting & Technology, Inc. and serves as the Executive Director of the Alliance of Rouge Communities (ARC). ARC is a nonprofit organization that encourages watershed-wide cooperation to restore beneficial uses of the Rouge River to area residents, while meeting water quality permit requirements. Her entire career has focused on the restoration of the Rouge River watershed. Her experience includes municipal stormwater permitting, green stormwater management, water quality monitoring, beach sanitary surveys, and project management. She oversees municipal stormwater permit compliance for more than 20 communities in the Rouge River watershed and has identified more than 200 illicit connections in southeast Michigan. In her role with the ARC, she has developed collaborative plans to reduce bacteria levels in the Rouge River by coalescing the efforts of 35 public agencies.

Brian James Egen is an award-winning film director and producer, Civil War historian, and lifelong student of history. He has been employed at The Henry Ford, in Dearborn, Michigan for the past 27 years. He currently serves as Executive Producer and Head of Studio Productions, overseeing the film department, and is a coordinator for the CBS television's award-winning *The Henry Ford's Innovation Nation*. He was appointed by the governor to the Michigan Historical Commission in 2012 and currently serves as its president and was chair of the Michigan Civil War Sesquicentennial Committee. He also serves as chair of the Monroe County Historical Commission and the City of Monroe's Commission on the Environment and Water Quality. In 2019, he became chair of the River Raisin Heritage Corridor Commission. In 2015, Egen coauthored *Michigan at Antietam: Wolverine State's Sacrifice on Ameri-*

ca's Bloodiest Day that chronicles Michigan's role during the Civil War's Maryland Campaign of 1862. Egen's dual interest in history and film-making has given him experience serving on many historical documentaries for the National Park Service, History Channel, and other outlets. Born in Monroe, Michigan, he lives there in a historic home with his "loves of life" wife, Jody, and daughter, Scarlett.

Orin G. Gelderloos is Professor of Biology and Professor of Environmental Studies, Emeritus at the University of Michigan–Dearborn (UM-D). He has been a resident of the Rouge River watershed and involved with Rouge River restoration programs since 1970. He has been engaged with the of Friends of the Rouge since its inception in 1986 and served on its Board of Directors. He initiated programs and served as Director of the University's Environmental Study Area and the Environmental Interpretative Center, which was added to the program in 2001. Among the more than 15 courses he taught were Watershed Analysis, with the Rouge River as its focus, and Field Biology in the floodplain on the UM-D campus. Professor Gelderloos continues research on the Rouge River's floodplain vegetation patterns and groundwater levels. He has taught "Ecology of the Indian Tropics" during January in Tamal Nadu, South India for students from North America and India. Among his honors, he has received awards for distinguished teaching, the Governor's Service Award for Service-Learning Educator of the Year, and a Green Leader of Michigan Award in 2010 from the *Detroit Free Press*.

Jim Graham is a former award-winning journalist and public relations consultant. He served as a reporter and editor for the *Detroit News*, where he was cited by United Press International for "Best Reporting Under Deadline Pressure" for coverage of an explosion that killed 17 men in the City of Detroit's water intake tunnel under Lake Huron. He also worked for newspapers in St. Louis, Ohio, and Georgia and contributed articles for the *New York Times*. In 1978 he was appointed Press Secretary to the Mayor of Detroit, the late Coleman A. Young. He also served as a consultant to the Wayne County (MI) Board of Commissioners. From 1992 to 2002 he was the Executive Director for Friends of the Rouge where he coordinated the annual volunteer Rouge Rescue cleanup and provided leadership in the development of citizen science programs and the school-based Rouge River Education Project. He is a veteran of the

United States Army and served in Vietnam during 1965–66 as founding editor of the 1st Air Cavalry Division's newspaper, the *Cavalair*. For his work he was awarded the Army Commendation Medal. He is a graduate of the University of Georgia and now lives in Asheville, NC with his wife, Gail Reagan, and their dogs.

John H. Hartig is an accomplished Great Lakes scientist who has written six books and more than 130 peer-reviewed, scientific publications. He serves as a Visiting Scholar at University of Windsor's Great Lakes Institute for Environmental Research, is a Board member of the Detroit Riverfront Conservancy, and chair of the Community Foundation for Southeast Michigan's Great Lakes Way Advisory Committee. Questioning how science fits into public decision-making for the Great Lakes and how he can personally make a difference in developing a stewardship ethic for the Great Lakes, his life journey has led him to become an award-winning nonfiction writer focused on accelerating the sustainability transition and inspiring the next generation of environmentalists, conservationists, and sustainability entrepreneurs in urban areas because that is now where most people on our planet live. He has received numerous awards, including a 2022 Notable Leader in Sustainability Award for Crain's Detroit Business, the 2016 Edward G. Voss Conservation Science Award from Michigan Nature Association, the 2015 Conservationist of the Year Award from the John Muir Association, and a 2010 Green Leaders Award from the Detroit Free Press. His recent book titled *Waterfront Porch* won a 2020 Next Generation Indie Book Award in the "nature/environment" category.

Kurt Kuban is an award-winning journalist, having served as a reporter and editor for several Michigan-based newspapers and magazines, including the *Canton Observer, South Lyon Herald,* and *Northville Record,* over the course of a career spanning more than two decades. He founded Journeyman Publishing in 2017, which produces the community-based magazines *The 'Ville* and *The Rock.* He also co-founded and was editor of Michigan's *Streamside Journal,* an independent magazine focused on outdoor pursuits in the Great Lakes State. He has been recognized for his reporting on environmental issues, and in 2005 was named Best Friend of the Rouge for spotlighting the plight of the river in his work. He also has been an active Rouge River volunteer, having coordinated

Rouge Rescue activities in the City of Wayne. He lives in the Rouge River watershed in Northville Township.

Betty Kay McGowan is a Native American of Choctaw and Cherokee heritage who received her PhD from Wayne State University in 1994 and serves as an adjunct professor of anthropology and sociology at Eastern Michigan University. She has served as vice-chair of the National Indian Youth Council, in Albuquerque, New Mexico, and has represented the interests of Indigenous Peoples at the United Nations, in the Working Group on the Declaration on the Rights of Indigenous Peoples, the Committee on the Elimination of Racial Discrimination, and the Expert Mechanism on the Rights of Indigenous Peoples. An active labor union supporter, she worked for years picketing with the United Farm Workers in California. In 1995, McGowan was a delegate to the Fourth World Conference on Women in Beijing. She has coauthored five books and written many academic articles, and in 2009 was inducted into the Michigan Women's Hall of Fame.

Dorothy McLeer is the Program Coordinator at the University of Michigan–Dearborn's Environmental Interpretive Center, where she has worked for nearly 30 years. She began her tenure at University of Michigan–Dearborn as an Environmental Studies major, under the tutelage of Dr. Orin Gelderloos. She earned undergraduate and graduate degrees in environmental studies, anthropology, and education. She currently teaches courses in environmental interpretation and environmental education. Over the years, the Rouge River has flowed through her formal and nonformal education with students, residents, and families in the Rouge River watershed. She is honored to work with other committed individuals and organizations working to improve the health and understanding, past, present, and future, of this storied local treasure that connects 48 communities in southeast Michigan.

Noel Mullett Jr. is the Department Administrator in the Environmental Services Division, Wayne County Department of Public Services. He has been actively involved in restoration of the Rouge River Area of Concern since the early 1990s, including all elements of the Rouge River National Wet Weather Demonstration Project. He has actively participated, on behalf of the County, in the Alliance of Rouge Communities as well as the Rouge River Advisory Council since their formations. He also coordinates implementation of the Wayne County's stormwater permit including illicit discharge elimination, public education, pollution prevention, and good housekeeping, as well as progress evaluation monitoring and reporting and grants administration within the Environmental Services Division. He holds a Bachelor of Science degree in Natural Resources from the University of Michigan, Ann Arbor.

Sally Petrella holds a master's degree in biology from the University of Michigan and serves as Monitoring Manager for Friends of the Rouge where she manages citizen scientists in collecting biological data, including benthic macroinvertebrates, calling amphibians, fish, and aquatic plants. She has been inspiring and training people to become stewards of the Rouge River for more than twenty years, sharing her knowledge of the natural world and passion for its restoration. She collaborates with local, state, and national agencies to collect the data needed to assess and guide the restoration of this degraded urban river. As water quality improved in the Rouge River, she initiated the development of a water trail to engage residents with the resource and build support for its restoration. Growing up in southeast Michigan near the Rouge River, she has always had a strong connection to the natural environment and a commitment to improving it for all. She and her husband are active in improving their neighborhood park, Rouge Park in Detroit. They spend their free time gardening, backpacking, and paddling.

Cyndi Ross serves as Restoration Manager of Friends of the Rouge where she leads a team that works to develop and implement education programs and hands-on activities to inform and engage the public in the restoration of the Rouge River. Through training courses such as "Rain Gardens to the Rescue" and "Master Rain Gardner," garden design, and hands-on installations, she helps Detroit and other Rouge River watershed residents reduce pollution from combined sewer overflows and urban stormwater runoff and even, as many participants proclaim, "improve their quality of life!" She has helped create lifelong river stewards as she engaged the community in installing hundreds of rain gardens, decades of river cleanup projects, and a new workforce development program. In her 21 years with Friends of the Rouge, she has developed many strong community partnerships and regularly collaborates with a myriad of partners from across the region. She values diversity and has made a sincere commitment to incorporating diversity, equity, inclusion, and justice into her work. She is an alumna of the University of Michigan–Dearborn, where she focused on Natural Resource Management and Policy in Environmental Studies. While away from work, she enjoys camping on the shores of our Great Lakes with her husband and spending weekends with her grandson.

Rick Simek was born in Detroit, Michigan. A wonderful part of his childhood was exploring nature every chance he got, including his parents' bird-friendly backyard and the playground across the street from his house. In his late teens he began leading bird walks for the Detroit Audubon Society. He spent the next several decades volunteering as a field trip leader for various local Audubon chapters. In 1989, he graduated from Northland College in Ashland, Wisconsin, with a BS in Naturalist/Outdoor Education. Soon after that he obtained a part-time job as a naturalist at the Metro Beach Metropark Nature Center and at Cranbrook Institute of Science. He was brought on staff at Cranbrook in 1990. Since 1994, he has served as the Program Supervisor and Natural Areas Manager at the University of Michigan–Dearborn (UM-D) where he oversees the planning, development, and implementation of a host of outdoor nature and science-oriented programs for school groups that come to the UM-D Environmental Interpretive Center and is also responsible for the stewardship of the Environmental Study Area on the university campus.

Alan VanKerckhove was born and raised on the eastside of Detroit, Michigan. He began his fascination with flowing water at age four playing along Girard Drain near the home of his grandparents in Harper Woods. At a young age, he enjoyed playing hockey on the frozen eastside canals of Fox Creek. Family drives would take him to relatives' farms in Macomb County where he experienced natural streams and wished he lived near them. He graduated from Cass Technical High School in Detroit and went on to get a BS degree in civil engineering and an Master's degree in environmental engineering from Wayne State University. In 1970, he attended the first "Earth Day" rally held at Wayne State University and met a group called "Rescue the Rouge." He immediately signed on to help clean up the Rouge River, which has now become a lifelong passion. From 1972 to 1995, he raised a family of four boys along the banks of the Rouge River in northwest Detroit. He had a 42-year career with the Detroit Water & Sewerage Department, working at the wastewater plant and in water system operations until retirement. For the last three years, he has served on the Friends of the Rouge Board of Directors.

INDEX

NOTE: Page numbers that are italicized indicate figures or tables.

Ableson, Kathy, 111
abolitionists, 28–29
Agricultural and Horticultural Society, 24
airplane factory, 28, *29*
Algonquins, 1
Alliance of Rouge Communities (ARC): Benthic Macroinvertebrate Program funding by, 119–20; building capacity of, 87; concrete channel partnerships and, 150; Murray and, 175; priorities of, 191–92; RRAC and, 192; watershed restoration and, 82–84
Ambassador Bridge, 30
American Agricultural Chemical Company (Agrico), 33–34
American Bell and Foundry Company, 28
Ann Arbor public schools, 132
Applied Science and Technology, Inc., 108–9
ArcGIS Online, 110, 111–12
Areas of Concern (AOCs): cleanup of, 73, 187, 188; funding to improve, 83–84; future delisting Rouge River as, 192; Rouge River as, 64. *See also* Rouge River revival
Areawide Water Quality Board, 175
Arsenal of Democracy, 36, 47, 186–87
Asian clams (*Corbicula fluminea*), 121
Assembly of Rouge Communities, 191
attitudes, environmental education and, 131

automobile industry, 34, 35–36. *See also* Ford, Henry
awareness, environmental education and, 131

Baby, Jacques Duperon, 26
Bagale, Edward, 150
baseflow, 10
Baudry, Jean Baptiste, 25
beautification, 98
beaver, 20, 24–25, *86*, 156–57, 171–72, 186
bedload, 10
benthic macroinvertebrates: community improvements, 76, *86*; FOTR monitoring, 107; funding for monitoring, 119–20, 124–25; monitoring findings, 120–21; monitoring partners, 118; monitoring program origins, 115–16; sampling protocol, 117; as stream health indicators, 73, 114, *115*; students and research on, 118–19; students sampling, 135–36, *135*; training for monitoring, 116–17; volunteer participation, 119
Benz, Karl, 35
biking trails, 170–73
biodiversity, along Rouge River, 154–55
bioswales, 94, 95–96, *96*
birds, 151–52, 155
Blanchard, James, 175
Blott, Kristina, 122
bone black production, 33–34

bones, bison, 33
Boundary Waters Treaty (1909), 188
Bovee Cider Mill, 29
Brennan Pool complex, 172
brick-making, 26, 33
bridges, 14, 31
buckskin, 25
bugs. *See* benthic macroinvertebrates;
    Fall Bug Hunts; Spring Bug Hunts
Bugs 'n' Pizza, 116
burials, waterway, 14–15
Burris, Valerie, 100
Burroughs, John, 50–51
Burroughs Corporation, 36–37
Butler, William F., 39

Cadillac, Antoine de la Mothe, 23–24,
    31
Canada, transport of goods between
    Michigan and, 30
canoes and canoeing, 19, 161–63, *163*,
    164–65
Carpenter Lake Nature Preserve,
    168–69
Carson, Rachel, 152, 153
Cassady, Erin, 140, 141–42
Cave, Kelly, 194
chemicals in the landscape, 104
Cherry Hill Mill, 38
Chippewa, 18–19
chloride testing, 117
citizen science: challenges, 124–25;
    early FOTR efforts, 106–7; fish sur-
    veys, 121–24; FOTR and, 191; future
    changes in, 126–27; river understand-
    ing and stewardship contributions by,
    125–26. *See also* benthic macroinver-
    tebrates; Frog and Toad Survey
Civil War, iron demand and, 34
Clark, Nelson and Frank, 32
Clean Water Act (1972), 4, 91, 94, 144–
    45, 194
cleanup: of Areas of Concern, 73, 187,
    188; Rouge Rescue, 154, 160; Rouge
    River, 1, 182; as school project, 137,
    138. *See also* Rouge River revival

climate change, 93, 106, 195–96, 198
Coleman, Hurley, 194
collaboration: Rouge River revival
    and, 87. *See also* Rouge River Basin
    Committee
combined sewer overflows (CSOs):
    controlling, 63–64, *67*; human-
    engineered infrastructure for, 93;
    progress in, 67–68; Rouge River
    improvements and, *85*; as solution
    that became a problem, 144; Water
    Resource Recovery Facility and,
    91–92
concrete channel: as flood control, 148;
    habitat improvement along, 149–50;
    of Lower Rouge River, 12–13, *13*; Mur-
    ray, Dingell, and McNamara visit to,
    178; oxbow at The Henry Ford and,
    54, *75*; partners managing, 150–51; as
    urban stream desert, 14
Coon's Grist Mill, 26, *27*
Cooperative Institute for Great Lakes
    Research, 121
copper extraction and manufacturing, 34
COVID-19 pandemic, 112, 126–27
Craves, Julie, 151
Critter Science Investigators, 119
cross-cultural environmental educa-
    tion, 139

dams: fish passages around, 79–80, *81*,
    192; hydroelectric power and, 37, 186;
    Newburgh Lake and, 29; removal
    projects, *67*, 79, *80*, *85*, 169; river
    revival and, 14–15, 122; on Rouge
    River, 13. *See also* Rouge River revival
Davis, William, 34
Davison Freeway, 31
Dearborn: Detroit Arsenal in, 26; Hines
    Park and, 39–40; Lower Rouge Water
    Trail and, 163–65; Rouge River pol-
    lution smell and, 4, 63, 187; walking,
    jogging, and biking trails in, 171. *See
    also* Ford Rouge Plant; industrial
    section of Rouge River; Lower Rouge
    River; Rouge River revival

Dearborn Guide, 3, 63
Deep Spring Water Company, 28
Delray, 17, 33
Detroit: First Peoples' mound in, 16–17; outward migration from, 61, 63; reduced forest and wetlands and, 12; Rouge Park in, 172; Straits of Detroit, 29–30; Water Resource Recovery Facility, 92
Detroit Car Wheel, 35
Detroit Copper and Brass Rolling Works, 34
Detroit Future City, 101
Detroit Heritage River Water Trail, 162
Detroit Horticulture Society, 24
Detroit River, 1, 30, 165–66
Detroit Steel and Spring Co., 34
Detroit Urban Railway, 29
Detroit Wastewater Treatment Plant, 193
Detroit Wheelman, 31
Detroit Windsor Tunnel, 30
DeWitt, Calvin, 146
Dingell, John D., 145, 176, 177, 194
discharges, illicit, 67, 83, 85
dissolved oxygen, 68, 69, 70, 80, 86
Dubuar, James A., sawmill of, 26–27
Dynamite Park, Wayne, 172–73

Eagle boats, 3, 46, 46
Earle, Horatio "Good Roads," 31
Earth Day, 129–30
Earth Force, 139–40, 141
Earth Summit (1992), Rio de Janeiro, Brazil, 197
Ebonex Corporation, 34
ecosystem: environment compared with, 187; First Peoples on living in, 196
ecosystem-based watershed management model: advocating for, 198; institutional arrangements for, 190–2; of remedial action plan, 64, 65–67, 187–90, 189
ecotourism, 57
Edinger, Grace, 141

Edison, Thomas, 50–51
Eisenman, Bill, 121
Endangered Species Act, 194
engine manufacturing, 35
Entwhistle, Frederick, 36
environmental education: continuing Stapp's vision for, 138–40; evolution of, 130–31; Rouge River degradation and, 133–34; Rouge River water-monitoring project creation, 134–38; Rouge River water-monitoring project today, 140–42; Stapp's vision for, 129–30; thinking globally, acting locally and, 131–33
Environmental Interpretive Center at UM–Dearborn, 152–53
environmentalism: Ford Motor Company and, 55–57, 56, 58; Ford on conservation and, 49–50, 59
EPA. *See* US Environmental Protection Agency
Erb (Fred A. and Barbara M.) Family Foundation, 100
Erie Canal, 30
Eureka Iron Co., 34
Eureka Iron Works, Wyandotte, 34
Europeans, water pollution and, 21
Evans Products Ditch, 195
Executive Steering Committee, 65–66

Fair Lane Estate, 49–50, 123, 144, 152
Fall Bug Hunts, 116
farming: ecosystem-watershed partnerships compared to, 64–65; for export, 24; fish, 31–32, 32; mineral deposits found during, 33; in Rouge River watershed, 25–26; transition to factories from, 29–31
fecal coliform bacteria, 132, 136. *See also* sewage
Feikens, John, 176, 189, 193–94
ferryboats, 30
fertilizer production, 33
Field Manual for Water Quality Monitoring (Mitchell et al.), 133

fire, in Lower Rouge River, 3, 48–49, 61, 189

Firestone, Harvey, 50–51

First Peoples: as inheritors of a bounty, 185; life along the Rouge River, 18–21; on living in an ecosystem, 196; Mound Builders, 16–17; perspective on the future, 155

fish: dam removal and, 122; fishway for, *81*, 192; health advisories, 70; kills, 4, *5*, *86*; Rouge River revival and, 76, 77–79, *79*–80, *86*, 195, 199. *See also* fishing

fish hatcheries, 31–32, *32*

Fish Hatchery Park, 32

fish surveys: citizen science and, 107; findings, 123–24; FOTR and, 121–22; funding, 122–23; sampling protocol, 122

fishing, 18, 166–70, *170*

flashiness or flashy flows, 12, 93, 164, 173

floodplains, 145–47, 148, 149–50, 195–96

Fochler, Corrie, 110, 112

Ford, Henry: auto industry and, 35; business along Rouge River and, 28; conservation and, 49–50, 59; Coon's Grist Mill and, 26; early childhood and formative years, 42–44; Four Vagabonds and, 50–51; The Henry Ford, 51–52, *52*, 150; hydroelectric power and, 37, 49–50, 186; industry and agriculture synergy and, 52–53; Middle Rouge Parkway and, 40; paradigm shifts by, 57–58; Village Industry Plants of, 27, 29, 37–38, 40, 50

Ford, William Clay, Jr. "Bill," 55, 58, 152, 198

Ford Field Streambank Buffer Project, 150

Ford Motor Company: citizen science data analysis and, 125; environmentalism of, 58–59; Ford Fund and Global Data Insight and Analytics Team, 121; Highland Park Plant, 35; Model T production, 43; native-plant

grow zones and, 99; oil-eating pontoon boat, 49

Ford Rouge Plant (Complex): as Arsenal of Democracy, 186–7; construction of, 44–45, *45*, 186; Ford's vision for, 197; immensity of, 35–36; kayaking through, 166; oil pollution from, 47, 48; as sustainable manufacturing model, 55–57, *56*, 59, 197

Fordson Island, 163, 166

forest, watershed and, 11, 12

Fort Pontchartrain, 25

Fort Rouge Gateway Project (FRoG), 163

Fort Street Bridge Park, 166

French pony owners, 3

French voyageurs, *coureurs des bois,* and fur trappers, 1, 3, 24, 25

Friends of the Rouge (FOTR): Alliance of Rouge Communities and, 83; citizen science programs and, 73, *75*, 76, 106–7; as citizen stewardship, 87; ecosystem-based watershed management and, 190–91; established (1986), 66; founding and community involvement by, 133; Frog and Toad Survey and, 108, 109, 110, 111; goals for, 103; kayaking on Detroit River and, 165–6; Land + Water WORKS Coalition, 101–2; Lower Rouge Water Trail and, 161; Murray and, 175, 193; Quality Assurance Project Plan, 118; rain gardens and, *82*, *94*; restoration projects, 98; Rouge education project and, 140–42; RRAC and, 192; signature programs, 153; volunteer activities, 99. *See also* benthic macroinvertebrates

Frog and Toad Survey: breeding call recordings, 111; challenges, 124; COVID-19 pandemic and, 112; data management, 111–12; determination of need for, 107–8; findings, 113; funding, 112–13; survey design, 108–9; survey management, 109–10; volunteer participation, 108, 109; volunteer stewardship, 114

Fulton Iron and Engine Works, 35
fur trade, 24–25, 30, 186
Fusaro, Abigail, 118–19

Gateway Partnership, 150–51
gelatin production, 33
Gelderloos, Orin G., 146
General Motors Corporation, 139
Geoform (ArcGIS Collector app), 112
German automobiles, 35
glaciers, 8–9, 23–24
glass manufacturing, 33
Globe Furniture Company, 28
Golding, Arthur, 196–97
Good Roads Movement, 30–31
Gotts, Mike, 161
gradients, Rouge River, 10–11
Granholm, Jennifer, 118
grass mowing, 104
Great Lakes: formation of, 8–9, 9;
    Straits of Detroit and, 29–30. See also
    Areas of Concern
Great Lakes Legacy Act, 192
Great Lakes Restoration Initiative, 73,
    84, 192
Great Lakes Water Authority, 83, 191
Great Lakes Works, 35
Great Mound of the Rouge River, 16,
    17, 17
Great Sauk Trail, 20
GREEN (Global Rivers Environmental
    Education Network), 139–40, 141, 142
green infrastructure: additional ben-
    efits, 97–98; anticipating climate
    change problems and, 196; descrip-
    tion, 93–94; examples, 95–97; Friends
    of the Rouge and, 99–100; home-
    owner actions and, 103–4; Land +
    Water WORKS Coalition, 101–2;
    Master Rain Gardeners and, 102–3;
    nonpoint-source pollution and, 93;
    public action effects on Rouge River,
    104; Rain Gardens to the Rescue,
    100–101; Rouge River revival and,
    80–82, 82, 85
green roofs, 56–57, 97

green streets, 96–97
grindstone quarries, 33
gristmills, 3, 26, 27, 33

habitats: benthic macroinvertebrates,
    117; concrete channel and, 149–50;
    contaminated sediment and, 70;
    destruction and degradation, 10, 62;
    goals for, 11; oxbow restoration and,
    54; progress in restoring and con-
    serving, 72–73, 74; stormwater runoff
    and, 12, 68
Haggerty, John S., 33, 39
Hamilton, Sandra, 111
Harding, James, 111
Harmon, Asa and John, 33
Hartig, John H., 177, 178
headwaters, Rouge River, 10
health, human, 98
health advisories, 70, 195
The Henry Ford, 51–52, 52, 150. See also
    oxbow at The Henry Ford
Henry Ford Academy, 54, 55
Henry Ford Company, 35. See also Ford
    Motor Company
Henry Ford Estate Dam Fishway, 81, 192
Henry Ford Estate Dam, 13
Heraclitus, 173
hiking trails, 170–73
Hindale, W.B., 17
Hines, Edward N., 31, 39
Hines Park, formerly Hines Drive: bike
    path, 172; development of, 38–40;
    fishing in, 167–68; on a floodplain,
    146; naming of, 31; paddling through,
    165; as popular hangout, 159; Village
    Industry Mills and, 38. See also New-
    burgh Lake
Holliday Forest and Wildlife Preserve,
    171
homeowners, green infrastructure and,
    103–4
Huron River, 132, 162
Huron River Watershed Council, 115–
    16, 117
Hurons, 1

hydroelectric power, 37–38, 49–50, 186. *See also* stream power; waterpower

ice age, 8–9, *9*
impervious surfaces, 12, 63, 72, 81, 196
industrial section of Rouge River, 166–67, 169–70
International Joint Commission, 188; Great Lakes Water Quality Board, 64
invasive species, fish surveys and, 123, 124
Invertebrate Analysis, 153. *See also* benthic macroinvertebrates
iron ore and manufacturing, 34
Iroquois, 24
Izaak Walton League, 117, 126

Jensen, Jens, 50, 152
Jo-Blocks, 38
jogging trails, 170–73
Johansson, Carl E., 38
John Clark Shipyard and Drydock, 34
John Kendall (fireboat), 49
Johnson Creek, 168
Journal of Conservation Planning, 94

Kahn, Albert, 50, 172
kayaking, 161–62, 164–65, 193
Kierkegaard, Søren, 185
Kimmerer, Robin Wall, 157–58
King, Brady, 35
knowledge, environmental education and, 131
Krabbenhoft, Corey, 118
Kuhn, Thomas, 57
Kukulski, Philip, 121, 122

"Lake Superior" iron and copper, 34
Lake Whittlesey, 23–24
lakebeds (lakeplains), 8, 11. *See also* floodplains
lakes, restoration projects implemented in, 67
Land + Water WORKS Coalition, 101–2
League of American Wheelmen, 31
Leopold, Aldo, 193

leptospirosis (rat fever), 4, 6, 63, 195. *See also* sewage
Livonia, 29
logjams, Lower Rouge Water Trail and, 161, 164–65
Louis XIV, King of France, 24
Lower Rouge River: average gradient of, 11; cleanup of, 1; concrete channel in, 12–13, *13*; contaminated sediment remediation, *71*, 72; dams on, 13; dissolved oxygen trends in, 68, *69*, 70; dredging (early 1900s), 3; fire in, 3, 48–49, 61, 189; fish in, *78*–*79*, 79, 169; meanders of, 146–47, *147*; shipping channel and, 186; walking, jogging, and biking trails along, 171; watershed, 2, 9–10
Lower Rouge River Water Trail Committee, 162
Lower Rouge River Water Trail, 160–65, 193, 195
lumber, 24

machine manufacturing, 35
Maguire, Tim, 119, 121
Main (or Mainstem) Branch: average gradient of, 11; canoeing or kayaking on, 165; cleanup of, 1; dams on, 13; dissolved oxygen trends in, 68, *69*, 70; watershed, 2, 9–10
maps, Frog and Toad Survey and, 110
Marathon Oil Corporation, 36, 163
Marine Pollution Control, 49
Master Rain Gardeners, 102–3
McCormack, Flora, 178–81
McCormick, Marie, 194
McCulloch, Bruce, 116
McDonough, William "Bill," 55, 197
McLouth, Donald B., 35
McLouth Steel, 35
McNamara, Ed, 177
meadows, 96
Mead's Mill, 28–29
meanders, of Lower Rouge River, 146–47, *147*
Meldrum, Vince, 140

Melvindale: boat launch, 166; Rouge River pollution smell and, 4, 63, 187. *See also* concrete channel

metal factories, 34–35

Michigan Car Company, 34

Michigan Carbon Works Company, 33–34

Michigan Central Railway Tunnel, 30

Michigan Clean Water Corps, 118

Michigan Department of Environment, Great Lakes, and Energy (EGLE), 118

Michigan Department of Environmental Quality, 108

Michigan Department of Natural Resources, 4, 6, 64

Michigan Department of Natural Resources Trust Fund, 162

Michigan Galvin Brass and Iron Works, 35

Michigan Good Roads Association, 31

Michigan Highway Department, 31

Michigan Nonpoint Source Program, 102–3

Michigan School Furniture Company, 27–28

Michigan United Conservation Clubs, 48

Michigan Water Resources Commission, 4, 6, 64

Middle Rouge Parkway, 38–40. *See also* Hines Park, formerly Hines Drive

Middle Rouge River: average gradient of, 11; cleanup of, 1; dams on, 13; dissolved oxygen trends in, 68, *69*, 70; Edward N. Hines Drive along, 31, 38; fish in, *78*, 79, 167–68; watershed, 2, 9–10; zebra mussels and Asian clams in, 120–21

Middlebrook & Post Manufacturing, 34

Miller, John, 26

mills, waterpower and, 26–29, 37–38

minerals, 23–24

Mitchell, Mark, 133

Model T, 43, *44*

Monroe, James, 30

moraines, formation of, 8

morphometry, as urban stream deserts, 14

Mound Builders, 16–17. *See also* First Peoples

Mulholland, Mathew, 164, *170*

Muller, Robert, 121, 122–23, 124

Murray, Jim: on the banks of the Rouge, *183*; career defined by water, 174–76; formative years, 176–77; FOTR founding and, 133; key lessons learned from, 181–82; leadership style, 178–81; legacy, 182–83, 194; major accomplishments, 193; proudest achievement, 181; provoking outrage and compelling action, 177–78

Nankin Lake, 167

Nankin Mills, 28, 37

National Environmental Policy Act, 148, 194

National Pin Company, 34–35

National Pollutant Discharge Elimination System, 91

National Science Foundation, 144, 153

National Steel, 35

Native Americans, 1, 24–25. *See also* First Peoples

native-plant grow zones, 96, 99

natural resources, 23–24

natural stream shape alteration, as urban stream deserts, 14

Newburgh Lake: Bovee Cider Mill dam and, 29; canoeing or kayaking on, 165; contaminated sediment remediation, *71*, 72; dam forming, 37, *38*; fishing in, 167, 168; PCBs in, 195

nonnative species, fish surveys and, 123, 124

nonpoint-source pollution, 92–93. *See also* green infrastructure

Norden bombsight, 36

North American Association for Environmental Education, 129–30

Northville area mills, 26–28

Northville Laboratories, 28

Northville's Fish Hatchery, 168

Northwest Territories, 25
Norwood, David, 164

Oakwood Commons Wildlife Committee, 148
Odawa, 18–19
odor, putrid, 4, 63, 187
Olds, Ransom E., 35
One Water Public Education Campaign, 83
outhouses, on Rouge River banks, 143–44
oxbow at The Henry Ford, 53–54, 55, 73, 75, 192
oxygen, dissolved, 68, 69, 70, 80, 86

Paris Climate Accord, 58
Park Trustees, 37, 39–40
participation: environmental education and, 131. See also volunteers
PCBs (polychlorinated biphenyls), 61, 70, 72, 195
People of the Three Fires, 18–19
permeable paving, 97
pet waste, 104
Phoenix Lake, 167
Phoenix Mill, 37–38, 39, 50
phytoremediation, 56
plants, domesticated by First Peoples, 19
Platt, R.H., 87
Plymouth, industry in, 27, 36
Pola, Andrew, 119
pollution: as cost of doing business, 61; Europeans and, 21; examples, 62; industrial, World War II and, 47–48, 187; of Lower Rouge River, 3–4, 5, 6; nonpoint-source, 92–93; point-source, 91–92; of Rouge River, scale of, 174; water-quality monitoring of, 136. See also stormwater runoff
Potawatomi, 18–19, 171
Power, Art, 20
prairie plantings, 96
Project Wet program, 140
Public Advisory Council, 120, 123

Quadricycle, Ford's, 35, 43, 44

racial justice movement, 126–27
railroad car manufacturing, 34
railroads, 186
rain gardens, 94, 94, 95–96, 99–100, 103–4
Rain Gardens to the Rescue program, 100–101
rat fever (leptospirosis), 4, 6, 63, 195. See also sewage
recreation, river-based: fishing, 166–70, 170; funding, 67; Lower Rouge Water Trail, 160–65; other paddling places, 165–66; walking, jogging, and biking trails, 170–73; warnings against, 159
recycling, at Ford Rouge Plant, 55–56
red swamp crayfish (Procambarus clarkii), 121
redside dace (Clinostomus elongatus), 122, 123
remedial action plan (RAP), 64, 65–67, 187–90, 189f. See also Rouge River RAP
Ridgway, Jim, 174, 176
river flows, 10, 12–13, 146–47
roads, 20, 26, 38–40
Roosevelt, Franklin D., 186–87
Rouge Park, 172
Rouge Plant. See Ford Rouge Plant (Complex)
Rouge RAP Advisory Council, later Rouge River Advisory Council (RRAC): Alliance of Rouge Communities and, 83; on fish and wildlife habitat impairment, 107–8; fish surveys and, 122; funding for benthic monitoring and fish surveys by, 120; habitat restoration projects supported by, 73, 74; purpose of, 192; remedial action plan and, 66
Rouge Rescue, 153, 160
Rouge River: delisted as Great Lakes AOC, 192; environmental education funding for, 133–34; exploring wonders of, 153–55; as fishable and swim-

mable, 4, 194–95, 199; formation of,
8–9, *9*; human disturbance of, 11–14;
Mound Builders and, 17–22; Murray
and, 176–77; oxbow at The Henry
Ford, 53–54, *55*, 73, *75*, 192; percep-
tion over time of, 186–87; personal
experiences on, 155; personal letter
to, 157–58, 198; as respected asset,
192–93; scale of cleanup, 1; water-
shed, 2, 9–11, 145; wen as description
for, 143–44. *See also* Lower Rouge
River; Main (or Mainstem) Branch;
Middle Rouge River; pollution; Rouge
River revival; Upper Rouge River
Rouge River Advisory Council, 83, 191
Rouge River Basin Committee, 65, 175,
190
Rouge River Gateway Trail, 163, 171–72
Rouge River National Wet Weather
Demonstration Project (Rouge
Project): Benthic Macroinvertebrate
Program funding by, 119; Dingell and,
194; Frog and Toad Survey and, 108;
Murray and, 175, 193; Newburgh Lake
and, 167; projects funded by, 66–67,
67; Rouge Program Office of, 190;
Rouge River Watch and, 107; wastewater treatment and, 144–45
Rouge River RAP, 66, 70, 191. *See also*
remedial action plan
Rouge River revival: Alliance of Rouge
Communities and, 82–84; beavers
and, 156–57; bird migrations and,
151–52; concrete channel and, 149–
50; contaminated sediment remediation, 70, *71, 71*, 72, *85*, 192; CSO controls and stormwater management,
67–68; dissolved oxygen and, 68,
69, 70, 80, *86*; ecosystem approach
and watershed partnerships, 64–65,
187–90, *189*; ecosystem health and,
198–99; ecosystem-based watershed
management model, 65–67; evidence
of success, 84, *85–86*; First Peoples'
perspective and, 185; fishery improvements, 76, *77*–79, *79*–80, *81*; Ford

Field Streambank Buffer Project, 150;
Gateway Partnership, 150–51; habitat
restoration and conservation, 72–73;
invertebrates in river sediments and,
73, 76; lessons learned from, 84, 86–
87; personal things you can do for,
198–99; post-construction stormwater controls, 80–82, *82*; tipping point
for, 63–64, 187
Rouge River Watch, 107
Rouge-a-Palooza, 164, 169
Roush Industries, 57
RRAC. *See* Rouge RAP Advisory
Council, later Rouge River Advisory
Council

safety stripe, on roads, 31
salmon, 169, *170*
sand paintings, First Peoples', 19
School Water-Quality Monitoring, 153
Schoolcraft College, 118, 125
schools. *See* environmental education
Scout Hollow Nature Trail, 172
sediment: contaminated, remediation
of, 70, *71, 71*, 72, *85*, 192; phosphorus
and heavy metals in, 93. *See also*
bedload
A Sense of Wonder (Carson), 152
sewage, 136, 175–76, 193. *See also* com-
bined sewer overflows; rat fever
shells, First Peoples' use of, 18
Sheuter, Beat, 150
Shiawassee Trail, 20
shipping, 23, 30–31, 36, 186
shipyards, 3, 26, 34
Sierra Club, 100–101
Simek, Richard A., 156, 171
smells, pollution-producing, 4, 63, 187
Smith, Gerald, 122
Sorensen Nature Trail, 172
Southeast Michigan Council of Govern-
ments, 64, 83, 191
Spring Bug Hunts, 116
St. Joseph Trail, 20
St. Suzanne Cody Rouge Community
Resource Center, 101–2

stagecoaches, public, 30
Stapp, William B. "Bill": continuing vision of, 138–40, 142; environmental education definitions and, 130–31; Murray and, 181; Rouge River water-monitoring project and, 134, 138; vision of, 129
steamboats, 30
steel industry, 34, 35–36
Stimpson Scale and Electric Company, 28, 29
Stinson airplane factory, 28, 29
Stone Bridge Nature Trail, 172
Stonefly Refresher, 117
Stonefly Searches, 116, 117, 119
stormwater runoff: controlling projects implemented, 66, 67; EPA lawsuit, 193; Ford Motor Company and, 57; Friends of the Rouge and, 99; as nonpoint-source pollution, 92–93; post-construction controls on, 80–82, 87; progress in, 67–68; Watershed-Based Stormwater Permit, 67. See also rain gardens
stove manufacturing, 34
STREAM Girls, 127
stream power, 10–11. See also hydro-electric power; waterpower
Stream Quality Index (SQI), 117
streambank stabilization, 67, 73, 85, 96, 99. See also Rouge River revival
sustainable development, 197
sustainable living, 198–99
swamp fever, 25
Swift, Marcus, 28–29
swimmable rivers, 4, 194–95, 199

tanneries, 25
Thayer, William W., 32
Thompson, Sue, 116
tile manufacturing, 33
Tonquish, Chief, 171
trading posts, 20
traditional knowledge, 21
trails, First Peoples', 20
Trappers Alley, Detroit, 25

trapping, 24–25. See also fur trade
Traugott Schmidt & Sons, 25
trees, 24, 96–97
Trip of a Drip learning experience, 153
Trout Unlimited, 127
Tuncay, Esma, 119

Underground Railroad, 28–29, 37
United States Steel, 35
University of Michigan: students as resource people for water-quality monitoring, 134; US Fish Hatchery and, 32
Upper Peninsula, iron ore and copper in, 34
Upper Rouge River: average gradient of, 11; cleanup of, 1; dams on, 13; dissolved oxygen trends in, 68, 69, 70; fishery improvements, 77–78; watershed, 2, 9–10
urban stream deserts, 14
urbanization: nonpoint-source pollution and, 92; Rouge River watershed and, 13–14. See also industrial section of Rouge River
US Army Corps of Engineers, 148, 150
US Bureau of Ethnology, 17
US Environmental Protection Agency: citizen science and, 106, 108, 125; Feikens' judicial leadership and, 193–94; FOTR's Quality Assurance Project Plan and, 118; National Pollutant Discharge Elimination System, 91; petitions sent to, 4; river restoration and, 64; on Rouge River cleanup, 182; teacher-education programs and, 153
US Fish and Wildlife Service, National Fish Hatcheries, 32
US Fish Commission, 32
US-Canada Great Lakes Water Quality Agreement, 188
utility stream crossings, 14

Village Industry Plants, Ford's, 27, 29, 37–38, 40, 50
volunteers: Benthic Macroinvertebrate

Monitoring Program, 115–16, 119; Frog and Toad Survey, 108, 109; logjam clearing and, 164–5; for the Rouge River ecosystem, 198. *See also* citizen science; Friends of the Rouge; participation

walking trails, 170–73
Walk-in-the-Water (steamboat), 30
Walled Lake branch, mills along, 26
wampum, 18
Wasko, Steve, 101–2
Watchfrogs, 114
water, as sacred to First Peoples, 21–22
water harvesting, 95
water pollution. *See* pollution
Water Quality Congress, 181
water quality monitoring: Huron River, 132–33; projects implemented, *67*; Rouge River, 134–38, *135, 137*; School Water-Quality Monitoring, 153, 181. *See also* benthic macroinvertebrates
water trails, 160–65, 191
Waterford Mill, 38
waterpower, 23, 25–29; hydroelectric, 37–38, 49–50, 186; stream power, 10–11
Watershed Alliance legislation (2003), 191
Watershed-Based Stormwater Permit, 67
watersheds: definition, 9; exploring wonders of, 153–55; partnerships, ecosystem approach and, 64–65; Rouge Project division of, 67; urban sprawl and, 63; urbanized eastern portion, 11, 13–14. *See also* Rouge River revival

Wayne County: mounds of, 16–17; Rouge River watershed in, 9
Wayne County Road Commission, 31, 39
Wayne Road Dam, 13
Wayne State University, 118, 123
Welch, Betty, 149
Welland Canal, 30
wen: Rouge River as, 143–44; unforgettable experience on, 144–45
wetlands: at Ford Rouge Plant, 56; Frog and Toad Survey findings about, 113; mapping, Frog and Toad Survey and, 110; as natural green infrastructure, 94; watershed and, 11, 12
wheat, French, 24
Wilcox Lake, 167
Wilcox mill-pond dam, 37
wildlife, 24, 97
Wiley, M.J., 10
Willow Run Airport, 36
Winter Stonefly Searches, 116, 120
Wisconsin Glaciation, 8
Wolf, Clancy, 136
Wolinski, Richard, 108–9
women, Phoenix Mill and, 37–38, 39, 50
World War I, 36–37, 45–46
World War II, 36–38, 47, 58, 186–87
Wyandots, 1, 18, 20
Wyandotte, 34

Yerkes Gristmill, 26

zebra mussels (*Dreissena polymorpha*), 120–21
Zug Island, 35, 166

Printed and bound by CPI Group (UK) Ltd, Croydon, CR0 4YY

13/04/2025

14656535-0001